A WORLD OF CURRIES

ALSO BY DAVE DeWITT

The Texas Monthly Guide to New Mexico
Hot Spots

With Nancy Gerlach
The Fiery Cuisines
Fiery Appetizers
The Whole Chile Pepper Book
Just North of the Border

With Mary Jane Wilan
The Food Lover's Handbook to the Southwest
Callaloo, Calypso and Carnival: The Cuisines of Trinidad and Tobago

With Paul Bosland
The Pepper Garden

A WORLD OF

Curries

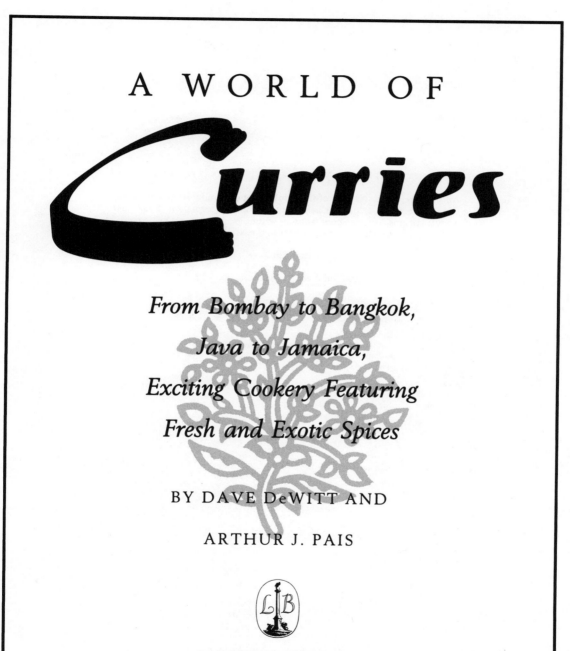

From Bombay to Bangkok,

Java to Jamaica,

Exciting Cookery Featuring

Fresh and Exotic Spices

BY DAVE DeWITT AND

ARTHUR J. PAIS

Little, Brown and Company

BOSTON   NEW YORK   TORONTO   LONDON

First Edition

Illustration credits appear on page 229.

Library of Congress Cataloging-in-Publication Data

DeWitt, Dave.
    A world of curries : from Bombay to Bangkok, Java
to Jamaica, exciting cookery featuring fresh and exotic
spices / by Dave DeWitt and Arthur J. Pais. — 1st ed.
        p.   cm.
    Includes bibliographical references and index.
    ISBN 0-316-18224-9
    1. Cookery (Curry)   I. Pais, Arthur J.   II. Title.
TX819.C9D49   1994
641.6'384 — dc20   93-29745

10 9 8 7 6 5 4 3 2 1

MAR

Published simultaneously in Canada by Little, Brown & Company (Canada) Limited

PRINTED IN THE UNITED STATES OF AMERICA

*For our wives and our companions in travel,
food, and life: Mary Jane Wilan and Betty Pais.*

"*Curries, with their vast partitioned platter of curious condiments to lackey them, speak for themselves. They sting like serpents, stimulate like strychnine; they are subtle, sensual like Chinese courtesans, sublime and sacred, inscrutably inspiring and intelligently illuminating, like Cambodian carvings.*"

ALEISTER CROWLEY,

BRITISH AUTHOR AND MYSTIC

Contents

Acknowledgments

Special thanks to Mark Preston, researcher par excellence, and to John Vittal of the Albuquerque Public Library for his assistance in acquiring books through interlibrary loan.

And our appreciation to the following people who also made this book possible: Retta Blaney, Partha and Vinita Bose, Sandi Brooks, Jane Jordan Browne, Pat Chapman, Sue Erwin, Averil and Harry Fernandes, Elizabeth Fernandes, Nancy Gerlach, Maria Ghadiali, Aziz Haniffa, Jennifer Josephy, Singh Lally, Linda Lynton, Joe and Lena Menezes, Ismail Merchant, Anita and Anna Miranda, Harry Morris, Violet Oon, Betty Pais, Alan and Priscilla Pais, Raphael Pais, Marie Permenter, Nancy Ramesar, Anura Saparamadu, Radhika Shankar, Jay Solomon, Robert Spiegel, Richard Sterling, Tommy Tang, and Mary Jane Wilan.

Introduction

This book seemed destined to be born. It was a writing project that took on a life of its own, that expanded in scope and gained significance as the research continued. There were so many occasions when we serendipitously stumbled onto information about curries in unlikely places that we were tempted to attribute them to karma.

Independently, before we ever met, both of us had been encountering curries for decades on our travels. Arthur found them in abundance in his native India, in London, in New York. Dave experienced them in Bangkok, Singapore, Malaysia, Trinidad, and Jamaica. The information about curries and the recipes we collected sat in our files for years, occasionally appearing in bits and snatches in magazine articles.

Then Arthur began writing for *Chile Pepper* magazine, which Dave edits, and a friendship ensued. It was Arthur who first proposed the idea of a book about worldwide curries, and after some delays because of other projects, Dave agreed that it was a culinary tale that had to be told.

Exploration, conquest, and constant collisions of cultures caused curries to spread far and wide from their native India. The worldwide trade in spices made the basic curry spices available in many lands, where they were combined with local spices and foodstuffs, thus transforming the nature of curries from locale to locale.

The story of the spread of curries around the world is also the story of Indian migration, and later emigration in the form of indentured servitude. The latter practice, called by historians "a new system of slavery," caused horrendous suffering among the Indian emigrants. However, it did carry Indian culture — and curries — to many parts of the globe.

Curry is everywhere these days. It is perhaps the favorite dish of Trinidad and Tobago. It is now the de facto national dish of the United Kingdom, served in more than seven thousand curry restaurants. And curry has even spread to Germany as "curry-wurst," a street snack of sausages slathered with ketchup and sprinkled with chile powder and curry powder!

We like a fairly liberal definition of "curry." As a noun, it is simply a blend of spices and other ingredients, or a dish containing them. As a verb, it signifies an international style of cooking, usually stewing, using combinations of spices.

A few explanations are in order. We have uncovered many different ways to spell, in English, various food terms in languages as varied as Malay and Tamil. For example, is the word for eggplant spelled *terong* or *terung* in Malay? We have endeavored to select the most commonly used spellings, but we do not claim that they are the only true spellings of the ingredient or technique.

Concerning chile peppers, we have tried to keep the recipes simple by suggesting chiles that are commonly available, regardless of their land of origin. In most cases, substitutions of chiles will not greatly affect the flavor of the curries.

The first chapter explores curry controversies and basics, and each of the subsequent chapters covers a region where curries have flourished. The chapters begin with a discussion of the culinary history of curries in the region, followed by recipes.

The organization of the recipes within each chapter is much like a regional menu, combining curry dishes with accompaniments, in the following order:

Curry Powders and Pastes
Appetizers/Pickles/Chutneys
Soups/Salads
Main Dishes
  Beef
  Lamb

INTRODUCTION

Pork
Game
Poultry
Fish and Seafood
Vegetable Curries
Curried Accompaniments
Non-Curried Accompaniments/Breads

Desserts have been omitted because they are not common in many of the regions covered in this book, where sweets are served mostly as snacks. The best desserts for curries are fruit, ice cream, and sorbet.

We have suggested some common curry condiments and accompaniments in chapter 1, and cooks are encouraged to mix and match the curries and their accompanying dishes from various regions. We have also provided a glossary in the form of "A Curry Pantry" (page 21), a list of Mail Order Sources (page 228), and a Bibliography (page 230).

We have collected recipes from around the world and have been assisted by many people who have given us their favorite curry recipes. These people include celebrity chef Tommy Tang; filmmaker Ismail Merchant; Singapore cooking star Violet Oon; world traveler Richard Sterling; England's "king of curry," Pat Chapman; and many other curry cooks we met on our travels.

Of course, it was not possible to include every known curry in the world in this book. However, we think it is the broadest survey of curries yet presented, and we hope that our readers will have fun cooking the curries that follow.

ONE

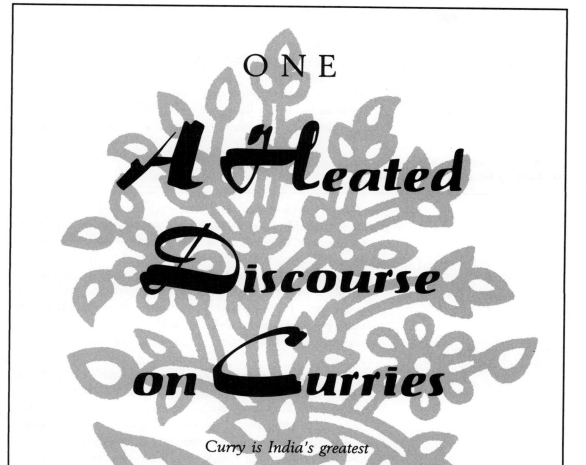

A Heated Discourse on Curries

Curry is India's greatest

contribution to

mankind.

NORMAN DOUGLAS,

BRITISH NOVELIST AND

TRAVEL WRITER

*W*e assume that Douglas's tongue was firmly planted in his cheek when he wrote the above assessment, but his comment hints at a wide range of opinion about the subject, from those people who believe, like cookbook author Manju Shivraj Singh, that "the tongue becomes a slave to the flavor of curry — it is an addiction," to critics who view curry as an insipid yellow powder that is turned into a floury yellow cream sauce.

The never-ending arguments about curry begin with its origin.

*C*urry *C*ontroversies

One of the most intriguing theories about the ancestry of curry was advanced by Captain Basil Hall, a traveler in India, Ceylon, and Borneo. "It will surprise most people — old Indians inclusive — ," he wrote in 1930, "to learn that the dish we call curry is not of India, nor, indeed, of Asiatic origin at all. There is reason to believe that curries were first introduced into India by the Portuguese." Hall reasoned that since the Portuguese had introduced chile peppers into India, and since hot peppers are a primary ingredient of curry, ergo they must have introduced curries as well.

Hall was dead wrong, of course. Currylike spice mixtures date back to at least 2500 B.C. In excavations of the ancient cities of Harappa and Mohenjo-Daro in the Indus Valley in what is now Pakistan, grinding stones were found that contained traces of mustard seed, cumin, saffron, fennel, and tamarind. Since all of these spices appear in curries, it is not unreasonable to assume that the ancient Indus Valley people were cooking with curry spices forty-five hundred years ago — although no recipes survive.

"Many people consider them [inhabitants of Mohenjo-Daro, called the Harappa culture] the world's first gourmets and creative cooks," writes William Laas in *Cuisines of the Eastern World*. "Their achievements may be measured by the fact that their seasonings were adopted by all who came after them." For the story of how curries evolved in India, see chapters 2 and 3.

One of the first written mentions of curry-style cookery is attributed to Athenaeus, a Greek miscellanist who lived about

A.D. 200. In his *Deipnosophistai* (The Gastronomers), a fascinating survey of classical food and dining habits, he quotes Megasthenes, the fourth-century-B.C. author of *Indica:* "Among the Indians at a banquet a table is set before each individual . . . and on the table is placed a golden dish, in which they first throw boiled rice . . . and then they add many sorts of meat dressed after the Indian fashion."

"The Indian fashion," as mentioned by Megasthenes, has sparked most of the curry controversies, because some writers and cooks believe that it has been stolen and ruined by the rest of the world, especially by the English. Other writers think that notion is nonsense, and they believe that cookery continues to evolve as the world shrinks. In fact, there are multitudinous definitions and beliefs about curry, and rarely do two writers agree on precisely what curry is.

"Curry in its twentieth century manifestation — a meat or occasionally vegetable stew flavoured with commercial curry powder — is essentially a British dish," writes John Ayto, author of *The Glutton's Glossary*. He takes the oversimplified stance that all curries are made with commercial curry powder, which simply is not true, despite a plethora of commercial curry powders and other products.

M.F.K. Fisher, the famous gastronome, disagrees with the curry-powder-stew concept, believing the preparation of curries to be a high art: "Books about curries, for instance," she writes,

> are published continually, with the success of a well-ticking clock. Special restaurants all over the world serve nothing but curries. Spice merchants grow rich on making their regional and private blends of curry powder. In other words, reputations can and do depend upon the authenticity of the recipe first and then of the powder that goes with the sauce, the skill with which the sauce is made, and in many cases the atmosphere in which the whole is served.

Some curry lovers carry things too far. "The word *curry* is magic," gushes William Kaufman in his book *The Art of India's Cookery*. "Its mention conjures up for us the romance and mystery of the far-off land of the Taj Mahal. The best way to create the Indian atmosphere is to perfume your house with curries."

His comment may have some truth, but the worship of curry irritates famed Indian chef and author Madhur Jaffrey, who writes in her book *An Invitation to Indian Cooking*: "To me the word 'curry' is as degrading to India's great cuisine as the term 'chop suey' was to China's. If 'curry' is an oversimplified name for an ancient cuisine, then 'curry powder' attempts to oversimplify (and destroy) the cuisine itself."

Although Jaffrey may call the word "curry" degrading, actually it is not meant to be insulting. The term reflects the evolution of language, and the need to designate, in English, dishes that were based on various spice mixtures. Indeed, "curry" has come to mean, in English, different spice mixtures that are used in a similar manner in countries throughout the world. "Curry," explains Yohanni Johns, author of *Dishes from Indonesia*, "is a word frequently used by foreigners to describe Indonesian dishes cooked with coconut milk." Santha Rama Rau, author of the Time-Life book about Indian cooking, says that the "proper sense" of the word is "a highly seasoned stew with plenty of sauce."

There is even controversy over the etymology of the word itself. Most sources attribute it to a British colonial corruption of the Tamil (South Indian) word *kari*, meaning sauce. Indian food expert Julie Sahni notes that *kari* is also a shortened version of *kari-pulia*, or *kari* leaves, meaning the leaves of the curry plant, *Murraya koenigii*, a common ingredient in Indian curry blends.

But other writers disagree with the *kari* origin of curry. Dharamjit Singh, author of *Classic Cooking from India*, writes that "curry is a word that comes from the Hindustani: *turcarri*. In the colloquial it is shortened to 'turri,' which in Anglo-Saxon usage is called 'curry.' " William Laas agrees with this etymology. Other authors believe that the word is derived from *karhai*, a woklike metal implement made of silvered brass in which curried dishes are cooked, or from *khari* (sometimes *khadi*), a soup made with buttermilk and chickpea flour.

Julie Sahni claims that curry is derived from *curryup*, an ancient Tamil word for blackened or crisp-fried, noting that *curryi* is Tamil for uncooked vegetables. She concludes: "Curry powder was thus originally the seasoning blend used for flavoring fried vegetables."

Perhaps the most unusual theory of the origin of the word

"curry" comes from Selat Elbis Sopmi of London's Punjab Restaurant, who writes in the *Curry Club Magazine* that some centuries ago an Irish sea captain married into a wealthy family. The captain's gambling led to the demise of the family, which kept a large stable of racehorses. They were forced to sell the best of the horses and eat the rest. The Irishman used the word *cuirreach*, Irish for racetrack, and told everyone he had been reduced to eating *cuirreach gosht,* or racetrack meat. "Over the ages, this has become, through usage," claims Sopmi, "the word as we know it, curry."

The *Oxford English Dictionary* prefers the Tamil *kari* as the word of origin and defines curry as "a preparation of meat, fish, fruit, or vegetables, cooked with a quantity of bruised spices and

Black pepper, a favorite curry spice for millennia.

turmeric, and used as a relish or flavouring, especially for dishes composed of or served with rice." A secondary definition says that curry powder may be used in the cooking process.

Interestingly enough, the English were already predisposed to accept the word "curry," regardless of its precise Indian ancestry. First, there was the influence all over Europe of Marco Polo, who in the late thirteenth century reported of the Asian origin of "ginger, galangal, spikenard, and many other kinds of spices" that were just starting to be used in the English kitchen.

Second, the word *cury*, with an Old French word *keurie* as its root, first appeared in English as *kewery*, meaning cookery and also the "concoction" of substances in alchemy. As early as 1390, a manuscript of the first English cookbook appeared, entitled *Forme of Cury* (Art of Cookery), and it was supposedly written by the master cook of King Richard II. *Forme of Cury* was not actually printed as a book until 1780, about thirty years after Robert Clive of the East India Company captured the fort of Arcot, west of Madras, and laid the basis for the British empire in India. Thus the first printed English cookbook was contemporaneous with the early rise of the British Raj — but that is not the only curry coincidence.

In *Forme of Cury*, hot spices were considered to be, according to culinary historian L. Patrick Coyle, an "essential luxury" because of the medieval belief in their digestive qualities and their ability to mask the tastes and odors of food spoilage. "Pepper was the most highly prized," writes Coyle, "followed by ginger and a related root called galangal, then cubeb, a berry whose taste suggests allspice and peppercorn, and clove, cinnamon, cardamom, cumin, and coriander." Given the fact that all of these spices appear in curries, it was inevitable that the English would warmly embrace Indian curries (see chapter 7 for that story).

As for the word "curry," it soon had its own variants through the British empire, including *currie, carrye, curree, kerry,* and *kerrie*. It was transferred to other languages, appearing as *poudre de cari* in French and *Indisches Currypulver* in German, but remaining simply *curry* in Italian and Spanish. The word has even crept into slang, as in the American and British phrase "currying favor" (which originally meant to please with cookery) and the Australian "to give curry," which means to abuse or rebuke someone.

During the research for this book, we have uncovered four primary myths about curry that need to be refuted.

Curry Myth Number 1: *Curry is a spice*. This fiction continues to spread despite numerous books about spices and Indian cooking. Curry leaf (*Murraya koenigii*) is a single herb used in some curries, but in reality there are dozens and dozens of herbs, spices, fruits, rhizomes, bulbs, pulses, nuts, and other ingredients that are combined to make curries. A quick glance at our "Curry Pantry" (page 21) will reveal the great number of ingredients used in curries worldwide.

Curry Myth Number 2: *All curries are the same*. Nothing could be further from the truth. "Contrary to popular belief," notes Sri Lankan food importer Anura Saparamadu, "there are about as many types of curries as there are spices." And given the total number of curry ingredients, the combinations and permutations of those ingredients provide a nearly infinite variety of flavors in curries. "Even the best Indian cooks will argue endlessly over the inclusion and exclusion of particular spices and herbs," adds Santha Rama Rau.

Curry Myth Number 3: *Authentic curries cannot be made outside their country of origin*. Purists often say that to enjoy genuine curries, one must travel to all the regions covered in this book. Arthur, who grew up in southern India, is often asked by his American friends if authentic Indian curries can be made here. The answer is a resounding yes. Virtually every exotic curry ingredient (and every one in this book) is available in the United States in Asian markets or by mail order. Besides, as Arthur points out, across the Indian subcontinent, as well as in other curry countries, cooks boldly experiment, and it is possible to get five or six variations on the same recipe. So cooks should use our recipes as a rough guide and feel free to experiment. In all cases, even with a few substitutions, our recipes will be authentic — meaning, as in the dictionary, reliable and genuine.

Curry Myth Number 4: *No self-respecting Indian cook would ever use commercial curry powder*. Virtually every writer on the subject of curry or Indian food falls for this falsehood, or some variation on the theme, as if to say that all commercial curry products are bogus. Expatriate Indians in other parts of the world, such as the United States and Canada, commonly use commercial powders, pastes, oils, and sauces. And in India, as Tom Stobart, author of *The Cook's Encyclopedia*, observes,

> books commonly say that Indians do not use curry powder. This may have been true in the days when even the servants had servants and the *masala* of fresh ginger, garlic, onion, coconut, green chile, and spices was ground on the stone freshly for each dish. But today [1980], a First World cost of servants has caught up with Third World households, and ready-ground spice mixtures are no longer beyond the pale.

This is not to say that Indian cooks now use commercial preparations to the exclusion of homemade curries, but rather that they now have the option because of the vast number of commercial products on the market.

Julie Sahni takes a liberal view of the most basic ingredients required to make a curry: "For a spice blend to be called a curry powder, the mixture must contain three core spices: coriander, turmeric, and pepper." Others will disagree, asking "Where's the cumin?" or any other of their favorite spices. The point here is that many spice blends not originally defined as curry powders, such as those from North Africa and the Middle East, can fit into the broad category of curries.

Curry Categories and Commercial Preparations

For years, food writers have been attempting to categorize curries. According to John Philips Cranwell, author of *The Hellfire Cookbook:* "Generally speaking curries are, like Burnside's army before Fredericksburg, divided into three grand divisions. They are: sweet curries, largely from Thailand, Burma, and Indonesia; dry curries; and liquid or sauced curries from India, Ceylon, parts of the Middle East, and Indonesia."

William Kaufman divides curries as follows: those with a picklelike flavor; stewy types; vegetables in a sauce; and lentil and gram curries. William Laas organizes them from wet to dry. "Curries of the poor," he suggests, include *saar*, a soup similar to mulligatawny. The thicker curries are *kadi*, like a puree; *sukke*, like a custard; and *korma*, a dry curry.

Since it is difficult to categorize the large number of curries that appear in numerous cuisines, we have organized curries according to regions around the world where they are commonly found and then have differentiated the types of curries within those regions in the chapter introductions.

Some people divide curries according to commercial, pre-packaged curry concoctions, such as powders, pastes, oils, and sauces. This practice has triggered a major curry controversy: that of fresh curries versus packaged ones. Many purists abhor commercial curry powders. "They are anathema to Indian cooking," writes Dharamjit Singh, "prepared for imaginary palates, having neither the delicacy nor the perfume of flowers and sweet-smelling herbs, nor the savour and taste of genuine aromatics." He adds: "Curry powders often contain inferior spices which with age become acrid and medicinal in taste. They not only mask the natural taste of foods, but lend a weary sameness to everything with which they are used."

Pat Chapman, the founder of England's Curry Club, notes another drawback to commercial powders. "The manufacturers," he writes, "often put in too much chile and salt, and in some cases, chemical colorings and preservatives. Undeclared additives can include husks and stalks, and other adulterations." (In India, salt is added to curry powder to delay the formation of mold.)

Noted gastronome Elizabeth David also dislikes prepared curry powders. "To me they are unlikeable," she writes, "harshly flavored, and possessed of an aroma clinging and all-pervading in its way as English boiled cabbage or cauliflower. Too much hot red pepper, too much low-grade ginger, too much mustard seed and fenugreek."

Juel Anderson, author of *Juel Anderson's Curry Primer*, has pointed out: "Through time, commercial spice mixtures have become so uniform a blend that most of us know curries only as yellow-colored foods with a standard aroma, often peppery-hot and as predictable in flavor as a Big Mac." Indeed, there is a sameness to commercial curry powders, especially those made in the United States to meet the 1977 U.S.D.A. standards for curry powder, which call for the following percentages of spices:

coriander, 36; turmeric, 28; cumin, 10; fenugreek, 10; white pepper, 5; allspice, 4; mustard, 3; red pepper, 2; and ginger, 2.

However, we should point out that there are many imported curry powders, especially from India, that vary in flavor considerably because they contain a wider variety of spices used in many different percentages.

Commercial curry powders are basically convenience condiments and should be treated that way. John Philips Cranwell suggests three reasons for using commercial curry preparations: they produce a uniform result with a given recipe; the individual spices necessary to make a certain curry may not be available at a given time; and buying commercial curry preparations saves kitchen time and work.

We believe that common sense must prevail. It may be true, as Dharamjit Singh suggests, that "once you have tried [separate spices] you will no more use the packaged curry powder than you would accept another person's taste in the choice of your clothes." But, on the other hand, is it considered bad taste to use a packaged Sri Lankan curry paste if the cook has run out of some of the necessary ingredients to prepare a fresh curry paste? Or, if fresh lemongrass is not immediately available for a Thai curry, should the cook substitute powdered lemongrass, or use a packaged curry paste containing fresh lemongrass? These are decisions only the cook can make, and there will certainly be times when convenience will triumph over authenticity.

Our recommendation is that, whenever possible, cooks should follow our recipes and use freshly ground or mixed ingredients for the curries. Prepared powders and other products can be a backup for cooks lacking the time or certain essential ingredients, but cooks should avoid the cheap American curry powders if they can.

Generally speaking, the commercial curry preparations fall into the following categories. **Masalas** are spice blends that usually lack turmeric. **Curry powders** contain turmeric (the yellower the powder, the more turmeric it contains) and a large percentage of coriander. Imported powders are generally superior to domestic ones. **Curry pastes** are sealed, moist blends of herbs, spices, and other ingredients such as coconut, onion, fresh chile, and ginger. They are imported from India, Thailand, Indonesia, and Sri Lanka. **Curry sauces** are available either in bottles or in mixes and are used as marinades or to make an "instant" curry gravy for meats. **Curry oils** are vegetable oils steeped in curry spices, and they are generally used as condiments to add a curry flavor to prepared foods.

Curry for Health!

Curry spices have a long history in Indian folk medicine as curatives. Mixtures of various combinations of black pepper, cumin, cloves, cardamom, nutmeg, ginger, and cinnamon were used to treat numerous conditions, including intestinal problems, asthma, anemia, jaundice, and even "tubercular leprosy," according to S. N. Mahindru, author of *Spices in Indian Life*. He also notes that nutmeg, cloves, and black pepper, when combined with camphor, "are the spicy components of the well known Ayurvedic aphrodisiac *chandrodaya makardhwaja . . .* a general tonic which increases virility." This revelation is encouraging for male curry lovers.

An Englishwoman who lived in India in the early 1800s, Harriet Tytler, wrote: "There was a time when doctors put all ills connected with the liver down to hot curries, till one doctor with more sense than the rest discovered that red chiles, not black pepper, were very good for sluggish livers."

Harvey Day, the witty author of *Curries of India*, seeks to dispute the notion, "difficult to eradicate, that curry eating is bad for you; that it causes dyspepsia, makes you evil-tempered and tends to shorten your life. This impression has been fostered by writers who depict purple-faced, curry-eating colonials who retire to rural England and vent their spleens on the natives."

Day, who was influenced by his studies of folk medicine, claims that curries are foods for health. He points out that nearly every herb and spice used in curries is a preservative, all of them have antiseptic values, and many are carminatives, which expel gas from the stomach and intestines. The addition of chile powders to curries not only increases their pungency but also has the benefit of producing gustatory sweating, which cools the body down. Freshly ground green chiles are high in vitamin C, while red chile powder contains significant amounts of vitamin A.

Some of Day's health claims for curries would hardly pass

modern medical scrutiny, but they are interesting nonetheless. Ginger, he says, long used as a medicine by Indians and Chinese, also has aphrodisiac qualities. Turmeric is a great cure for skin diseases. Garlic and onions are "blood cleansers" and ward off colds in the winter because they are "potent germ destroyers." Both cinnamon and coriander too are "powerful germicides," nutmeg oil aids digestion and cures insomnia, and black pepper has been used to treat fevers. Other curry spices, such as mustard seed, fennel, and cardamom, also have numerous medicinal uses.

The total effect of curries, says Day, is ultimately good for the body. "First," he writes, "there is anticipation, caused by the appetizing *aroma* of the curry. Digestive juices are secreted in the mouth. Then follows the real pleasure of eating with enjoyment. Contentment, naturally, is the result, and in its train, sound health."

Of course, since Day's book was written in the 1960s, medical science has discovered that some ingredients used in curries — particularly coconut derivatives — are high in saturated fats, which are considered to be a primary cause of coronary artery disease. We recommend the moderate use of curries that contain coconut or coconut milk; however, in the recipe for Coconut Milk Substitutes in this chapter (page 20), we suggest a more healthful replacement that will allow cooks to retain the flavor of coconut milk, but not the fat.

On the other hand, science has determined that curry powders have some useful properties. "They should not be neglected," writes spice expert J. S. Pruthi of the Central Food Technological Research Institute in Punjab, India, "since they stimulate secretion of the digestive fluids in the stomach. They are carminative, digestive, and antiflatulent. Thus," he concludes, "curry powders play a significant role in the culinary arts and add flavor to otherwise dull foods." We couldn't agree more.

Making Freshly Ground Curry Powders

Since the process of making a powder exposes more surface area of a spice as it is ground, the spice oxidizes more quickly in powder form, quickly losing volatile oils and flavor components. We advise cooks to make only enough powder for one meal and to avoid storing leftover powder. However, we realize that some cooks will make quite a volume of powder and, being frugal, will store it. In this case, we advise using as small a jar as possible and sealing the top tightly.

Curry pastes store better than powders because the moisture in them retards oxidation and traps the spice oils. But the moisture is also a breeding ground for fungi and bacteria, so curry pastes should always be refrigerated. Some cooks place a thin layer of vegetable oil over the paste to reduce oxidation even more.

The first step in making curry powder is to roast the spices. This is accomplished by placing the raw spices in a dry skillet on top of the stove, in a dry electric frying pan, or on a baking sheet placed under the broiler or in the oven. The goal is to heat the spices with medium heat until they release their distinct aromas. Except in the cases of some dark curry blends, such as those from Sri Lanka, the spices should not be blackened. Also, they should not be heated for too long, or the volatile oils will be lost. Practice is the only way to learn how long to roast the spices. The oily and volatile spices, such as cloves, cinnamon, cardamom, and mace, are usually not roasted — but there are exceptions in some recipes.

The next step is grinding the spices. Cooks have several options, including the original method of grinding between two stones, which in this day and age is a bit obsolete. A mortar and pestle can be used, but it takes a lot of muscle power to grind the spices fine enough to make a powder. Blenders, coffee grinders, and food processors may also be used, but by far the best solution is to use an electric spice mill that is dedicated only to spices. Grind the roasted spices in small quantities so as not to burn out the motor. Avoid grinding whole dried ginger or turmeric without first pulverizing them manually (with a hammer), because they are very fibrous and difficult to grind with home equipment. Some cooks find it easier to use powdered ginger and turmeric.

Freshly ground spices can be stored for later use, but not for long periods of time. Two or three months is the maximum for most ground spices (and again, be sure to store them in small bottles that are tightly capped). Store the spices in a dark place, since sunlight can degrade their flavors.

Blending the roasted and ground spices is simple. Either use the spice mill or place the spices in a shallow bowl and blend them thoroughly with a fork. Use a food processor or blender to make curry pastes, following the individual recipe directions. Often, pastes must be made in two or three batches and then further mixed by hand. Some pastes must be fried in oil before they are added to the recipe. This procedure removes water from the onions and other paste ingredients and cooks the spices again to remove their raw flavor. Just take care not to burn the paste.

Cooking and Serving Curries

Some cooks suggest that curry spices actually take a secondary role to the other ingredients. "Although the dish is called curry," observes Julie Sahni, "the most characteristic ingredient in all classic curries is the slowly cooked, caramelized onions not unlike those used in French onion soup." Indeed, in many cuisines, the curry spices used provide only a portion of the flavor of the dish. Additional tastes are contributed by ingredients such as lemongrass, galangal, coconut, papaya, tamarind, or other exotic ingredients. And finally, the chosen meats, fish, or vegetables in the curry also add their unique flavors.

Most curries are cooked in large skillets or in woks, so the curry cook is advised to have a selection of shallow, nonaluminum cookware with lids. Wooden spoons are the best utensils for stirring curries, since they do not conduct heat very well.

Because most curries can easily be prepared ahead of time and reheated just before serving, they are convenient to cook for parties. They also freeze well, which is a great convenience. Cooks should remember that some curries, such as salads, can be served cold and make good outdoor summer food.

And what other dishes should be served with curries? Most curries are paired with some form of rice, and plain white rice is an excellent accompaniment to most recipes. We have given recipes for some exotic rices found in various parts of the world. We have also included some non-curried side dishes that go well with curries and some chutneys, relishes, breads, and simple condiments. These side dishes can accompany curries from all over the world, and cooks are encouraged to experiment with various combinations.

The condiments are usually either served in bowls, so that guests may sprinkle them over the curry, or are placed on the side of the individual dishes. Additionally, here is a general list of basic condiments often served with curries worldwide: fried eggplant, tamarind jam, candied coconut, candied ginger, pickled vegetables (such as onions), mango chutney, grated fresh coconut, grated roasted coconut, chopped peanuts or almonds, grated or sliced hard-boiled eggs, chopped crisp bacon, chopped tomatoes, and salted fish.

Curry and Beverages

The curry controversy continues with the subject of what drinks to serve with curries. Of course, many nonalcoholic drinks can be partnered with curries, including milk to cool them down. But it's the question of which alcoholic beverage to choose that engenders the real debate.

"Curries present a perplexing problem," writes John Philips Cranwell. "Most of them come from countries whose population is predominantly Muslim or Hindu. To both alcohol is forbidden, hence little indigenous wine exists. I enjoy beer, or ale with curry, or even a rough red wine." Cranwell was right about Muslims but wrong about Hindus, who have no laws regarding alcoholic beverages.

Many writers believe that wine and curries simply do not work together. William Templeton Veach and Helen Evans Brown, authors of *A Book of Curries and Chutneys*, warn: "It is a mistake to serve wine with curry. Wine is quite foreign to the nature of the dish, and even if the combination were perfectly digestible, the spices of the curry would completely mask the bouquet and flavor of the wine."

Noted oenologist André L. Simon agrees: "I do not know of any wine that can be happily partnered with curry." Another wine expert, Roy Andries de Groot, explains:

The most exotic menus reach their climax with the incendiary, mouth-burning torrid curries in which the black, green, and red chiles are the masters. When the dish is a Malaccan Devil's Curry . . . we are whistling in the dark to hope that wine can be anything more than secondary. Yet the right wine, if it has a clear enough character to cut through the heat, will refresh the mouth and help separate and balance the flavors.

De Groot goes on to recommend sparkling wines from California and the Alps.

Harvey Day generally agrees with the wine prohibition, although he concedes that a good champagne is acceptable on "a very special occasion." He is supported in this contention by English curry expert Pat Chapman, who writes: "The facts are simple: wine, red or white, is perfectly acceptable with curry. The more delicately spiced the dish, the more sophisticated can be the wine. My personal favorite with curry is pink champagne or sparkling wine." He does acknowledge, however, that "fine wines are wasted . . . their subtlety is overpowered even by mild spicing." Chapman concludes succinctly: "Wining and dining is for enjoyment — rules are for fools."

New York wine connoisseur Peter Grieg throws a ringer into the debate: "Although I am quite sure that curry in any form is too pungent a flavor for all wines, why should not a long rum drink complement the dish excellently well, especially in spring and summer?"

The British in India commonly drank ginger beer with curries, and beer of all kinds seems to be the universally accepted alcoholic drink to accompany curries worldwide. "Generally speaking," observes Harvey Day, "light beers are the best beverages to drink with or after curries." He also notes: "If you fancy a Guinness before, and a vintage port after your meal of curry and rice — and if it agrees with you — then to perdition with the Food and Wine Society!"

Later studies indicate that Day is correct. Statistics collected in 1991 by the Curry Club, a British organization devoted to curry, show that the favorite beverages ordered by diners at curry restaurants were as follows: lager, 45 percent; wine, 21 percent; beer, 20 percent; nonalcoholic, 14 percent. In fact, beer is so popular with curries in the United Kingdom that Cobra Indian

Lager is a major sponsor of a guide to the best curry restaurants.

For curry purists, there is one possible solution to the problem of what to drink: Turtle Lady Curzon. This beverage was named for Lady Curzon, vicereine of India from 1899 to 1905, and consists of 1 cup turtle consommé, 1/2 teaspoon curry powder, and cream to taste. It was a popular drink aboard the *Queen Elizabeth*, but, not surprisingly, is hardly ever served today.

Anyway, not all the curry controversies can be definitively resolved. The ultimate decision as to what curries are, how to cook with them, and what to serve with them is up to the individual cook. We simply hope that the recipes in this book will encourage cooks to develop their own strong opinions about the nature of curries.

Basic Recipes

Following are recipes for two curry ingredients that are called for many times in this book, ghee and coconut milk (or cream).

 ## *Ghee*

Yield: 1 3/4 pounds (about 3 cups)

2 pounds unsalted butter

Ghee is clarified butter; that is, the milk solids and moisture have been removed. It imparts a unique flavor to curries and has a higher smoking point than many vegetable oils, such as olive oil. When cooled, ghee will keep for about a year without turning rancid. Although some sources say it does not need to be refrigerated, just to be safe we recommend refrigeration. For a vegetarian version of ghee, simply substitute a high-quality margarine for the butter. There are a surprising number of ways to make ghee, including boiling the butter in water, but we believe the following recipe is the easiest. Some people add a curry leaf or bay leaf when cooking for added flavor.

Melt the butter in a heavy saucepan, then increase the heat slightly to just below the simmering point of the butter. Cook for 45 minutes, stirring any foam that rises back into the butter.

Gathering coconuts, Ceylon, c. 1890.

Remove the pan from the heat and allow the butter to cool to lukewarm. Carefully pour off the top layer of clarified butter, allowing the solids on the bottom to remain in the pan. Strain the butter through muslin cloth or through a sieve lined with paper towels.

Store in the refrigerator in a widemouthed jar with a screw lid.

Note: Never use salted butter for this recipe.

 ## Coconut Milk and Cream

Yield: 2 cups

4 cups freshly grated coconut
2 1/4 cups boiling water or hot milk

Both of these liquids are extracts from coconut, and it is important to differentiate them from the highly sweetened, canned coconut cream (or syrup) that is used to make drinks called piña coladas. The canned cream is not a substitute and should not be used in any recipe in this book. Coconut milk is used extensively in curries, and it is best when made from freshly grated coconut meat. But if that is not available, use frozen grated coconut or desiccated, unsweetened coconut flakes and substitute cow's milk for the water. Coconut milk powder, now available in some specialty markets, mixes well with water to make coconut milk. Canned coconut milk is also commonly available, but cooks should check the label to make certain that sugar has not been added.

Coconuts are widely available in Asian markets and large supermarkets across America. Look for a coconut without cracks or any sign of mold. The fresher the coconut, the more liquid it has. To break a coconut open, heat the oven to 350 degrees. Puncture a hole through one of the "eyes" and drain the liquid. (This coconut water makes an excellent drink and can be consumed straight or mixed with rum or scotch.) Place the coconut in the oven for 20 minutes, then remove it and allow it to cool. Break it open with a hammer; the meat should fall away from the shell. If some meat still clings to the shell, carve it out using a small knife. Use a vegetable peeler to remove the thin brown skin from the meat and then grate the meat on a metal grater or carefully chop it in a food processor using the pulse mode.

In a bowl, cover the grated coconut with the boiling water (or milk, for a thicker coconut "cream") and let it steep for 15 minutes. Using a strainer, drain the coconut and reserve the "milk." The coconut meat may be squeezed through muslin cloth or a double layer of cheesecloth to collect the rest of the milk.

Store the milk in the refrigerator (it has about the same shelf life as whole milk), and the cream will rise to the top.

Variation: For a thicker milk, approaching cream, instead of steeping the grated coconut in hot water, puree it in a blender with the water and then strain it through cheesecloth.

Yield: 1 cup

1 cup milk (whole or low-fat), yogurt, or evaporated skim milk
1/2 teaspoon coconut extract

🌸 *Coconut Milk Substitutes*

One cup of coconut milk contains — depending on its thickness — between 45 and 60 grams of fat, quite a bit in today's world of low-fat diets. Fortunately, a low-fat coconut milk is now available that reduces the fat level to about 12 1/2 grams. To lower the level even further, we suggest the very simple recipe below, which combines whole or low-fat milk, yogurt, or evaporated skim milk with coconut flavoring. Several companies manufacture coconut flavoring, or extract, which in this recipe concentrates the flavor while removing nearly all the fat. Two brands of coconut extract on the market are Nielsen-Massey Coconut Extract and Wagner's Coconut Flavor — they are available at gourmet shops and by mail order. By combining such extracts with whole milk, the amount of fat is decreased to 8 grams; when combined with low-fat milk, that figure is further reduced to 5 grams. These substitutes may not be perfect, but they are a lot healthier than the high-fat version. Since the consistency of coconut-flavored milk is thinner than that of canned coconut milk, cooks may need to add more of the substitute than is called for in a recipe and cook it a bit longer to achieve good results. Yogurt can also be combined with coconut extract; the consistency will be thicker, the taste will

A WORLD OF CURRIES

be different and interesting, but the fat count will be even lower, about 3 grams. Evaporated skim milk will also give a thicker consistency.

Combine the ingredients in a bowl and stir.

A Curry Pantry

In this glossary of curry ingredients, we have eliminated most of the more common foods that are curried, such as meat, seafood, fruit, and vegetables, and have concentrated on seasonings, flavorings, and unusual condiments.

Ajowan *(Carum copticum)*
Called bishop's-weed in some parts of Africa, it is a hairy herb with pungent seeds; an occasional spice in some African curry mixes.

Almonds *(Prunus amygdalus)*
The familiar cultivated nut; an occasional ingredient in curries around the world.

Allspice *(Pimenta dioica)*
The dried berries of a tropical tree, grown mainly in Jamaica, which suggest the aroma of cinnamon, nutmeg, and cloves. An ingredient in West Indies curries and some commercial curry powders.

Amchar
In India, powdered mango; in the West Indies, a *masala* used to curry mangoes.

Anise *(Pimpinella anisum)*
The licorice-flavored seeds of an annual herb. An occasional ingredient in Indian curry powders.

Annatto *(Bixa orellana)*
An orange-colored extract of the seeds of the annatto tree. Also called *achiote*, it is used as a coloring agent and seasoning. An ingredient in some commercial curry pastes.

Asafoetida *(Ferula asafoetida)*
A gum resin from the giant fennel plant, used as a seasoning in home and commercial Asian curry pastes.

Basil *(Ocimum basilicum)*
A common herb native to Central Asia. Fresh basil is an ingredient in curries from the Malaysian state of Selangor and in curried butters in Ethiopia.

Bay leaf *(Laurus nobilis)*
The leaf of the sweet bay, or laurel tree. An ingredient in Indian and South African curries and some commercial curry powders.

Black pepper *(Piper nigrum)*
The pungent berry that is perhaps the most famous spice in the world. It is ubiquitous in curry blends all over the world.

Bombay duck
This ingredient is not duck at all, but rather a small salted dried fish that accompanies curries in India and is a curry ingredient in Malaysia. Substitute anchovies.

Buttermilk
A low-fat milk treated with bacteria, this could be called a thinner version of yogurt; remove the butter from milk, and you have buttermilk. Buttermilk is used in curries in southern India. It is also made into a refreshing summer drink, with green chiles, black pepper, and salt thrown in.

Candlenuts *(Aleurites moluccana)*
Fleshy nuts of the candleberry tree of Southeast Asia, used as a thickening agent in curries. Substitute macadamia nuts, Brazil nuts, almonds, or cashews.

Cardamom *(Elettaria cardamomum)*
The seeds of a relative of ginger, primarily grown in India and Guatemala. Unripe (green or white) cardamom pods are also sold; the seeds must be removed before using. A common ingredient in home and commercial curry powders.

Cashews *(Anacardium occidentale)*
Nuts of a small evergreen tree (cashew apple) that are laden with fat, up to 48 percent. They are commonly used in South Indian curries and snacks. They are an occasional ingredient in Nepalese curries.

Cassia *(Cinnamomum cassia)*
The scraped, dried bark of a relative of cinnamon. It is often used in place of cinnamon in the curries of Malaysia and elsewhere in Southeast Asia.

The cashew, an occasional curry ingredient.

Cayenne *(Capsicum annuum)*
One of the hotter dried chiles; its powder commonly appears in curries worldwide. See CHILE PEPPERS.

Celery seed *(Apium graveolens* var. *dulce)*
The seed of the common salad vegetable. An ingredient in some commercial curry powders.

Chile peppers *(Capsicum* spp.*)*
The fruits of the *Capsicum* genus, they provide most of the heat in curries. They are found all over the world and are used dried in commercial and home powders and both fresh and dried in curry pastes. We have suggested appropriate chiles and substitutions in the recipes.

Cilantro *(Eryngium foetidum)*
Coriander leaf, often used as a garnish for curries, either whole or chopped. An ingredient in some curry pastes.

Cinnamon *(Cinnamomum zeylanicum)*
The bark of an evergreen tree that grows in western India and Sri Lanka. It is a common ingredient in curry powders and pastes from all over the world.

Cloves *(Eugenia caryophyllata)*
The dried, unopened flower buds of an evergreen tree native to the Moluccas; the spice is now grown extensively in Zanzibar. Cloves are a common ingredient in curry powders and in curry pastes from Malaysia, Indonesia, and other parts of Southeast Asia.

Coconut *(Cocos nucifera)*
The fruit of the *Cocos* genus of palms, found in tropical regions all over the world. The grated flesh, and milk extracted from it, appear in tropical curries from around the world.

Colombo
The name for curry in the French West Indies.

Congo peppers *(Capsicum chinense)*
Extremely hot chiles that are commonly added to Trinidadian curries.

Coriander *(Coriandrum sativum)*
The seed of a Mediterranean herb; one of the most common ingredients in curry powders.

Cumin *(Cuminum cyminum)*

The seed of a common annual herb native to Egypt; another common ingredient in curry powders.

Curry leaf *(Murraya koenigii)*

The aromatic leaf of the curry leaf tree (or curry plant), which grows on the Indian subcontinent. The leaf is used primarily in Indian home curry powders and usually does not appear in commercial powders and pastes.

Dal

The term usually means lentils, but it can refer to a number of dried pulses. See GRAM.

Dill *(Anethum graveolens)*

The seed of a biennial herb native to southern Europe; an ingredient in some commercial curry powders.

Fennel *(Foeniculum vulgare)*

The seed of a perennial herb native to southern Europe; an ingredient in some commercial curry powders.

Fenugreek *(Trigonella foenumgraecum)*

The seeds of an annual herb native to the Mediterranean area and India, often available in powdered form. A common ingredient in Indian curry powders.

Fish sauce

Called *nam pla* in Thailand and *nuoc cham* in Vietnam, this salty, fermented fish sauce is found in Southeast Asian curries.

Five-spice powder

A blend of star anise, *fagara* (Chinese prickly ash), cassia, fennel, and cloves; popular in Southeast Asia, it occasionally appears in curries.

Galangal *(Alpinia galanga)*

A close relative of ginger, this rhizome appears in curry pastes from Malaysia, Indonesia, and other parts of Southeast Asia.

Garam masala

A powdered blend of basic Indian spices that may be considered the beginnings of curry powder. The usual ingredients are cumin, coriander, peppercorns, cloves, cinnamon, and sometimes mace.

Garlic *(Allium sativum)*
A perennial herb that appears in curries and curry pastes all over the world.

Ginger *(Zingiber officinale)*
A rhizome that appears in curries, curry powders, and pastes all over the world.

Gram
Certain plants of the pea family, especially chickpea. Gram flour is known in India as *besan*. Gram most commonly appears in Indian curries. Greengram, known as *moong dal*, can be found in Asian markets.

Jackfruit *(Artocarpus heterophyllus)*
A tropical fruit, its seeds and flesh are cooked, pickled, and roasted. In southern India, jackfruit curries are popular in the summer months, when the fruit is abundant. The jackfruit flesh is also ground with rice and turned into fritters.

Kaffir lime leaf *(Citrus hystrix)*
The leaf of a Southeast Asian citrus tree; used in curries and curry pastes of the region.

Lemongrass *(Cymbopogon citratus)*
The bulbs and lower stalk of this perennial plant have a strong citrus flavor. It is used in Malaysian, Indonesian, and other Southeast Asian curries and curry pastes. If fresh lemongrass is used, cooks should remove the upper two thirds of the stalks and cut the rest, including the bulb, into small bits. Dried lemongrass should be soaked in warm water for 90 minutes before use, then drained and chopped. Lemongrass is available fresh in some gourmet supermarkets and fresh or dried in Asian markets.

Mace *(Myristica fragrans)*
The outer, fibrous covering of the nutmeg seed; occasionally appears in curry powders.

Malagueta peppers *(Afromomum malagueta)*
Also called grains of paradise and false cardamom, these seeds of a ginger relative appear in African curry powders.

Mango *(Mangifera indica)*
A tropical fruit that is used both as a dessert and key ingredient in the curries of southern India and the West Indies.

Mint *(Mentha arvensis)*
A common perennial herb and an ingredient in some Singaporean curries and such North African spice blends as *harissa*.

Nigella *(Nigella sativa)*
Also called black cumin, this plant is native to North Africa. Its black seeds have a lemon-carrot aroma, and they are used in some North African curry powders.

Nutmeg *(Myristica fragrans)*
The seed of an evergreen tree native to the Moluccas; a common ingredient in world curry powders and pastes.

Okra *(Hibiscus esculentus)*
The pods of an annual vegetable; an occasional ingredient in Malaysian curries, often used as a thickening agent. It is widely used in curries and soups *(sambhar)* in southern India.

Onion *(Allium cepa)*
A common ingredient in curry pastes and dishes around the world. It appears in some commercial curry pastes.

Orange leaf *(Citrus aurantium)*
From the common orange tree; an ingredient in South African curries.

Orrisroot *(Iris germanica)*
The dried root of the German iris, which has a violetlike aroma. An ingredient in some North African spice mixtures.

Pandan
See SCREW PINE.

Papaya *(Carica papaya)*
A widely used tropical fruit. Green papayas are common in curries in India; the ripe papayas are used as desserts.

Poppy seed *(Papaver somniferum)*
The seed of the opium poppy; an ingredient in North African curry pastes and some Nepalese curries.

Prawn paste
Called *blacan* in Malay, this strong-smelling paste is made with fermented prawns and salt. The fishy odor dissipates during cooking. It is sold in blocks and cakes in Asian markets. Substitute SHRIMP PASTE, or FISH SAUCE as a last resort.

Saffron *(Crocus sativus)*
The dried stigmas of a variety of crocus flower, used in Moghlai curries. Regarded as the most expensive spice in the world, it is available whole, powdered, or in liquid essence form.

Salam *(Eugenia polyanza)*
A laurel leaf that dries to a very dark color, almost black; used in Malaysian curries. It is not a bay leaf, but bay leaves may be substituted for it.

Screw pine *(Pandanus odoratissimus)*
Leaves that are used to flavor rice in India and Malaysia. Available in leaf form or essence in some Asian markets.

Sesame seeds *(Sesamum indicum)*
The seed of an annual herb indigenous to Indonesia; an occasional ingredient in Indonesian and Malaysian curries.

Shallots *(Allium ascalonicum)*
This onionlike bulb is an ingredient in Malaysian, Thai, and Singaporean curries and curry pastes.

Shrimp paste
Called *hei-ko* in Chinese and *petis* in Malay, this paste combines shrimp and salt, which are allowed to ferment. It is milder than PRAWN PASTE and is an ingredient in some commercial Thai curry pastes.

Shrimp powder
Dried powdered shrimp; available in Asian markets.

Silver foil
A bright, edible foil used in some Indian curries; available in Asian markets.

Tamarind *(Tamarindus indica)*
The five-inch pods of this tree contain seeds and a sour pulp. The pulp and seeds can be rehydrated in warm water and then strained. Tamarind can also be found in specialty markets in a variety of forms: pastes, concentrates of pulp, and whole pods dried into bricks or ground into powders. (In the recipes that follow, we tell you how to substitute for tamarind if you're unable to find it.)

Turmeric *(Curcuma longa)*
The yellow rhizome of a relative of ginger; one of the most common ingredients in world curries, curry powder, and curry pastes.

Yogurt
Fermented and coagulated milk; an occasional ingredient in South African curries but used more frequently in northern Indian curries.

TWO

South Indian Curries

With spices freshly ground and individually blended, the flavours

amalgamated and smoothed out with coconut milk or dahi, it

was possible to produce an infinite range of sauces to ring the

changes on the staples that have always formed the life-support of

the Indian peoples.

REAY TANNAHILL,

AUTHOR OF *FOOD IN HISTORY*

Curry's oldest tradition, of course, is in India. We have seen in the previous chapter that some of the spices used in curries — namely cumin, saffron, and fennel — were being ground on stones as early as 2500 B.C. in the Indus Valley. Eventually this Harappa culture of the Indus Valley declined, and since its seals have never been translated, we have no idea if the spices they ground were actually used in currylike dishes. We also do not know if the spices were cultivated, collected in the wild, or acquired through trade with other peoples.

Although there is no definitive proof, we suspect that curries originated in the south of India because the Malabar Coast of Kerala became India's first spice-growing region. Black pepper, cinnamon, turmeric, and cardamom first grew wild there and then were cultivated for centuries before they spread throughout the subcontinent.

A Spicy History

Although curries per se are not described until much later, curry spices such as black pepper and turmeric are mentioned in the Vedas, the ancient sacred literature of the Hindus, which date from approximately 1500 B.C. (Some authorities claim an earlier date, of about 5000 B.C.) Nutmeg, mace, saffron, and cardamom were ingredients in candies and perfumes used in early Indian nuptial ceremonies. In Epic Period literature, dating from around 2000 B.C., curry spices such as black pepper and mustard are mentioned in the preparation of young buffalo for banquets. The buffalo were served "floating in a spicy sauce," according to Jeanine Auboyar, author of *Daily Life in Ancient India*.

From about 500 B.C. on, the Malabar Coast of Kerala became renowned for its black pepper, cinnamon, ginger, and cardamom as growers there sold the spices to the Phoenicians and the Arabs. As legend holds, Saint Thomas visited the region soon after Christ's crucifixion and was to stay only a few days. But after he tasted the shrimp curries and tasted the beverages, he decided to stay for quite a while.

Most of the Malabar's spices were carried to Alexandria, Egypt, for reexport around the Mediterranean. But interestingly enough, the cultivation of the spices was somewhat haphazard, and some experts believe that they were collected in the wild rather than actually farmed. "Even pepper and cardamom and other spices much demanded by the Arabs and Europeans," writes Dr. K.K.N. Kurup of Calicut University,

> were not cultivated or produced in a systematic manner. From an early period of history, pepper had become the staple commodity of trade between India and Europe. However, the efforts of man in its production were very little. The only human effort involved in the production of spices was the gathering of the commodity from the plants.

According to S. N. Mahindru, author of *Spices in Indian Life*,

> After 700 B.C., the Indian spice trade saw a boom never seen before, because the rich clove- and cinnamon-growing areas of Ceylon and Moluccas came under the sovereignty of Bengal kings. The principal traders and shippers were the Arabs, the Dravidians, and the Phoenicians, who shipped spices to their respective markets of good profits.

Indian traders also imported spices and other goods from the Moluccas, or the Spice Islands, China, and Cambodia for reexport.

India supplied ginger to Romans by way of the Arabs, and also black pepper, cassia, cinnamon, and cardamom. The Arabs cleverly concealed their Indian connection, spreading rumors that the spices were from Ethiopia. The Romans eventually discovered the "monsoon route" to India and did some trading directly. Whatever their method, they paid dearly for their spices, and the only currencies acceptable to the Indians and their Arab intermediaries were wine, gold, and silver. The Roman historian and poet Pliny observed: "No year passes in which India does not impoverish us of fifty million sesterces." The huge payments for spices triggered an economic crisis in Rome, which was unable to pay its armies. Without an army, Rome was at the mercy of the "barbarian" invaders. Thus the

Vasco da Gama.

Roman lust for spices was one of the factors that brought about the fall of the Roman empire.

The first specific mention of curry in Indian literature that we could find comes from the longest epic poem in any language (eighty-eight thousand couplets), the *Mahabharata*, written about A.D. 400 (some sources say the first century A.D.). In one section of the poem Bhima addresses Yudhishthira about how he planned to live in disguise in the kingdom of King Virata: "I shall appear as the ex-cook of King Yudhishthira as I am well-versed in the culinary art. I shall prepare King Virata's curries and shall supersede even those experts who used to make curries for him before."

The spice trade boomed in medieval India (roughly A.D. 600 to 1500). Calicut was the center of it all, a city eight miles in circumference that was described by the Indian traveler Niccolò de' Conti in 1430 as the "spice emporium of the East . . . a notable emporium for the whole of India, abounding in pepper, aloe, ginger, a larger kind of cinnamon, and zedoary." The Arab chronicler Abder-Razzakm described Calicut in 1442: "One of the greatest shipping centers in the world in this period, from where vessels are continually sailing for Mecca which are for the most part laden with pepper." Other spice products available in Calicut were turmeric and cloves.

These were the riches that awaited the Europeans, who had finally ignored the Arabs' continuing rumors of Africa as the origin of spices and had sailed on to India. The Portuguese were the first to arrive, led by Vasco da Gama, who reached Calicut and anchored nearby in 1498. Pedro Alvarez Cabral followed soon after and began capturing Arab ships laden with spices. But the local *nairs* fought back, destroying much of his armada.

Da Gama returned in force to the Malabar coast in 1502, fought with the coastal principalities, and finally made peace with the maharaja of Cochin, Unni Rama Verma. A deal was soon struck. "In my country, there is abundant cinnamon, pepper, cloves, and nutmeg," said the maharaja. "What I need from your country is gold, silver, coral, and scarlett [cloth]."

The Portuguese captain was allowed to load five ships with pepper, cardamom, and other spices, and before he left he demanded Portuguese exclusivity for the spice trade and the right to build factories and garrisons. A treaty was finally approved in

1513, and the people of Calicut agreed to a Portuguese monopoly on the spice trade from the Malabar Coast. But the Portuguese sailors deserted to the ships of private merchants, and the Portuguese fell behind on their payments for pepper and other spices.

The Portuguese forever changed curries by introducing chile peppers, which became the principal hot spice in curries from then on. Christopher Columbus brought chile peppers and their seeds back from the New World in 1493, and they were grown mostly by monks. Portuguese explorers carried the chiles to their ports in Africa and Goa, India, shortly thereafter. Although the exact date of their introduction into India is not known, most experts believe it was in the early 1500s.

Garcia Orta, a Portuguese chronicler, wrote in 1593: "This Capsicum or Indian pepper is diligently cultivated in castles by gardeners and also by women in their kitchens and house gardens." Nowadays, India is the world's largest producer of chiles, with over two million acres under cultivation and a yield of more than seven hundred thousand dry equivalent tons.

Chiles became an integral part of Indian cooking and religious lore. They are believed to ward off the evil eye, and in many houses and offices, chiles are hung for just such a purpose. In the home, chiles are burned in the kitchen to intimidate the evil eye and protect children. "The smoke of a burning chile pepper," writes Julie Sahni, "assures me that I am at home, warm and secure in my own culture wherever I may be."

The Portuguese remained in India for 450 years; although they colonized only a small part of the subcontinent, they created a world market for Indian spices. The story of the British influence on Indian spices and curries is told in chapter 3.

The Essentials of Southern Indian Curries

In addition to the numerous spices found in the curries of southern India, there is one other enormously important ingredient: the coconut. It is difficult to imagine a social function in many southern Indian states where the auspicious coconut is not present. At wedding ceremonies and the breaking of ground at construction sites, a coconut is broken. According to tradition, the act is a powerful but bloodless sacrifice to invoke the blessings of the gods. In thousands of temples across southern India, priests break a coconut before representations of the gods and distribute its kernel (the meat) to devotees as a sort of communion.

The Hindu scriptures refer to the coconut as the *sriphala* — the holy or sacred fruit. In fact, many Hindus call it the *kamadhenu*, the source of life. The three "eyes" on the coconut, some Hindus believe, represent the Hindu trinity of Brahma, Vishnu, and Shiva. However revered the coconut is in Hindu society, it is also an integral part of Muslim, Christian, Jewish, Buddhist, and Jain cuisines as well.

The milk and puree derived from the coconut transform hundreds of ordinary fish, meat, and vegetable dishes into memorable treats. Although canned coconut milk is now available in Asian markets, we suggest that cooks prepare their own by following the suggestions and recipes in chapter 1 (pages 19 and 20).

Another essential ingredient in the curries of southern India is tamarind, the tangy, sun-dried pods that often are sold in the form of a dried cake. Tamarind is also available in markets as paste, jars of concentrated pulp, syrup, and even powder.

The food of southern India is hardly known to most non-Indians who visit Indian restaurants outside India. Most of these restaurants serve what is known as Moghlai and Punjabi foods, from India's north and northwest regions. Many restaurant owners have told us that the bias for this northern food is due largely to the fact that most of the early restaurant owners were from those regions, and their success was widely emulated.

Even in India, northerners have a limited idea of the incredible variety of delicacies found in the south. Most northerners (and non-Indians too) believe that the majority of southerners are vegetarians. Even Pat Chapman, England's curry expert, states: "Over eighty percent of the population of India are vegetarians; and the southern half of India is almost exclusively so."

Such statements are simply not true and have been fueled by articles in newspapers and magazines that perpetuate this myth, spread (perhaps unwittingly) by people from the two Indian states that *are* predominantly vegetarian. In Gujarat, in India's northwest, and in its neighboring state Rajasthan, at least 75 percent of the people are vegetarians because of the lingering influence of the Jain religion; with the rest of India, only 25 percent are vegetarians. The myth about Indians' food habits owes a lot to the Gujaratis, the largest group of Indian immigrants in North America and Britain.

According to the Hindu religion, which includes 80 percent of India's 850 million people, only cow meat is expressly forbidden because the cow (*go-mata*) is a sacred animal. Other meat is perfectly permissible. Hinduism also forbids Brahmins from eating meat and fish, but Brahmins constitute only a tiny fraction of India's population.

So, contrary to popular belief, South Indians excel in preparing hundreds of meat and fish dishes. They even have a basic, all-purpose curry powder that will suffice in these dishes and others from around the world: *Bafat*, or Hurry Curry (page 40). In Karnataka, in the southwest, pork and fish are part of the staple diet of Christians along the coast, where such dishes as *Bajjali Masli Bafat* (page 49), a fish curry, are eaten with white rice and Mango Curry (page 53). Another seafood dish, Seafood Combo Curry (page 50), was invented by Arthur and his wife, Betty, based on the ingredients and techniques of the state. Also from Karnataka is the tasty Pork and Yam Curry (page 46) and *Koli Kochupu*, Dry Chicken with Coconut (page 47). Egg Curry with Cashews (page 52) is a vegetarian specialty from the state, as is Tomato *Palya* (page 53). A vegetarian curry from the Mangalore region of southwestern India is *Batate Palya*, Potato Curry with Lima Beans (page 55).

Visitors to Madras, the capital of Tamil Nadu, are often intrigued by the phrase "Military Hotel" on restaurant signs. Many Indians use the word "hotel" to denote a restaurant, and "military" indicates a nonvegetarian restaurant. The story goes that many butcher shops were located near military barracks during the British Raj, and that caused restaurateurs to label nonvegetarian dishes military food.

Of course, millions of Indians are vegetarians. Vegetarian establishments serving southern fare are called *udupi* restaurants, because Udupi is a temple town that trained its temple cooks to prepare vegetarian food in mass quantities to be given away at festivals. Some of the cooks left the temples and opened their own restaurants, and today there is hardly a city in India where *udupi* vegetarian dishes, such as our *Vangi Bhat* (page 59), are not available.

Another southern state with a considerable consumption of meat and fish is Kerala. Two interesting seafood curries from that state are *Erachi Kootu*, Shrimp and Eggplant Curry (page 51), and Shrimp and Crab Curry (page 52). A vegetarian curry from the state is Pineapple *Kalan* (page 54). More than half the residents of Kerala are either Muslim or Christian, and they are voracious beef eaters, so naturally some of the best local curries are made with beef, such as *Gaychi Indad* (page 43), which is also made in Karnataka. Another Karnatakan beef dish is *Keema Bafat* (page 44).

It is a common misconception that because cows are sacred in India, no beef is served there. Although cow slaughter is banned in most Indian states, Kerala and West Bengal — both long ruled by communists elected by ballot — have refused to enact legislation banning beef. Elsewhere in India, the meat of the water buffalo is substituted for beef. It should be pointed out that across India cows are clandestinely slaughtered all the time, and the resulting minced beef, appearing in curries, is passed off as the more expensive lamb.

Pork is also popular in curries, especially in the state of Goa, a former Portuguese colony. Goan pork *sorpotel* and *Shikar Vindaloo* (page 46) are so fiery from red and green chiles that they are traditionally eaten with strong swigs of *fenni*, a sweet, home-made alcoholic beverage made from cashews, to cool the dish down. Another Goan specialty using pork is Curried Sausages (page 45).

Vegetable curries do, of course, abound in Kerala and Tamil Nadu, and not all of them are hot and spicy. In our recipe *Masala Dosai*, a type of pancake (page 60), for example, chiles play a minor role. The pancake is usually served with *Sambhar* (page 61), a soupy lentil curry. *Vangi Bhat*, Eggplant Rice (page 59), is a vegetarian dish served at any time of the day. Another popular vegetarian curry from Tamil Nadu is *Keere Kootu*, Spinach Curry (page 54). Some vegetarian curries, such as *moru kolambu*, are cooked in buttermilk; in our version of this dish (page 57) we substitute yogurt diluted with water, as do many Indians living in North America. The best place to have *moru kolambu*, Arthur remembers, was in Brahmin homes. For even though non-Brahmins cook excellent vegan meals, the Brahmins have mastered the art of turning even the plainest of vegetables into curry feasts.

Although non-Brahmins love Brahmin preparations, they would rather eat in a Brahmin restaurant than in a Brahmin home. Many Brahmins, very conscious of caste distinction, keep a separate set of plates and spoons for their non-Brahmin guests, so there is always an implied insult when they bring them out at dinnertime.

However, many young Brahmins who stealthily partake of nonvegan curries in their friends' homes have no problem using their cutlery. On Sundays, Arthur remembers, his Brahmin friends would drop by to savor pork and beef curries.

"Don't give us the meat," some of them would say, "give us just the gravy."

Like most Christians across India, Arthur would eagerly wait for Sunday. For soon after the mandatory Mass ended, the feast would begin. As men sat around imbibing liquor made from cashews or bananas, women chopped mounds of onion, crushed garlic and green chiles, and cubed sweet potatoes for the pork dish. They would also cook vegetables such as cabbage or green bananas as accompaniments. Two other excellent accompaniments for any of the curries in this chapter are Eggplant Pickle (page 41) and Mango and Coconut Chutney (page 42).

Red, White, and Black Curries

Sri Lanka, formerly known as Ceylon, the Isle of Gems, has a very rich culinary tradition that has been influenced by traders, immigrants, and conquerers from India, Arabia, Malaysia, Portugal, the Netherlands, and Britain. Many people believe that Sri Lankan food is the same as southern Indian food, but there is one very large difference: the heat level.

According to Sri Lankan food importer Anura Saparamadu, no self-respecting Sri Lankan cook would ever buy Indian products, because they are too mild. "Their curries are cumin- and coriander-based," he says, "while our Sri Lankan curries are chile-based."

Food writer Tina Kanagaratnam, who grew up in Sri Lanka, agrees: "Hotter and more robustly flavored than Indian curries, the curries of Sri Lanka get their distinctive flavor from the roasting of whole spices until they are dark brown before grinding — and from extra chiles."

Sri Lanka's reputation for extremely hot curries rests with its red, white, and black curries. The color of the red curry is derived, not surprisingly, from huge amounts of red chile pods. In one recipe for a Sri Lankan curry powder for fish and beef, Doreen Peiris, author of *A Ceylon Cookery Book*, calls for an entire pound of small dried red chiles.

White curries are considerably milder because the chiles are tempered with coconut meat and milk. Another unusual Sri Lankan recipe, Tamarind Chicken in White Curry Sauce (page 48), combines the tartness of tamarinds with the heat of chiles and the pungency of shallots, garlic, and spices.

But it is the black curries, featuring darkly roasted curry spices, that give better aroma and flavor, according to Sri Lankan cooks. Typically, a Sri Lankan black curry is made as follows: coriander, cumin, fennel, and fenugreek seeds are roasted separately, then combined with whole cinnamon, cloves, cardamom seeds, and leaves from the curry tree. This mixture is then finely ground with mortar and pestle. The finishing touch is the addition of no fewer than three types of chiles. Medium-hot yellow wax chiles are ground together with bush-ripened dried red chiles called *valieche miris*, plus the tiny but deadly-hot "bird's eye" chile, a relative of chiltepins. The result is our Ceylon Dark Curry Powder (page 41), which is used in our recipe for Black Lamb Curry (page 45).

Sri Lanka is one country composed of two different peoples. The Tamils, a majority of whom are Hindus, constitute about 20 percent of the population and live mostly in the northern part of the island. They cook in a style similar to their relatives in India, across the Palk Strait. A typical Tamil dish is *Meenu Kootu* (page 48), a fish curry that is served year-round.

The Sinhalese, the majority of whom are Buddhist, have no compunction about eating meat and fish, and make very hot, dark curries. Beef *Smoore* (page 44) is a typical Sinhalese meat dish. Both Sri Lankan peoples are great fish lovers, and some of their curry recipes call for dried and powdered maldive fish (also known as Bombay duck), which is found around the Maldive Island seas.

Fruits such as mangoes are commonly curried in Sri Lanka, in both unripe and ripe forms. Another favorite fruit is jackfruit, the largest fruit that grows on trees — it weighs as much as seventy pounds. The unripe jackfruit meat is brined for about a month; then the salt is squeezed out and the jackfruit is fried in lard and red chile powder. Jackfruit seeds, with a chestnutlike taste, are boiled and then curried. Both the fruit and the seeds are available canned in Asian markets. A popular vegetarian curry from Sri Lanka is the eggplant curry called *Brinjal Pohie* (page 56).

Accompaniments to Sri Lankan and southern Indian curries include Colombo's Greengram Milk Rice (page 58) and Cucumber *Raita* (page 42), which is a spiced cucumber salad with coconut milk.

The flesh and seeds of the jackfruit, the world's largest fruit, are often curried in Sri Lanka.

Tina Kanagaratnam has observed: "Sri Lankan curries are a rare treat. Hardly ever found outside of home, the treasured recipes are passed down from mother to daughter, with no written record and certainly no measurement." Fortunately we have been able to track down a number of Sri Lankan curry recipes — complete with measurements.

Again, we should point out that many of these recipes from South India and Sri Lanka call for coconut milk. For suggestions and substitutions for this delicious but fat-laden ingredient, see Coconut Milk Substitutes, page 20.

Bafat

Yield: About 2 cups

1/3 cup coriander seeds
1/4 cup cumin seeds
2 tablespoons mustard seeds
2 tablespoons whole peppercorns
2 tablespoons whole cloves
1 tablespoon fenugreek seeds
2 tablespoons ground cardamom
2 tablespoons ground cinnamon
2 tablespoons ground turmeric
1/2 cup freshly ground hot red chile powder, such as cayenne

HURRY CURRY

There are scores of curry powders on the market today. Purists may frown on curry powders, but they are indeed useful for making curries in a hurry. Even in India, prepared curry powders have become an integral part of middle-class family life. The following curry powder, called Bafat, is from the southwestern region of India. It can be used for a meat, fish, or vegetable dish. It can even be used the same day for two completely different dishes, each with its own unique flavor! For example, it is found in Keema Bafat (page 44) and Shrimp and Crab Curry (page 52). Traditionally, the spices are sun-dried for 3 days and then roasted.

Dry the whole spices in the oven at 200 degrees for 15 minutes, taking care that they do not burn. Remove them from the oven, cool, and grind them together with the ground spices in a spice mill.

🌸 Ceylon Dark Curry Powder

Yield: About 1 cup

Some Sri Lankan curries are quite dark — almost black — because the various seeds that are used are toasted or roasted to a dark brown color. They are also quite hot, as is this basic southern powder.

Roast the chiles on a cookie sheet in the oven at 350 degrees until they turn very dark. Remove and allow them to cool.

In a dry skillet, roast the rice, coconut, cinnamon, and the coriander, cumin, fennel, cardamom, fenugreek, and mustard seeds over medium heat, stirring often, until they turn dark brown, almost black.

Combine the chiles, roasted spices, cloves, and curry leaves in a spice mill and blend to a fine powder.

10 small dried hot red chiles, such as piquins, seeds and stems removed
1 tablespoon uncooked rice
1 tablespoon freshly shredded coconut
1 two-inch piece cinnamon
2 tablespoons coriander seeds
1 tablespoon cumin seeds
1 tablespoon fennel seeds
1 teaspoon cardamom seeds
1 teaspoon fenugreek seeds
1 teaspoon mustard seeds
6 whole cloves
5 curry leaves

🌸 Eggplant Pickle

Yield: 3 to 4 cups

Indian pickles, unlike the American and European versions, are heavily spiced. Some are hot, and some are both hot and sweet. The following pickle, which can accompany a meal or can be used with crackers or bread rolls as a snack, owes its inspiration to Arthur's friend Radhika Shankar.

Grind the chiles, ginger, turmeric, cumin, and fenugreek seeds, and peppercorns with the vinegar to make a smooth chile paste. Make a separate paste of just the garlic.

Heat the oil in a skillet over medium heat, add the curry leaves and the chile paste, and cook for 2 minutes. Add the garlic paste, mix well, and continue frying for 2 minutes. Add the sugar for a sweeter pickle.

Add the eggplants to the combined pastes, then the water, and cook, uncovered, for 20 minutes, stirring occasionally. Add the salt.

Cool and refrigerate in an airtight jar. This pickle keeps for at least a month in the refrigerator.

10 fresh red chiles, such as serranos, seeds and stems removed
1 four-inch piece ginger, peeled and minced
1 teaspoon ground turmeric
1 teaspoon cumin seeds
1 teaspoon fenugreek seeds
1/2 teaspoon whole peppercorns
2 cups vinegar
20 cloves garlic, peeled
1 cup vegetable oil
1/2 cup curry leaves
1 cup sugar (optional)
2 pounds long, thin eggplants, peeled and diced
2 cups water
Salt to taste

🌺 Cucumber Raita

CUCUMBER SALAD

Raitas *are combinations of vegetables or fruits with spiced yogurt or coconut milk. In some cases the ingredients are pureed together to make a thick drink. This fragrant version is more like a salad and can be enjoyed with any main dish — and throughout the year. It is widely served across Sri Lanka with coconut milk; in northern India, it is prepared with yogurt and smaller amounts of spices. An option here is to add 1 chopped tomato and increase the yogurt or Coconut Milk by 1/3 cup.*

In a large bowl, combine all the ingredients and refrigerate for 1 hour before serving.

l thin
e
ound coriander
poon ground cumin
1/2 teaspoon ground ginger
1/2 teaspoon fenugreek seeds
2 tablespoons freshly squeezed lime juice
1 cup yogurt or Coconut Milk (page 19)
Salt to taste

Yield: 4 to 6 cups

1 lime-size ball tamarind pulp
1/2 cup warm water
2 cups freshly shredded coconut
1 one-inch piece ginger, peeled
4 green chiles, such as serranos, seeds and stems removed, halved
4 cloves garlic, peeled
1/2 cup cilantro leaves, chopped
6 large green mangoes
1 teaspoon cumin seeds
1 teaspoon fenugreek seeds
4 tablespoons vegetable or olive oil
1/2 teaspoon mustard seeds
1 teaspoon moong dal (greengram, available in Asian markets)
1 teaspoon asafoetida
1 teaspoon red chile powder, such as New Mexican
1 teaspoon ground turmeric
1/4 cup curry leaves
1/2 cup cilantro leaves
Salt to taste

🌺 Mango and Coconut Chutney

This chutney from the southwest coast of India can be served with any curry in this book and can be used as a dip for any kind of chip, including fried plantains.

Soak the tamarind in the 1/2 cup warm water for 10 minutes, then squeeze the pulp, discard, and save the liquid (see Note).

Grind the coconut, ginger, chiles, garlic, and cilantro into a fine paste. Combine the paste with the tamarind liquid. Set aside.

Peel the mangoes, discard the seeds, and grind the pulp in a food processor or blender along with the cumin and fenugreek seeds into a smooth paste.

Heat the oil in a large skillet over medium heat for 2 minutes. Reduce the heat, add the mustard seeds, *moong dal*, and asafoetida. When the seeds begin to pop, add the mango paste, chile powder, turmeric, and coconut-tamarind paste. Add a little water, mix well, and cook over low heat for 10 minutes, stirring occasionally.

Remove from the heat and add the curry leaves, cilantro leaves, and salt. Place in a jar in the refrigerator; this chutney keeps for at least 3 months.

Note: 1 teaspoon freshly squeezed lime juice can be substituted for the tamarind liquid.

🌸 *Gaychi Indad*

BEEF INDAD

Serves: 4

This is a sweet and hot dish popular among the Christians in the Goa and Mangalore regions, on India's southwest coast. It is particularly popular during the monsoons. The people drink the locally brewed alcohol, play some folk music, and savor the indad *dish (preferably made the previous day) with a bowl of plain rice.*

Soak the tamarind in the 1 cup warm water for 15 minutes. Squeeze the pulp, discard, and retain the liquid (see Note).

In a blender, grind the chiles, raisins or dates, onion, ginger, garlic, and cumin seeds to a coarse paste in the vinegar.

Heat the oil over medium heat for 2 minutes, add the Ghee (if using) and the chile paste, and fry over low heat for 1 minute. Add the sugar and the tomatoes and cook for about 8 minutes or until the tomatoes turn into a smooth pulp.

Add the beef, water, and turmeric, mix well, and cook over medium heat for 25 minutes. (If you are using chicken, cook for 10 minutes.) Add the potatoes and cook for another 10 minutes. Add the reserved tamarind liquid and the salt and garnish with the cilantro leaves.

Note: 2 teaspoons freshly squeezed lime juice can be substituted for the tamarind liquid.

1 lemon-size ball tamarind pulp
1 cup warm water
4 small fresh red chiles, such as serranos, seeds and stems removed
2 small green chiles, such as serranos, seeds and stems removed
1/4 cup raisins or dates
1 large onion, chopped
1 one-inch piece ginger, peeled and minced
4 cloves garlic, peeled and minced
1 teaspoon cumin seeds
1 teaspoon vinegar (or more as needed)
2 tablespoons vegetable or olive oil
1 tablespoon Ghee (page 17) (optional)
1 teaspoon sugar
4 large tomatoes, chopped
1 pound stewing beef (or substitute lamb or chicken), diced
1 cup water
1/2 teaspoon ground turmeric
4 medium-size potatoes, peeled and cut into quarters
Salt to taste
1/2 cup cilantro leaves for garnish

Serves: 4

4 pounds beefsteak (filet mignon preferred)
2 onions, finely chopped
6 cloves garlic, peeled and finely chopped
1 two-inch piece ginger, peeled and finely chopped
1/4 cup Ceylon Dark Curry Powder (page 41)
6 bay leaves
1 one-inch piece cinnamon, crushed
1/2 cup rice or white vinegar
3 limes, pickled in brine (available at Asian markets)
2 large tomatoes, chopped
4 cups Coconut Milk (page 19)
Salt to taste
1 tablespoon vegetable or olive oil
1 large onion, finely chopped
1/2 cup cilantro leaves

🌸 Beef Smoore

A delicious curry prepared during festivals, this is one of Sri Lanka's signature dishes. The recipe is courtesy of Aziz Haniffa, a journalist colleague of Arthur's.

Using the tip of a sharp knife, puncture the steaks all over. Place the steaks in a large skillet. Combine the onions, garlic, ginger, Ceylon Dark Curry Powder, bay leaves, cinnamon, vinegar, limes, tomatoes, and 2 cups of the Coconut Milk in a bowl. Pour this mixture over the steaks and cook, covered, for about 40 minutes on low heat.

Add the remaining 2 cups of Coconut Milk and cook, uncovered, for 15 minutes. Add the salt and let simmer for 2 minutes.

Remove the meat, let cool, and cut into thin slices. Reserve the curry gravy, remove the bay leaves, and keep warm.

In a skillet, heat the oil for 2 minutes, add the onion, lower the heat, and cook for 2 minutes. Add the meat and fry for 3 minutes.

Place the meat pieces in a serving dish, pour the curry gravy over them, and garnish with the cilantro leaves.

Serves: 4

2 tablespoons vegetable oil
1 tablespoon Ghee (page 17) (optional)
1 large onion, chopped
6 cloves garlic, peeled and minced
1 one-inch piece ginger, peeled and minced
1 tablespoon Bafat (page 40)
1 pound minced meat (beef or lamb, or substitute chicken)
Salt to taste
1/4 cup cilantro or mint leaves

🌸 Keema Bafat

MINCED MEAT CURRY

This is a popular dish from the coastal region of Karnataka using the basic Hurry Curry powder. It is traditionally prepared with beef or lamb, but chicken may be substituted and the cooking time reduced by 7 minutes.

In a skillet, heat the oil for 1 minute, add the Ghee (if using) and the onion, and cook over medium heat until the onion wilts, about 1 minute. Add the garlic and the ginger and fry the mixture for 1 minute. Add the Bafat, lower the heat, and simmer for 1 minute.

Add the minced meat, mix well, and cook for 20 minutes over low heat. Sprinkle with cold water from time to time. Add the salt. Garnish with the cilantro or mint leaves.

✿ *Black Lamb Curry*

Serves: 4

Sri Lanka is famous for its fiery cuisine, and this is one of the hottest of all Sri Lankan dishes.

3 tablespoons Ceylon Dark Curry Powder (page 41), or less for a milder curry
1/2 cup water
1 pound lamb, cut into 1 1/2-inch cubes
4 yellow wax hot chiles, seeds and stems removed, chopped
1 onion, chopped
2 tablespoons vegetable oil
2 cups water

Place the Ceylon Dark Curry Powder and the 1/2 cup water in a blender and puree to a smooth, thin paste. Toss the lamb cubes in the mixture and marinate, covered, for 1 hour at room temperature.

Sauté the chiles and the onion in the oil until soft. Add the lamb with its marinade and the 2 cups water. Bring to a boil, reduce the heat, and simmer, covered, until the lamb is tender, about 1 hour, or until the lamb starts to fall apart. Add more water if necessary.

✿ *Curried Sausages*

Serves: 3

Except in large cities, sausages are rarely eaten in India. But in Goa, a former Portuguese colony, pork sausages are very popular. Arthur has added his own touches to the following dish, which he has often cooked for his friends Anna and Anita in America. Salt is not needed, since both the soy sauce and sausages are heavily salted.

12 pork link sausages
2 cups water
1/2 cup olive oil
2 large onions, chopped
6 cloves garlic, peeled and minced
1 two-inch piece ginger, peeled and minced
1 teaspoon cayenne
1 teaspoon ground cumin
1 teaspoon ground coriander
1 tablespoon soy sauce
4 large tomatoes, cut into quarters
1 bell pepper, seeds and stem removed, diced
1/4 cup cilantro or mint leaves

Boil the sausages in a large skillet in the water for about 5 minutes. Drain, cut each in half, and set aside. Wipe the skillet dry.

In the same skillet, heat the olive oil over low heat for about 2 minutes, then add the onions and cook until they wilt, about 1 minute. Add the garlic, ginger, and dry powders, mix well, and cook for 2 minutes. Add the soy sauce, mix well, and cook for 1 minute. Add the tomatoes and cook for about 5 minutes. Add the sausages and the bell pepper, mix well, and cook for 5 minutes. Garnish with the cilantro or mint leaves.

🌸 Shikar Vindaloo

GOAN PORK CURRY

The tiny state of Goa, on the west coast, is known for its fiery pork dishes. This is one of the very few regions in India where pork is the most popular meat. One reason for this is that one third of Goa is Christian, and Christians are the only people in India who do not have religious taboos about food.

Soak the chiles in the 1/4 cup vinegar for 20 minutes. Roast the spices in a skillet for about a minute and then place them in a food processor or blender with the onion, garlic, ginger, red chiles in vinegar, 1/8 cup of the oil, cider vinegar, sugar (if using), and salt, and puree to a smooth paste.

In a large bowl, combine the meat and the spice paste and marinate, covered, overnight in the refrigerator.

Heat the remaining 3/8 cup oil in a large skillet. Remove the meat from the marinade, reserving the marinade. Add the meat to the skillet and fry over medium heat for 5 minutes. Add the marinade, mix well, add the bay or curry leaves, and cook over low heat for 20 minutes. Remove the bay or curry leaves before serving.

🌸 Dukor Ani Batate

PORK AND YAM CURRY

This curry is pure dynamite. In the coastal region around Mangalore, it is a traditional Sunday afternoon dish for the large Catholic population. People return home from Sunday morning Mass and pop open bottles of home-brewed liquor, while being tantalized by the aroma from the kitchen.

Serves: 4

4 fresh red chiles, such as serranos, seeds and stems removed
1/4 cup vinegar
3 tablespoons cumin seeds
2 tablespoons mustard seeds
1 teaspoon ground turmeric
1 teaspoon freshly ground black pepper
1/2 teaspoon ground cinnamon
1/2 teaspoon cardamom seeds
1/2 teaspoon ground cloves
Pinch ground nutmeg
1 large onion, chopped
12 cloves garlic, peeled
1 one-inch piece ginger, peeled
1/2 cup vegetable or olive oil
3/4 cup cider vinegar
1 tablespoon sugar (optional)
Salt to taste
2 pounds boneless pork, cut into 1-inch cubes
1/4 cup bay or curry leaves

Serves: 4

2 teaspoons whole black peppercorns
4 fresh red chiles, such as serranos, seeds and stems removed
4 green chiles, such as serranos, seeds and stems removed
1 teaspoon ground cumin or cumin seeds

In a food processor or blender, combine the peppercorns, red and green chiles, cumin, coriander, ginger, turmeric, garlic, cloves, cinnamon, and cardamom seeds, and puree to a fine paste.

Place the pork in a large skillet, add 2 cups of the water, stir in the paste, and cook, covered, over low heat for 20 minutes.

Add the yams or sweet potatoes, onions, bay or curry leaves, and the remaining 1 cup of water, and mix well. Cook, covered, for 15 minutes on low heat. Stir in the nutmeg and the vinegar. Simmer for 1 minute. Add the salt and remove the bay or curry leaves before serving.

1 teaspoon ground coriander or coriander seeds
1 three-inch piece ginger, peeled
1/2 teaspoon ground turmeric
2 cloves garlic, peeled
1 teaspoon whole cloves
2 one-inch pieces cinnamon
1 teaspoon cardamom seeds
2 pounds boneless pork, cut into 1-inch-thick pieces
3 cups water
1 pound yams or sweet potatoes (or substitute yucca or green bananas), peeled and diced
5 large onions, chopped
1/4 cup bay or curry leaves
Pinch of ground nutmeg
2 tablespoons white vinegar
Salt to taste

🌸 Koli Kochupu

DRY CHICKEN WITH COCONUT

This spicy chicken is from Karnataka, and its heat is tempered by fresh, creamy coconut. Arthur often makes this dish with fresh coconut, since coconuts are easily available in large supermarkets. But unsweetened shredded coconut can be substituted.

In a food processor or blender, grind the chiles, peppercorns, cloves, turmeric, the coriander, cumin, and fenugreek seeds, and garlic into a smooth paste. Set aside.

Heat the oil in a large skillet over medium heat for 1 minute, add the Ghee (if using) and the onions, lower the heat, and fry until the onions wilt, about 1 minute. Add the chicken and fry for 4 to 5 minutes. Add half of the paste, mix well, and continue cooking for 10 minutes. Add the rest of the paste and stir. Add the tomatoes and the coconut and cook over low heat for 5 minutes. Add the cardamom, nutmeg, and vinegar, and simmer for 2 minutes. Add the salt just before serving.

Serves: 4

2 fresh red chiles, such as serranos, seeds and stems removed
6 whole black or green peppercorns
1 teaspoon whole cloves
1/2 teaspoon ground turmeric
1 teaspoon coriander seeds
1 teaspoon cumin seeds
1 teaspoon fenugreek seeds
6 cloves garlic, peeled
2 tablespoons vegetable or olive oil
2 tablespoons Ghee (page 17) (optional)
6 large onions, sliced
2 pounds boneless chicken, cut into 1-inch pieces
4 large tomatoes, chopped
2 cups fresh or dried shredded coconut
1/2 teaspoon ground cardamom
Pinch ground nutmeg
1 teaspoon vinegar
Salt to taste

Serves: 4

1 lemon-size ball tamarind pulp
1 cup warm water
8 green chiles, such as jalapeños,
   seeds and stems removed, sliced
   into rings
1 cup chopped shallots
5 cloves garlic, peeled and minced
2 tablespoons finely chopped ginger
3 tablespoons vegetable oil
1 teaspoon cayenne
1 three-pound chicken, skinned,
   boned, and cut into 1 1/2-inch
   cubes
1 1/2 cups Coconut Milk (page
   19)
4 green New Mexican chiles,
   roasted and peeled, seeds and
   stems removed, chopped

❧ *Tamarind Chicken in White Curry Sauce*

White curries with a coconut milk base are the mildest of the Sri Lankan curries — but still are hot by American tastes.

Soak the tamarind in the 1 cup warm water for 15 minutes. Mash the tamarind and then strain. Discard the pulp and reserve the liquid (see Note).

In a skillet, sauté the chile rings, shallots, garlic, and ginger in the oil until soft. Stir in the cayenne and the chicken and mix well. Add the Coconut Milk and bring to a boil. Reduce the heat and simmer, covered, stirring occasionally, for 20 minutes. Add the chopped chiles and cook for an additional 5 minutes. Stir in the tamarind liquid and cook, uncovered, for 10 minutes or until the sauce is thickened, stirring occasionally.

Note: 2 teaspoons freshly squeezed lime juice can be substituted for the tamarind liquid.

Serves: 4

2 pounds cod, tilefish, or mackerel,
   cut into 1-inch-thick pieces
1/2 teaspoon ground turmeric
1 lemon-size ball tamarind pulp
1 cup warm water
1/4 cup vegetable or olive oil
2 large onions, chopped
8 tomatoes, quartered
1 teaspoon ground coriander
1 teaspoon ground cumin
1 green chile, such as serrano,
   seeds and stem removed,
   chopped
1 cup water
1 cup fresh or dried shredded coconut

❧ *Meenu Kootu*

FISH CURRY FROM SRI LANKA

The cuisine of the Tamils in Sri Lanka is heavily influenced by that of the Tamils in India. This curry is tangy, hot, and delicious.

Rub the fish pieces with the turmeric. Soak the tamarind in the warm water for 15 minutes, squeeze the pulp, and pour the liquid over the fish (see Note).

Heat the oil in a large skillet over medium heat for 1 minute, add the onions, and fry until they wilt, about 1 minute.

Add the tomatoes, coriander, cumin, and chile. Lower the heat and simmer, covered, for 10 minutes. Add the 1 cup water and stir in the coconut.

Add the eggplant and cook, covered, for 12 minutes over medium heat.

Gently add the fish, cover, and cook for 3 minutes before serving. Add salt to taste.

Note: 2 teaspoons freshly squeezed lime juice can be substituted for the tamarind liquid. If using the lime juice, rub it over the fish after you've rubbed on the turmeric.

1 eggplant, peeled and cubed
Salt to taste

 # *Bajjali Masli Bafat*

FRIED FISH CURRY

This is one of the signature fish curries from the coast of Karnataka. It is popular during the monsoon season because it warms up the body. The most popular fish used is kingfish, a large variety of mackerel that is not commonly available in the United States.

In a food processor or blender, grind the chiles, cumin and coriander seeds, ginger, and the 2 large onions to a smooth paste.

Heat the oil in a deep frying pan over medium heat. Add the mustard seeds after 2 minutes; when the seeds begin to pop, reduce the heat and add the garlic and sliced onion. Cook until the onion wilts, about 1 minute.

Slightly increase the heat and add the fish, 4 steaks at a time, and fry for 2 to 3 minutes, turning once. Remove and drain on paper towels. Repeat until all the fish steaks are cooked.

Meanwhile, pour the Coconut Milk into a large skillet and stir in the curry paste, turmeric, and vinegar; mix well and cook over low heat for about 3 minutes.

Add the fried fish and simmer, uncovered, for 5 minutes. Add salt to taste.

Serve hot, garnished with the cilantro or mint leaves.

Serves: 6 (2 quarter-pound steaks each)

4 fresh red chiles, such as serranos, seeds and stems removed
1 green chile, such as serrano, seeds and stem removed
1 teaspoon cumin seeds
1 teaspoon coriander seeds
1 one-inch piece ginger, peeled
2 large onions, chopped
4 cups vegetable or olive oil
1 teaspoon mustard seeds
4 cloves garlic, peeled and minced
1 medium onion, sliced
12 mackerel steaks (or substitute salmon or tuna) (3 pounds fish)
4 cups Coconut Milk (page 19)
1 teaspoon ground turmeric
1 teaspoon vinegar
Salt to taste
1/2 cup cilantro or mint leaves for garnish

Seafood Combo Curry

6 lemon-size balls tamarind pulp
3 cups warm water
Water
12 cherrystone clams
5 pounds mussels
1 teaspoon fenugreek seeds
1 teaspoon whole peppercorns
1 teaspoon coriander seeds
1 teaspoon cumin seeds
4 large tomatoes, chopped
1/4 cup olive oil
1 teaspoon mustard seeds
1 teaspoon Ghee (page 17)
   (optional)
1/4 cup cilantro or mint leaves
1 large onion, chopped
6 cloves garlic, peeled and minced
1 two-inch piece ginger, peeled and
   minced
2 cups water
1 teaspoon paprika
1 teaspoon cayenne
1/2 teaspoon ground turmeric
Salt to taste
2 green chiles, such as serranos,
   seeds and stems removed, finely
   minced
1/2 teaspoon ground cardamom
2 pounds large uncooked shrimp,
   shelled and deveined
5 cups Coconut Milk (page 19)
1 pound roe (shad or any other
   fish), chopped fine

This is another dish that Arthur and his wife, Betty, have devised, taking inspiration from their southwest Indian culinary roots. They have prepared this for their special guests who love seafood. It is one of the most fragrant and colorful dishes in their repertoire.

Soak the tamarind in the 3 cups warm water for 20 minutes, then squeeze the pulp, discard, and reserve the liquid (see Note).

Soak the clams in 5 cups cold water for 15 minutes. Rinse well and set aside.

Scrape the mussels, cover them with cold water, soak for 10 minutes, and rinse well. Bring 10 cups of hot water to a boil and add the mussels. After a few minutes, the good mussels will open up. Remove the opened ones from the pot, let cool, and remove the flesh from the shells. Set aside. (Some people like to leave the shells on and use a larger skillet for the remainder of the recipe.)

Heat a small frying pan and roast the fenugreek seeds, peppercorns, and coriander and cumin seeds for 1 minute. Remove from the heat and grind in a food processor or blender with the tomatoes until a smooth paste is obtained.

Heat the oil in a large skillet over medium heat for 2 minutes and add the mustard seeds. As soon as the mustard seeds begin to pop, stir in the Ghee (if using) and add the cilantro or mint leaves. Stir a few times and add the onion, garlic, and ginger, and fry until the mixture is lightly browned.

Add the 2 cups water, paprika, cayenne, turmeric, salt, chiles, fenugreek paste, cardamom, and tamarind liquid. Heat to a boil, stirring constantly. Reduce the heat and simmer for 5 minutes.

Add the mussels and stir well. Two minutes later, add the shrimp and cherrystone clams, mix well, and cook over low heat for 5 minutes. Throw away the clams that don't open.

Add the Coconut Milk and mix gently but thoroughly. Add the roe. Cook, covered, over low heat for 10 minutes before serving.

Note: 1/4 cup freshly squeezed lime juice can be substituted for the tamarind liquid.

🌸 *Erachi Kootu*

Serves: 6

SHRIMP AND EGGPLANT CURRY

The small state of Kerala on India's southwest coast offers a tremendous variety of seafood, meat, and vegetable dishes. Kerala's cuisine reflects its religious diversity. The recipe below is one of the most popular dishes not only in Kerala but also across the southwestern coast.

Sprinkle a little salt and the turmeric on the shrimp and set aside.

In a food processor or blender, make a smooth paste of the chiles, peppercorns, coriander and cumin seeds, and ginger.

In a large skillet, heat 1 tablespoon of the Ghee over low heat for 1 minute, add the shredded coconut, and fry for 2 minutes. Set aside.

Wipe the skillet dry and heat the rest of the Ghee for 2 minutes. Add the onion and the garlic and fry for 2 minutes. Add the tomatoes and cook for 2 minutes. Add the eggplant and the Coconut Milk to the skillet. Mix well and cook, covered, over low heat for 15 minutes.

Add the shrimp, mix well, and cook for 8 minutes over low heat. Add the salt.

Garnish with the fried coconut and the cilantro leaves. Sprinkle with the lime juice just before serving.

Salt to taste
1 teaspoon ground turmeric
1 pound uncooked large shrimp, shelled and deveined
4 fresh red chiles, such as serranos, seeds and stems removed
1 tablespoon whole peppercorns
1 tablespoon coriander seeds
2 tablespoons cumin seeds
1 two-inch piece ginger, peeled
4 tablespoons Ghee (page 17)
4 tablespoons freshly shredded coconut
1 large onion, sliced
4 cloves garlic, peeled and minced
2 large tomatoes, chopped
1 medium eggplant, peeled and cubed
4 cups Coconut Milk (page 19)
Salt to taste
1/2 cup cilantro leaves
1/4 cup freshly squeezed lime juice

Shrimp and Crab Curry

Serves: 4

2 tablespoons vegetable or olive oil
2 large onions, chopped
6 cloves garlic, peeled and minced
2 tablespoons Bafat (page 40)
4 large tomatoes, chopped
2 cups Coconut Milk (page 19)
16 large uncooked shrimp, shelled and deveined
1 cup fresh or canned crabmeat
1/2 teaspoon ground turmeric
1 teaspoon rice vinegar
1/4 cup bay or curry leaves
Salt to taste

This is one of the most popular dishes found along the southwest coast of India. It is cooked only on special occasions, because shrimp and crab are very expensive.

Heat the oil in a large skillet for 2 minutes over medium heat. Add the onions and the garlic and fry over low heat for 1 minute.

Add the *Bafat*, stir well, and fry for 2 minutes. Add the tomatoes and the Coconut Milk and cook over medium heat for 8 minutes.

Add the shrimp, crabmeat, turmeric, vinegar, and bay or curry leaves, and cook for 15 minutes. Add salt to taste. Remove the bay or curry leaves before serving.

Tantiychi Kadi

Serves: 4

2 tablespoons vegetable or olive oil
1 large onion, chopped
1 large tomato, chopped
2 teaspoons cayenne
1/2 teaspoon ground cardamom
1/2 teaspoon ground turmeric
6 cloves garlic, peeled and minced
1 one-inch piece ginger, peeled and finely minced
4 cups Coconut Milk (page 19)
2 cups frozen lima beans
1 cup unsalted, unsweetened cashews, preferably raw
1 cube beef bouillon (optional)
8 hard-boiled eggs, halved
Salt to taste

For Garnish:
1/2 cup cilantro leaves
10 black olives, pitted
10 green olives, pitted

EGG CURRY WITH CASHEWS

Here is an easy-to-prepare dish that is aromatic, rich, and filling. Arthur has made it for many of his American friends. It is served in a shallow dish to show off the yellow of the eggs. The yellow, green, and black colors make this one of the most visually pleasing of Indian dishes.

In a large skillet, heat the oil over low heat for 1 minute and fry the onion until it wilts, about 1 minute. Add the tomato, cayenne, cardamom, turmeric, garlic, and ginger, and cook over medium heat for 3 minutes. Add the Coconut Milk, lower the heat, stir well, and simmer for 3 minutes. Add the lima beans and the cashews and cook over medium heat for about 10 minutes. Stir occasionally and add a little water if necessary. Add the bouillon cube (if using) and cook for 2 minutes.

Add the eggs and gently stir the curry. Simmer for 1 minute and then add the salt.

Serve hot, garnished with the cilantro leaves and the olives.

🌸 *Ambyachi Kadi*

MANGO CURRY

Serves: 4

The coastal city of Mangalore, where Arthur grew up, is known for its hearty fish and meat dishes. The region is abundant in cashews and mangoes, which are often curried.

In a food processor or blender, make a smooth paste of the garlic, ginger, peppercorns, Coconut Milk, and red and green chiles. Set aside.

In a large skillet, heat the oil over medium heat for 2 minutes. Add the mustard seeds. When the seeds begin popping, lower the heat, add the Ghee (if using), and cook for 1 minute. Add the paste, mango pulp, sugar (if using), and turmeric. Stir well and cook for 5 minutes. Add the salt just before serving.

6 cloves garlic, peeled
1 two-inch piece ginger, peeled
4 whole black peppercorns
1 cup Coconut Milk (page 19)
4 small fresh red chiles, such as serranos, seeds and stems removed
2 small green chiles, such as serranos, seeds and stems removed
1 tablespoon vegetable or olive oil
1 teaspoon mustard seeds
2 tablespoons Ghee (page 17) (optional)
12 ripe mangoes, skins and seeds removed
4 tablespoons sugar (optional)
1 teaspoon ground turmeric
Salt to taste

🌸 *Tomato Palya*

TOMATO CURRY

Serves: 4

A popular dish across the southern Indian coastal state of Karnataka, this curry is eaten at breakfast with breads and as a side dish with meat curries.

In a skillet, heat the oil over medium heat for 1 minute, then add the mustard seeds. When they begin to pop, add the onion and cook for 1 minute. Add the garlic and fry for 1 minute.

Stir in the cumin, black pepper, coriander, and turmeric; mix well and fry for 1 minute. Add the tomatoes, mix well, and cook, covered, for 10 minutes over low heat. Add the peas, mix well, and cook for 5 minutes.

Add the ginger, chile, and salt. Mix well and simmer for 3 minutes.

2 tablespoons vegetable or olive oil
1 teaspoon mustard seeds
1 large onion, chopped
6 cloves garlic, peeled and minced
1 teaspoon ground cumin
1 teaspoon freshly ground black pepper
1 teaspoon ground coriander
1/2 teaspoon ground turmeric
8 tomatoes, sliced
1 cup fresh peas
1 one-inch piece ginger, peeled and crushed
1 green chile, such as serrano, seeds and stem removed, finely chopped
Salt to taste

🌸 *Pineapple Kalan*

PINEAPPLE CURRY

Serves: 4

1 cup freshly shredded coconut
4 fresh red chiles, such as serranos, seeds and stems removed
4 green chiles, such as serranos, seeds and stems removed
1 teaspoon cumin seeds
1/4 teaspoon mustard seeds
1/4 teaspoon fenugreek seeds
1 large pineapple, peeled, cored, and diced
1/2 teaspoon ground turmeric
1 cup water
1 cup plain yogurt
1/4 cup curry or bay leaves
1 pound large uncooked shrimp, shelled and deveined (optional)
2 tablespoons Ghee (page 17)
1/4 teaspoon mustard seeds
1 fresh red chile, such as serrano, seeds and stem removed, halved
1 small onion, chopped
Salt to taste

This is a hot and sweet dish from Kerala. Arthur has prepared the traditional version, which is given below; on some occasions, he has added 1 pound of raw shrimp to the dish and cooked it for an extra 6 to 8 minutes.

In a food processor or blender, grind the coconut, red and green chiles, and the cumin, mustard, and fenugreek seeds into a paste. Set aside.

In a medium-size skillet, place the pineapple, turmeric, and 1/2 cup of the water. Cover and cook for 6 to 8 minutes.

Put the yogurt in a blender, add the other 1/2 cup water, and make a smooth mixture. Add this to the pineapple along with the spice paste and the curry or bay leaves and cook, covered, over low heat for 3 minutes. Add the shrimp (if using) and cook for 6 to 8 more minutes.

Heat the Ghee in a skillet over low heat for 2 minutes and add the mustard seeds, chile, and onion. Fry for 1 minute, then pour into the curry, add the salt, and serve.

🌸 *Keere Kootu*

SPINACH CURRY

Serves: 4

1 pound fresh spinach leaves or 2 ten-ounce packages frozen spinach leaves
2 teaspoons vegetable or olive oil
2 large onions, chopped
1 one-inch piece ginger, peeled and minced
6 cloves garlic, peeled and minced
1 teaspoon ground cumin
1 teaspoon ground coriander
1/2 teaspoon ground turmeric
4 large tomatoes, sliced
2 green chiles, such as serranos, seeds and stems removed, finely chopped
Salt to taste

Spinach is a year-round favorite across India. This recipe, from the state of Tamil Nadu in southern India, is usually made with fresh spinach, but frozen spinach also works well. For those who grew up hating soupy canned spinach, we recommend the dish — it will change your mind.

Wash the spinach leaves and dry them. If using the frozen spinach, let thaw.

In a skillet, heat the oil over medium heat for 1 minute, add the onions, and fry them until they wilt, about 1 minute.

54

Stir in the ginger and the garlic and cook for 1 minute. Add the ground spices, mix well, and simmer for 1 minute.

Add the tomatoes and the chiles and cook, covered, over low heat for 10 minutes. Gently add the spinach leaves, mix well, and cook, covered, for 2 minutes. Add the salt just before serving.

Batate Palya

POTATO CURRY WITH LIMA BEANS

Use this pungent curry to spice up a breakfast or to accompany the main meal. This simple dish from the Mangalore region in southwestern India makes a colorful, tasty addition to any meal.

In a skillet, heat the oil over medium heat for 1 minute, add the onions, and fry them for about 1 minute. Add the garlic and the ginger and continuing frying for 1 minute.

Add the ground spices, mix well, and then add the potatoes and the tomatoes, along with the water, and cook, covered, for 12 minutes. Add the lima beans, mix well, and cook for 5 minutes. Just before serving, add the salt and garnish with the cilantro leaves.

1 tablespoon vegetable or olive oil
3 large onions, chopped
4 cloves garlic, peeled and minced
1 one-inch piece ginger, peeled and minced
1 teaspoon ground cumin
1 teaspoon ground coriander
1 teaspoon cayenne
1/4 teaspoon freshly ground black pepper
1/2 teaspoon ground turmeric
6 large potatoes, peeled and diced
4 large tomatoes, sliced
1/2 cup water
2 cups frozen lima beans
Salt to taste
1/2 cup cilantro leaves for garnish

Serves: 6

2 large eggplants, skin on, cut into
   1-inch cubes
Salt to taste
1 teaspoon ground turmeric
4 tablespoons vegetable oil
1 teaspoon Ghee (page 17)
   (optional)
1/4 cup sliced lemongrass, including the bulbs
1/2 teaspoon fennel seeds
1/2 teaspoon fenugreek seeds
1 cup freshly shredded coconut
4 cloves garlic, peeled and minced
1 teaspoon coriander seeds
1 teaspoon cumin seeds
3 fresh red chiles, such as serranos, seeds and stems removed
1 two-inch piece cinnamon,
   crushed
1 tablespoon vegetable or olive oil
1 cup Coconut Milk (page 19)
Dash salt
1 tablespoon sugar

🌸 Brinjal Pohie

EGGPLANT CURRY

*Here is another popular Sri Lankan dish that has traveled well
beyond Sri Lanka. Ask anyone who has eaten with a Sinhalese
family in America or Britain, and this curry is bound to be mentioned.*

Toss the eggplant cubes in the salt and the turmeric.

Heat the oil in a large skillet for 1 minute, add the Ghee (if
using), and fry the eggplant over medium heat for about 10
minutes. Set aside.

In a large skillet, roast the lemongrass, fennel and fenugreek
seeds, coconut, garlic, coriander and cumin seeds, chiles, and
cinnamon for about 3 minutes. When these ingredients cool,
put them in a blender and make a smooth paste, adding a bit
of water.

Wipe the skillet dry and, over medium heat, heat the oil for
2 minutes. Add the spice paste, mix well, and lower the heat.
Add the Coconut Milk, salt, and sugar; mix well and simmer
for 2 minutes.

Add the fried eggplant, mix gently, and cook for 5 minutes
before serving.

❧ *Moru Kolambu*

VEGETABLES IN YOGURT

This dish is a favorite among the vegetarian people of Kerala and Tamil Nadu, the two southernmost states of India. Arthur has served it along with a meal consisting of rice, meat, and fish dishes from other parts of India.

In a food processor or blender, combine the yogurt and the 2 cups water and blend into a smooth mixture. Set aside.

Clean the food processor or blender and make a smooth paste of the Coconut Milk, cumin seeds, ginger, red chiles, and asafoetida. Set aside.

Cook the potatoes and the yams or sweet potatoes in the 6 cups water in a large pot over medium heat for 8 minutes. Add the turmeric, green beans, cauliflower, carrots, lima beans, and the coconut-spice paste from the food processor or blender. Mix well and cook over low heat for 8 minutes. Add the yogurt mixture and bring the dish slowly to a boil. Remove the dish from the heat.

In a frying pan, heat the oil over medium heat for 2 minutes, add the mustard seeds, and when they begin to pop, add the *urad dal*, curry or bay leaves, and green chiles. Add the chopped tomatoes and fry for 1 minute. Add this mixture to the vegetables and stir. Add salt to taste.

5 cups plain yogurt
2 cups water
2 cups Coconut Milk (page 19)
1 tablespoon cumin seeds
1 one-inch piece ginger, peeled
4 fresh red chiles, such as serra-nos, seeds and stems removed
1/4 teaspoon asafoetida
2 cups potatoes, cubed
4 cups yams or sweet potatoes, peeled and cubed
6 cups water
1/2 teaspoon ground turmeric
2 cups green beans, cut into 1-inch lengths
2 cups cauliflower, separated into florets
2 cups carrots, peeled and chopped
2 cups cooked lima beans
2 tablespoons vegetable oil
1 teaspoon mustard seeds
1 teaspoon urad dal (white split gram beans, available in Asian markets)
1/4 cup curry or bay leaves
4 green chiles, such as serranos, seeds and stems removed, halved
2 large ripe tomatoes, chopped
Salt to taste

1 cup moong dal *(greengram, available in Asian markets)*
4 cups water
2 green chiles, such as serranos, *seeds and stems removed, finely minced*
4 curry leaves or *1/4 cup cilantro leaves*
1 cup uncooked rice
1 tablespoon vegetable oil
6 red onions, sliced
2 cups Coconut Milk *(page 19)*
1 teaspoon Ceylon Dark Curry Powder *(page 41)*
Salt to taste

✿ *Colombo Mungatta Kiribath*

COLOMBO'S GREENGRAM MILK RICE

A favorite dish among the Buddhists in Sri Lanka, it is popular around Colombo.

Soak the *moong dal* in 2 cups of the water for about 2 hours. Transfer the mixture to a saucepan and cook the *moong dal*, covered, over low heat for about 10 minutes. Add a little water if needed. Add the chiles and half of the curry or cilantro leaves, remove from the heat, and set aside.

In a saucepan, boil the remaining 2 cups water, lower the heat, and add the rice. Mix well and cook, covered, for 12 minutes. Remove from the heat and set aside.

In a large skillet, heat the oil over medium heat, lower the heat, and fry the onions until they wilt, about 2 minutes, stirring occasionally.

Add the rice and the *moong dal* to the skillet and mix well; add the Coconut Milk, stir gently, and cook, covered, for about 3 minutes. Add the Ceylon Dark Curry Powder, mix well, and add the remaining curry or cilantro leaves and the salt.

Serve with a meat or fish dish, a pickle, and a chutney.

🌸 *Vangi Bhat*

EGGPLANT RICE

Tamil Nadu, in India's southeast, is renowned for its vegetarian dishes. The Tamils are great rice eaters, and the grain is ever present in different guises at breakfast, lunch, and dinner.

In a food processor or blender, grind the chiles, coriander, asafoetida, cinnamon, and cardamom into a paste. Set aside.

In a saucepan, boil the 2 cups water; add the rice, mix well, lower the heat, and cook, covered, for 12 minutes. Remove from the heat and set aside.

In a large saucepan, heat the Ghee or oil over medium heat for 1 minute. Add the mustard seeds and, when they begin to pop, lower the heat, add the *dals*, and cook for 1 minute. Add the eggplant, 2 cups water, and spice paste. Mix well and cook, covered, for 10 minutes over medium heat, stirring occasionally.

Add the rice, cashews, almonds, and coconut, mix well, and cook, uncovered, for 3 to 5 minutes over medium heat. Sprinkle a little water over the dish if it becomes too dry. Add the salt and top with the cilantro or mint leaves before serving.

2 fresh red chiles, such as serranos, seeds and stems removed
2 tablespoons ground coriander
1/4 teaspoon asafoetida
1/2 teaspoon ground cinnamon
1 teaspoon ground cardamom
2 cups water
1 cup long-grain rice
6 tablespoons Ghee (page 17) or olive oil
1 teaspoon mustard seeds
2 tablespoons urad dal *(white split gram beans, available in Asian markets)*
2 tablespoons chana dal *(dried split chickpeas, available in Asian markets)*
1 large eggplant, peeled and cubed
2 cups water
1/2 cup chopped cashews, preferably raw
1/2 cup slivered almonds
1 cup freshly shredded coconut
Salt to taste
1/2 cup cilantro or mint leaves for garnish

2 cups uncooked rice soaked overnight in 4 cups water
2 cups urad dal (*white split gram
   beans, available in Asian markets*) and 1 teaspoon fenugreek
   seeds, soaked overnight in 2 cups
   water
1 teaspoon baking soda
1/2 cup water
2 tablespoons vegetable oil
1 teaspoon mustard seeds
3 medium onions, finely chopped
2 large tomatoes, chopped
8 medium potatoes, peeled, boiled,
   and mashed
1 green chile, such as serrano,
   seeds and stem removed, finely
   chopped
1/4 teaspoon ground turmeric
Salt to taste
4 tablespoons Ghee (page 17)
6 bay or curry leaves
1/2 cup vegetable oil for frying

🌸 Arthur's Masala Dosai

PANCAKE WITH STUFFING

The masala dosai, *which originated in Madras, has become one
of India's most popular dishes in the past two decades. It is eaten
as a breakfast snack, a meal in the afternoon, or a snack in the
evening. It is always served with a chutney and a soupy dish
called* Sambhar *(facing page). Hot coffee or tea accompanies the*
dosai. *Traditionally, this pancake is served with a potato, but
Arthur has served it for many years with his favorite meat dish,*
Gaychi Indad *(page 43). A shortcut: Asian markets and Indian
grocery stores in large cities carry a* dosa *mix,* sambhar *mix, and
ready-to-use chutneys.*

Drain the rice that has soaked overnight and save 1/2 cup of
the soaking water. Grind the rice in a blender and add the
water to facilitate the blending.

Take the *urad dal* and the fenugreek seeds that have soaked
overnight, along with the soaking water, and grind together in
a blender.

In a bowl, mix the rice and *urad dal* pastes, add the baking
soda and 1/2 cup water, and keep in a warm place for 6
hours. Stir the batter once every 2 hours.

In a large skillet, heat the 2 tablespoons oil until it begins to
smoke. Add the mustard seeds and, when the seeds pop, add
the onions and fry until they wilt, about 1 minute. Add the
tomatoes, potatoes, chile, turmeric, and salt, and cook, uncovered, for 10 minutes. Stir in the Ghee and the bay or curry
leaves. Set aside.

Grease a medium-size frying pan with some of the vegetable oil. Pour in 3/4 cup batter and, with a wooden spoon,
spread the batter in the pan. Cover and cook for 1 minute.
Flip the pancake and cook for about 1 minute. Remove the
pancake and fill it with about 4 tablespoons of the vegetable
stuffing. Fold the *dosa* over the stuffing and keep it warm in a
serving dish. Repeat the process until all the batter and stuffing are used, taking care to regrease the skillet each time.

 **Sambhar**

This soupy South Indian vegetable dish can be served with rice or any unleavened bread. Serve it with Arthur's Masala Dosai (preceding recipe) or as a side dish with any other curry in this book.

1 cup fresh or frozen green peas
2 cups water
1 lime-size ball tamarind pulp
1/2 cup warm water
4 fresh red chiles, such as serranos, seeds and stems removed
6 whole peppercorns
1/2 teaspoon fenugreek seeds
1/2 teaspoon cumin seeds
1/4 teaspoon asafoetida
1 cup toovar dal (yellow split peas, available in Asian markets)
2 cups water
1/2 teaspoon ground turmeric
Salt to taste
1 tablespoon vegetable oil
1 teaspoon mustard seeds
2 large onions, finely chopped
6 curry or bay leaves

Boil the green peas in the 2 cups water for 15 minutes. Drain and reserve.

Soak the tamarind in the 1/2 cup warm water for 10 minutes, squeeze the pulp, discard, and save the liquid (see Note).

In a large skillet, roast the chiles, peppercorns, fenugreek and cumin seeds, and asafoetida on low heat for 3 minutes. Let cool. Place in a food processor or blender and make a smooth powder. Set aside.

Soak the *toovar dal* in the 2 cups water for 15 minutes and then boil the mixture for 8 minutes with the turmeric and the salt. Remove from the heat and reserve.

In a skillet, heat the oil for 2 minutes and add the mustard seeds. When they begin to pop, lower the heat, add the onions, and fry until they wilt, about 1 minute. Add the powdered spices, *toovar dal*, tamarind liquid, and green peas, and simmer for 10 minutes. Add the curry or bay leaves, let simmer for 1 minute, and remove just before serving.

Note: 1 teaspoon freshly squeezed lime juice can be substituted for the tamarind liquid.

THREE

The Migration of Curries

Foods having a bitter,

acidic, saltish, hot,

pungent, and piquant

burning taste are liked by

those hankering after

worldly pleasures,

epicureans included.

BHAGAVAD GITA

*C*urries have never stayed in one place. As a natural result of trade, migration, and foreign invasions, they first spread through India and then into neighboring countries. As they moved, changes in ingredients and methods of cooking were inevitable.

Moghuls and the British Raj

From the eighth through the sixteenth centuries A.D., India was subjected to a series of Muslim invasions. Turkish tribes swept through India from the west, and the Moghuls invaded from the northwest and settled across most of northern India. There were periodic Muslim kingdoms established in northern India, but not until 1526 did Babur, a descendant of Genghis Khan, conquer the Punjab and declare himself emperor of India. So began the Moghul rule of India, which lasted until the beginning of the nineteenth century.

During the sixteenth century, land routes across India began to connect the spice-growing south with northern India, Central Asia, Afghanistan, Tibet, and Bhutan. During the rule of Akbar (1556–1605), the greatest of the Moghul emperors, the cultivation of spices was encouraged all over India, and especially in Punjab, where mustard, ginger, poppy seed, sesame, turmeric, coriander, cumin, and chile peppers were grown. Interestingly enough, despite the fact that Portuguese missionaries attended Akbar's court in Delhi, the Moghuls hardly knew of the Europeans' lucrative spice trade along the Malabar Coast.

The Moghuls not only constructed some of the most beautiful buildings in the subcontinent — including the Taj Mahal — they were also great patrons of musicians, artists, and cooks. Feasts in the Moghul courts included classical music of the time, great storytelling sessions, and food fit for — well, emperors.

Akbar's prime minster, Abul-Fazl, in his book *Ain-i-Akbari* (1602), compiled a list of numerous dishes and the curry spices used in them; the book is notable for containing the first mention of chile peppers in Indian cookery. One of the favorite dishes of Akbar's court was a Mughlai curry called *do-piyaza*, or two

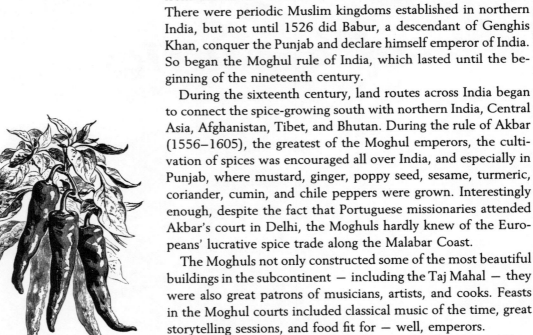

After 1500, chiles became the dominant pungency in Indian curries.

A WORLD OF CURRIES

Transport carts carrying food and spices, Pakistan.

onions, which combined 4 pounds of onions with 20 pounds of meat, seasoned with crushed red chiles, cumin, coriander, cardamom, cloves, and black pepper.

In an interesting section of his book, Abul-Fazl recorded the market rates of the various spices; from most to least expensive, they were saffron, cloves, cardamom, cinnamon, chiles, black pepper, turmeric, dried ginger, coriander, aniseed, fresh ginger, and cumin. Saffron was two hundred times more expensive than cumin. Today, saffron is still the most expensive spice in the world.

Meanwhile, farther south, the British had watched with envy as both the Portuguese and the Dutch were growing rich from the spice trade in India and the Moluccas, or the Spice Islands. The British East India Company was founded in London in 1600, with Queen Elizabeth I of England granting the company the sole British right to trade with India. The first Company ship, the *Hector*, arrived in India in 1608, landing at Surat, north of Bombay. The captain of the *Hector*, William Hawkins, searched the interior for jewels and spices and was greeted at the Moghul court by the emperor Jahangir, probably the world's most powerful and wealthy ruler. Jahangir promptly made Hawkins a member of his court and presented him with the most beautiful woman in his harem. He also eventually signed a trade agreement with the East India Company, which allowed the Company to establish trading depots near Bombay. The British had finally established a toehold in India, and by 1640 they had trading centers on both coasts.

By 1664, the Dutch had driven the Portuguese out of the Malabar Coast, and they competed with the British in buying spices and selling them in Europe. The Dutch attempted to monopolize the spice trade but were unable to compete successfully with the British and were forced to abandon their Indian interests by the end of the eighteenth century, when they concentrated on their holdings in the Spice Islands (see chapter 5 for that story).

The British influence in India grew stronger after the Dutch left. As early as 1694, the British had established their main pepper factory at Tellicherry because of its "proximity to the finest pepper and cardamom lands of the Malabar," as the Company stated. Around 1740, the East India Company undertook the creation of large pepper, coconut, and cinnamon plantations. Although the Company's motto was Trade, Not Territory, the unstable political situation in India caused the Company to extend its political influence. But it was not unopposed.

As soon as Siraj-ud-daula took the throne of the Moghul empire in 1756, he marched his troops to Calcutta and captured Fort William from the British. That victory led to the imprisonment of British soldiers in a tiny cell — the infamous "Black Hole of Calcutta" — in which supposedly all but twenty-three of the 150 prisoners died. The numbers vary from source to source, but the horrible suffering of the soldiers inspired generations of Englishmen with a desire to "civilize" India.

The British struck back in 1757 under the leadership of Robert Clive. With an army of about three thousand men, he regained Calcutta, soundly defeated the Moghul forces of fifty thousand, and — in effect — became the king of Bengal. So began the British control and plunder of India.

By 1800, the Company had taken the Malabar Coast by force

and also controlled Bengal and Madurai. The British established "Spice Gardens" in what is now Tamil Nadu, in South India, to encourage the cultivation of cinnamon and nutmeg in a more scientific manner. They also introduced the production of cloves into India.

During this time, the British government realized the enormous potential for wealth in India and, disturbed by the abuses and plundering of the East India Company, took control of India. In 1818, the British empire of India was established, and by 1833 the East India Company had lost its monopoly over trade in India. The British would control India until its partition, in 1947.

Englishmen and Englishwomen who were stationed in India in the early days of the Raj had no choice but to eat native foods because of the difficulty of obtaining British imports. Jennifer Brennan, the author of *Curries and Bugles*, notes that

the cooks were talented, mostly. Goanese, Nepalese, Madrassi or Bengali, they had served long apprenticeships with a variety of families and were well used to the idiosyncrasies of British tastes. [They] all could, naturally, produce a wide range of Indian food, accented by the regional tastes of their home provinces.

Many of those regional tastes were curries. "If any of my readers desire to make a real, good, Indian curry, get a Mohammedan woman to make one for you," advised Harriet Tytler in her nineteenth-century memoir, *An Englishwoman in India*. She added: "Only warn her not to make it too hot, for the English traveler does not consider it good manners to weep over his meals, especially after just giving thanks for what one is about to receive."

Tytler also complained that the curries of her later days in India (around 1858) were deteriorating as compared with the ones thirty years earlier, when they were eaten three times a day. "Most assuredly, curries are no more the curries of former days either; there were at least a dozen different kinds then. It is no longer the fashion to eat curry at dinner in India; it is now purely a breakfast dish, and no Indian chef deigns to know of any variety." We suspect that Ms. Tytler had somehow managed to hire some untalented cooks.

The British may have looted India to a great extent, but they also did some good, since India has become the largest producer of spices in the world. After satisfying the spice demand at home, it not only leads the world in chile production, it accounts for 20 percent of the world's black pepper, 50 percent of its dried ginger, and 90 percent of its cardamom, plus copious amounts of turmeric, saffron, cumin, cloves, fenugreek, cinnamon, and fennel.

The British, of course, brought Indian food customs back with them to England and spread them throughout the Commonwealth. That story is told in chapter 7.

No National Dish Here

Americans who have eaten Indian food in restaurants often stun an Indian when they ask: "What is the national dish of India?" That's like asking an Italian: "What is the national dish of Europe?"

For India is like Europe multiplied several times. It is a culture with five thousand years of history whose civilization has been constantly altered by outsiders. India's people profess more than six religions and speak fifteen national languages and more than 250 dialects. A country so diverse cannot possibly have a national dish. Likewise for Pakistan; it has six national languages and more than a hundred dialects. Bangladesh, however, is another story. Predominantly composed of Bengali-speaking Muslims, it is a country that loves fish, and half a dozen fish dishes vie for the honor of a national title.

But forget a national dish for India. The country is so varied that there is no such thing as a signature dish even in its smallest state. Throughout the country, spice combinations, diets, and food habits vary from district to district, town to town, and village to village.

A joke in India goes that when two Indians meet there are three opinions, four temples, five cuisines, and six different desserts. And since Hindus have more than thirty million gods and goddesses in their pantheon, the joke continues, there must be as many curry combinations, too.

Curries of the North, West, and East

Curries in northern India and the neighboring countries tend to be drier and milder in heat than their counterparts in the south of the country. This cuisine favors yogurt over the coconut of the southern states. Also, in the curries of Pakistan there is a preponderance of nuts and dried fruits. And because these curries are fairly dry, diners use unleavened bread such as *Naan* (page 102) to scoop up the thick gravy. Other breads to accompany curries are a deep-fried bread from Punjab called *Bhatura* (page 101), *Chapatti* (page 103), and *Palak Paratha* (page 104), a spicy spinach bread.

The most famous curries of the north are the Moghlai curries, which are a subtle blend of Indian and Central Asian cuisines, and which are the heritage of the courts of the Moghul emperors.

Moghlai meat curries often feature lamb, as with *Sindhi Gosht* (page 79) with cashews and almonds, from the Sind region of Pakistan, and *Kichida* (page 83), an unusual dish of lamb curried with wheat and rice. Fried Spareribs with Potatoes (page 78) allows the cook to use lamb or beef. Chicken also makes an appearance in Moghlai cooking; it is curried with lime and cashews in *Nimbu Masala Murgh* (page 86).

Eggplant figures prominently in Moghlai curry cookery. We have two examples, eggplant curried with tamarind and coconut, *Baingan Mewaa Ke Saath* (page 98), and *Baingan Burtha* (page 98), smoked eggplant with a tomato curry.

The best Moghlai food is found in such cities as Karachi and Islamabad in Pakistan, and in New Delhi, Meerut, Agra, Lucknow, and Kanpur in India. Some of the finest food in these cities can be had near the mosques; the restaurants nearby are dingy and their hygiene leaves much to be desired, but the food is out of this world. Visitors to Lucknow enjoy its *sheekh kababs*, made with ground meat, and the *shami kababs*, with ground meat and lentils. Moghlai cooking is very well known for its mouthwatering *kababs*, and since many *kababs* use the key ingredients of a curry, we have included recipes for *kababs* with fruit and lamb, *Mewaii Kabab* (page 80), and *Bangri Kabab* with *Prantha* (page 77), which features potatoes and minced beef.

And then there are the *biryanis*, those rich and elaborately prepared rice treats flavored with curry spices. Two examples are our *Peshawari Biryani* (page 97) and Biryani (page 87). Although cooks in northern Indian and Pakistani cities specialize in rich, aromatic, and spicy *biryanis*, this dish can be found all over Pakistan and India. Indian cities such as Bombay, Hyderabad, and Bangalore have scores of restaurants where *biryanis* are lovingly prepared using beef, lamb, or chicken. There are many varieties of vegetarian *biryanis*, too. As accompaniments to these Moghlai curries, *kababs*, and *biryanis*, we suggest Spicy Yogurt Salad (page 76), Prune Chutney (page 75) or Banana Chutney (page 76), and *Murgh Achar* (page 74), a chicken pickle.

Of all the cuisines of the Indian subcontinent, Moghlai and Punjabi foods are those most commonly available in Indian restaurants in the United States, Britain, and Europe. Most of these restaurants are owned by Pakistanis and Bangladeshis, but since the region of Punjab is divided between India and Pakistan, for someone on the Pakistani side of the border to start a restaurant and call it an Indian restaurant is not a problem. And for a Bangladeshi, who might have worked for a Pakistani chef before his country became independent more than twenty years ago, starting a Moghlai-style restaurant is, well — to coin a phrase — a curry-walk.

Farther north, in Tibet and Nepal, curries are still quite popular. The mild Tibetan curries usually contain goat, chicken, or water buffalo. Tibetans dry the entire buffalo carcass, treat it with curry spices, and eat the dried meat along with vegetables. The Tibetans, who are devout Buddhists, eat meat with impunity, like Buddhists in Sri Lanka, Burma, Thailand, and Vietnam.

"Buddha said not to kill animals, but he never said anything about not eating them," a Buddhist monk once told Arthur. The Buddhists often depend on Christian or Muslim butchers to do the sinful work!

We have three interesting recipes from the far north: a Tibetan meatball curry known as *Shabril* (page 78); Gurkha Pork Curry (page 84), from Nepal; and Kabul Tomato Chutney (page 75), from Afghanistan. These are much milder than the curries prepared elsewhere in the subcontinent.

In Kashmir, a predominantly Muslim state, too, the curries are not only mild, many of them do not call for chiles at all. So the story goes that when an unwelcome guest invites himself to dinner, the host doesn't worry if he has a limited supply of cooked food in his kitchen. He just tells his wife to add a scoop of extra-hot chile powder to the curry that is served to the guest. The guest usually declines a second helping.

The Kashmiris love their sweets, and even their curries tend to be sweetish because of the use of yogurt, milk, fruits, and nuts. *Yakhni* (page 82) features beef or lamb ribs spiced with saffron and cooked with yogurt. *Kashmiri Gosht* (page 82) is one of the simplest lamb curries. Two Parsi curries from the northwest are also included: *Bhinda Gharbano Patio* (page 94), fish roe curried with okra; and *Chutney Machi* (page 92), fish baked in a spicy chutney.

Arthur, who grew up in the southwestern state of Karnataka, began to enjoy the diversities of Indian cuisine when he went to Bombay for his postgraduate studies. There he sampled the rich, creamy, and milder curries from the northwestern region, including *Raan Shahnshahi* (page 81), traditionally made with an entire leg of lamb but simplified in our version to lamb shanks. He also visited West Bengal, in the far eastern part of India, and tasted their drier, mustard-based curries.

The Bengalis in West Bengal and in Bangladesh have great political and religious differences; most of the former are Hindus, and the latter are predominantly Muslims. Traditionally, the Hindus shun eating beef, while the Muslims eat it with great relish. And then there are many disputes relating to river water; the Ganges flows from India into Bangladesh, where it is called the Padma, and the Bangladeshis say that India hampers the flow of its water.

But despite these differences, the two peoples agree on one thing: their passion for fish. Even the Brahmins eat fish as a part of their daily fare, calling it the fruit of the sea to avoid the stigma of eating flesh.

A popular story in Calcutta illustrates the Bengali passion for fish. Swami Vivekananda, a well-known Indian philosopher and monk, continued eating fish even after joining a religious order that forbade it. His detractors went to his superior, Swami Ramakrishna Paramahamsa, and complained that Vivekananda was not a true ascetic. "Don't watch what goes into his mouth," Paramahamsa replied, "listen to what comes out of it."

Three Bengali fish curries are *Elish Macher Paturi* (page 90), a lightly curried fish cooked in banana leaves; *Masala Dum Machchi* (page 91), which is baked; and a Bangladeshi fish specialty, *Macher Jhol* (page 90). Another seafood curry is *Dahi Chingree* (page 96), shrimp curried with raisins and almonds in yogurt. A Bengali vegetable curry, *Shukto* (page 99), features bitter gourds.

The Bengalis also have a great sweet tooth. According to one story, a mother tried to get her son to stop eating so many sweets, but nothing seemed to work. So she asked a famous religious teacher to help her out. He said, "Fine, I will tell him how to stop, but give me a month." A month later, the holy man met with the mother and her son. He told the boy in a simple but kind way that eating too many sweets would spoil his teeth and make him vulnerable to many diseases.

The woman was puzzled. "It took you just a minute to tell him that. Why couldn't you have done that a month ago?"

The holy man smiled. "I wanted to test myself to see if I could stay away from sweets for at least a month before I could advise the young man."

Perhaps the oddest curry story we heard from India involved a Methodist minister who was visiting Nagaland, India's predominantly Christian state, which is largely tribal. The village leader was named Hitler — being the son of a rich man who had hated the British and hence named his oldest son after the German leader — and he welcomed the minister to his house and offered him a rice beer. The minister accepted. Then, a few minutes later, Hitler asked the minister if he cared to have a hot dog. The reverend was so happy at the thought of American food that he did not even bother to ask if the hot dog came with mustard or relish. A few minutes later, Hitler brought the minister a platter of curried dog meat, and the minister fled the village in disgust. The Nagas, like the Chinese, Filipinos, and Koreans, enjoy dog meat. No, there are no such recipes from Nagaland in this book! But there are plenty of politically correct regional Indian curries that follow.

Classic Indian Curry Powder

Yield: About 1 cup

6 dried red New Mexican chiles,
  seeds and stems removed, or 4
  small hot dried red chiles, such
  as piquins, seeds and stems removed
1/4 cup cumin seeds
1/4 cup coriander seeds
2 tablespoons whole black peppercorns
1 tablespoon mustard seeds
1 teaspoon cardamom seeds
1 teaspoon whole cloves
1 teaspoon fenugreek seeds
1 tablespoon ground turmeric
1 tablespoon dried powdered curry
  leaves

Here is a basic curry powder that makes use of the most common spices grown in India for centuries. Although this particular powder uses a large amount of fairly mild New Mexican chiles, cooks may substitute lesser amounts of hotter chiles. Traditionally in India, such spice mixtures are sun-dried, but these days the oven works quite well.

Preheat the oven to 250 degrees.

Place the chiles, cumin and coriander seeds, peppercorns, mustard and cardamom seeds, cloves, and fenugreek seeds in a baking pan and place in the oven. Roast for 15 minutes, taking care that none of the spices burn. Grind these spices in a spice mill to a fine powder.

Mix the ground spices with the turmeric and the curry leaves and seal in an airtight jar.

Turmeric, a relative of ginger, is both a curry spice and a dye.

4 pounds boneless chicken,
   chopped fine
2 cups white vinegar for marinat-
   ing
1 two-inch piece ginger, peeled
10 cloves garlic, peeled
3 tablespoons vegetable or olive oil
1/4 cup each almonds, cashews
   (preferably raw), and raisins
1 teaspoon each ground cloves,
   cardamom, nutmeg, mace, and
   cayenne
1 tablespoon vinegar
1 teaspoon saffron
Salt to taste

🌸 Murgh Achar

CHICKEN PICKLE

This delightful pickle, popular with the early Moghul rulers and used among the aristocratic families of Punjab and Kashmir, can also be made with lamb, fish, or shrimp. If lamb is used, it must marinate for at least 50 minutes. If you choose fish or shrimp, follow the steps below, but cook the fish or shrimp marinade for only 10 minutes.

Marinate the chicken in the 2 cups vinegar for 10 minutes.

In a food processor or blender, grind the ginger and the garlic into a smooth paste. Heat 1 tablespoon of the oil in a skillet for 1 minute, add the ginger-garlic paste, and fry for 2 minutes over low heat. Set aside.

In a skillet, heat the remaining 2 tablespoons oil over medium heat for 1 minute, lower the heat, and fry the nuts and raisins. Set aside.

Use a blender and finely mix the dry spice. Set aside.

Heat the 1 tablespoon vinegar and add the saffron to it.

In a large saucepan, combine the chicken with its marinade, ginger-garlic paste, fried nuts and raisins, blended spices, saffron and vinegar, and salt. Cook, uncovered, over low heat for 20 minutes, stirring occasionally. Remove from the heat.

When the pickle is cool, pour into a large, dry, airtight jar. This pickle stays in good condition in a refrigerator for at least 3 months.

🌸 *Prune Chutney*

Yield: 1 cup

This chutney is a popular dish in the rugged regions of Pakistan, where fruits play an important role in the cuisine.

Combine the water with the prunes and the raisins and let sit for 15 minutes.

In a food processor or blender, puree the prunes and the raisins with the cumin and the cayenne. Add the lime juice and the saffron or rose essence and garnish with the nuts and the silver foil.

4 cups lukewarm water
1 cup pitted prunes
1 cup raisins
1 tablespoon ground cumin
1 tablespoon cayenne
1 tablespoon freshly squeezed lime juice
1/4 teaspoon saffron or rose essence (available in Asian markets)
1 tablespoon almonds, crushed
1 tablespoon cashews, preferably raw, crushed
Handful edible silver foil (available in Asian markets), crushed

🌸 *Kabul Tomato Chutney*

Yield: 1 cup

This chutney originated in Kabul, Afghanistan, but it is found in many homes and restaurants in neighboring Pakistan, too.

Soak the tamarind in the warm water for 10 minutes. Strain the pulp, discard, and reserve the liquid (see Note).

In a food processor or blender, puree the tomatoes and the nuts. Add the tamarind liquid, chiles, sugar (if using), salt, and dried spices to the food processor or blender, mix well, and continue grinding for 5 minutes.

Add the saffron essence and the rose petals and continue processing for 2 minutes.

Note: 1 teaspoon freshly squeezed lime juice can be substituted for the tamarind liquid.

1 lime-size ball tamarind pulp
1/2 cup warm water
3 large tomatoes, sliced
1/4 cup each cashews (preferably raw), almonds, and walnuts
6 green chiles, such as serranos, seeds and stems removed
1 teaspoon sugar (optional)
1 teaspoon salt
1/2 teaspoon ground coriander
1/2 teaspoon ground cumin
1/4 teaspoon ground cloves
1/4 teaspoon ground nutmeg
1/2 teaspoon saffron essence (available in Asian markets)
1/2 cup fresh rose petals

Yield: 4 to 6 cups

1/2 cup dates
1/2 cup raisins
6 ripe bananas, chopped
1 cup water
2 tablespoons sugar
2 tablespoons ground ginger
1 tablespoon freshly ground black
  pepper
1 teaspoon red chile powder, such
  as New Mexican
1 tablespoon ground coriander
1/4 cup slivered almonds
1/4 cup crushed cashews, preferably raw
1/4 cup chopped walnuts
1 green chile, such as serrano,
  seeds and stems removed,
  minced
1 tablespoon Ghee (page 17)
  (optional)
Salt to taste

🌼 *Banana Chutney*

Chutney, usually a fine, spicy puree, is served with most Indian meals. Scoop up the chutney with a piece of unleavened bread or mix it into rice. Chutneys can also be a snack — dip a bread roll or cracker into it and enjoy the combination of flavors.

In a food processor or blender, puree the dates, raisins, and bananas.

Combine the water and the sugar and boil in a skillet over medium heat for 1 minute. Add the dried spices and, as the sugar water thickens, add the nuts, chile, Ghee (if using), and salt, and simmer for 1 minute. Add the date mixture and simmer for 5 minutes.

This chutney can be served hot or cold and can be refrigerated for several weeks.

Serves: 4

2 tablespoons vegetable or olive oil
1 teaspoon mustard seeds
1 teaspoon cumin seeds
1/2 teaspoon fenugreek seeds
1 fresh red chile, such as serrano,
  seeds and stem removed, minced
1 cucumber, peeled and cut into
  thin slices
2 tomatoes, sliced
1 onion, chopped
1 one-inch piece ginger, peeled and
  finely minced
2 carrots, peeled and cut into
  1-inch-long julienne
1/4 cup sour cream
1/4 cup plain yogurt
1 teaspoon salt
1/4 cup cilantro or mint leaves for
  garnish

🌼 *Spicy Yogurt Salad*

Arthur came across this delicious spicy salad in a small, inexpensive New Delhi eatery; the cook traded the recipe for a bottle of beer and fried chicken in a nearby ritzy restaurant.

Heat the oil in a skillet over medium heat for 1 minute. Add the mustard seeds, and when they begin to pop, after about 1 minute, lower the heat, add the cumin and fenugreek seeds and the chile, and fry for 30 seconds. Set aside.

In a bowl, combine the cucumber, tomatoes, onion, ginger, carrots, sour cream, yogurt, and salt; mix thoroughly.

Pour the mixture from the skillet into the salad and mix well. Garnish with the cilantro or mint leaves.

Bangri Kabab with Prantha

KABABS WITH PRANTHA BREAD

A rustic dish from the Punjab region, this is a year-round favorite. The term kabab, *as used in India, refers to meatballs as well as skewered meats. Commercial pita bread may be substituted for the* prantha.

For the *kababs*, in a large skillet, combine the potatoes, beef, water, *moong dal*, cumin, ginger, garlic, onion, cloves, cardamom, chile powder, and black pepper, and cook, covered, over medium heat for about 15 minutes. Remove from the heat and let cool.

Add the cilantro or mint leaves and the chiles. Place in a food processor or blender and grind into a smooth paste. Make 2-inch-thick patties (*kababs*); there should be about 24.

Beat the eggs, add the salt, and roll the *kababs* in the mixture.

Heat the oil in a deep skillet for 3 minutes, lower the heat, and fry a few *kababs* at a time for about 3 minutes, turning once halfway through the cooking time. Repeat the process until all the *kababs* are fried. Set aside.

For the *prantha*, combine the flours, add the eggs and the salt, and knead the dough well for several minutes. Divide the dough into 6 lime-size balls and roll each into a pancake shape about 1/4 inch thick.

Place a skillet over medium heat. Take 1 *prantha* at a time, sprinkle oil on both sides, and fry it in the skillet; flip it after 2 minutes and then cook for another 2 minutes, making sure the *prantha* does not burn. Repeat the process until all the *prantha* are fried.

The *prantha* are served hot, with 4 *kababs* inside each one.

For the Kababs:
2 potatoes, peeled and diced
1 pound minced beef
4 cups water
1/2 cup moong dal (greengram, available in Asian markets)
2 teaspoons ground cumin or cumin seeds
1 two-inch piece ginger, peeled and minced
6 cloves garlic, peeled and finely chopped
1 onion, finely chopped
1/2 teaspoon ground cloves
1/2 teaspoon ground cardamom
1/2 teaspoon red chile powder, such as New Mexican
1 teaspoon freshly ground black pepper
1/2 cup cilantro or mint leaves
2 green chiles, such as serranos, seeds and stems removed, finely chopped
2 eggs
Salt to taste
1/2 cup vegetable or olive oil

For the Prantha:
1 cup all-purpose flour
2 cups whole wheat flour
2 eggs, beaten
Salt to taste
2 tablespoons olive or corn oil

Serves: 4

2 pounds ground beef
1/4 cup vegetable oil
1 teaspoon fenugreek seeds
1 large onion, chopped
2 cloves garlic, peeled and minced
1 one-inch piece ginger, peeled and
    minced
1/4 teaspoon ground turmeric
1 teaspoon cayenne
4 teaspoons soy sauce
2 cups thinly sliced mushrooms
1 cup thinly sliced radishes
Salt to taste
1 cup sour cream

🌸 Shabril

MEATBALL AND RADISH CURRY

The Tibetans eat meat mostly on festive occasions. This is a classic dish from Tibet, and exiled Tibetans have taken it to India and beyond. The Indian version is hotter and requires 3 minced chiles.

Fashion the beef into 1-inch meatballs.

Heat the oil in a skillet for 1 minute over medium heat, lower the heat, and add the fenugreek seeds. When the seeds turn brown, add the onion and fry until it wilts, about 1 minute. Add the meatballs and stir gently.

Add the garlic, ginger, turmeric, cayenne, and soy sauce, and cook, covered, for about 15 minutes over low heat. Add the mushrooms and continue cooking for 15 more minutes. Add the radishes and cook for 5 minutes. Add the salt.

Remove from the heat, add the sour cream, and stir gently before serving.

Serves: 6

1 pound spareribs (beef, pork, or
    lamb), cut into 1-inch-long pieces
1 teaspoon ground cardamom
1 one-inch piece cinnamon,
    crushed
12 whole black peppercorns,
    crushed
2 onions, finely chopped
6 cloves garlic, peeled and finely
    minced
1 cup water
4 large potatoes
Pinch salt
1 teaspoon cayenne
1 teaspoon ground cumin
1 teaspoon ground coriander
1 teaspoon ground turmeric

🌸 Fried Spareribs with Potatoes

This is a moderately spicy dish that can be eaten as a snack. It originated in the Punjab region and traditionally is cooked with lamb, but it is equally delicious with pork or beef. It can also be served as an appetizer before a rice and meat curry.

In a large covered skillet, combine the spareribs, cardamom, cinnamon, peppercorns, onions, garlic, and 1 cup water, and cook for 15 minutes over medium heat. Make sure all the water has evaporated.

Meanwhile, boil the potatoes for about 12 minutes, then peel them and mash them well. Add the salt, cayenne, cumin, coriander, turmeric, chiles, and cilantro or mint leaves. Mix well.

78

Divide the potato mixture into portions that equal the number of spareribs. Take each portion of the mashed potatoes and flatten it lightly. Coat each sparerib with the potato mixture.

Beat the eggs well with salt; add the bread crumbs.

Heat the oil in a deep skillet for about 3 minutes; lower the heat. Take a few spareribs at a time, dip them into the egg batter, and fry them on all sides until they turn golden-brown.

2 green chiles, such as serranos, seeds and stems removed, finely minced
1/2 cup cilantro or mint leaves
4 eggs
Salt to taste
1 cup bread crumbs
4 cups vegetable or olive oil

❀ Sindhi Gosht

NUTTY CURRIED LAMB FROM SIND

The region of Sind, in Pakistan, is well known for its many lamb and beef dishes. This dish is marinated for at least 6 hours in a fragrant paste of onion, garlic, ginger, and dried spices.

In a food processor or blender, grind the onions, tomatoes, garlic, chiles, ginger, cumin, coriander, turmeric, cayenne, and vinegar. Set this paste aside.

Puncture the lamb or beef with a sharp knife in many places and marinate, covered, at room temperature in the paste for at least 6 hours.

In a skillet, cook the meat and the fennel seeds, covered, over low heat, for about 1 hour or until the meat is tender. Sprinkle with water from time to time.

Remove the lid, add the cashews, almonds, and salt to taste. Raise the heat and cook until all the liquid evaporates.

Add the oil to the skillet, reduce the heat, and simmer for about 5 minutes before serving.

Serves: 6

3 large onions, chopped
2 large ripe tomatoes, chopped
8 cloves garlic, peeled
2 green chiles, such as serranos, seeds and stems removed, halved
1 two-inch piece ginger, peeled
1 tablespoon ground cumin
2 teaspoons ground coriander
1 teaspoon ground turmeric
1 teaspoon cayenne
2 tablespoons vinegar
3 pounds boneless lamb or beef, cut into 1-inch cubes
2 teaspoons fennel seeds
1/4 cup cashews, preferably raw
1/4 cup almonds
Salt to taste
6 tablespoons vegetable oil

Serves: 6 (about 5 *kabab*s each)

2 pounds lamb, minced or ground
4 cups water
6 tablespoons vegetable or olive oil
1 two-inch piece ginger, peeled and
  finely chopped
6 cloves garlic, peeled and chopped
1 large onion, finely minced
2 green chiles, such as serranos,
  seeds and stems removed, finely
  minced
1 cup almonds
1/2 cup cashews, preferably raw
1/2 cup raisins
1/2 cup pistachios
1 teaspoon ground cumin
1 teaspoon cayenne
1/2 teaspoon ground nutmeg
1/2 teaspoon ground cloves
Salt to taste
2 eggs
1/2 teaspoon saffron essence
  (available in Asian markets)
1 cup bread crumbs
6 tablespoons heavy cream
1/4 cup cilantro leaves
1/4 cup mint leaves

Mewaii Kabab

CURRIED DRIED-FRUIT KABABS

Kababs, made of cubed or minced meat, are popular throughout Pakistan and northern India. This dish is adapted from a recipe from Pakistan's northwestern region, bordering Afghanistan, where the use of dried fruits is very popular.

Cook the lamb in the water, uncovered, for about 30 minutes or until all the water evaporates. Make sure the meat is dry. Remove from the heat and set aside.

Meanwhile, heat 1 tablespoon of the oil in a skillet for 1 minute, add the ginger, garlic, onion, and chiles, and fry over low heat for about 3 minutes. Remove from the heat and set aside.

In a food processor or blender, grind the almonds, cashews, raisins, pistachios, cumin, cayenne, nutmeg, and cloves together.

Add the mixtures from the skillet and the food processor or blender to the minced meat, along with the salt. Knead the meat mixture into about 30 lime-size balls (*kabab*s) and reserve.

Beat the eggs with the saffron essence. Set aside.

Combine the bread crumbs with the cream. Set aside.

Heat the remaining 5 tablespoons oil in a frying pan for about 1 minute. Lower the heat. Dip the *kabab*s in the beaten eggs and then roll them in the bread crumb mixture. Fry the *kabab*s in the oil until they are golden-brown on all sides.

Drain and serve garnished with the cilantro and mint leaves.

Raan Shahnshahi

CURRIED LAMB SHANKS

Traditionally, an entire leg of lamb is marinated in the masala overnight and cooked over low heat for 2 or 3 hours. A simplified version follows.

Combine the saffron with the milk in a blender and puree into a smooth paste. Set aside.

In a food processor or blender, grind all the nuts along with the raisins, poppy seeds, and Coconut Milk into a smooth paste. Reserve.

In a food processor or blender, grind the ginger, garlic, papaya, nutmeg, mace, coriander, cumin, and chiles into a separate paste. Combine this paste with the yogurt, add the salt, and reserve.

In a large saucepan, combine the nut paste, yogurt paste, and lamb shanks, and marinate for 30 minutes.

Heat the Ghee or oil in a large skillet over medium heat for about 1 minute, add the onions, cook for 1 minute, then add the shanks with their marinade and cook, covered, over low heat for 45 to 50 minutes. Stir occasionally, adding cold water if the mixture is too thick. Add the saffron mixture and continue cooking, covered, for another 10 minutes.

Serves: 6

1 tablespoon saffron
4 tablespoons warm milk
1 tablespoon each *almonds, walnuts, cashews (preferably raw), peanuts, and raisins*
1 teaspoon poppy seeds
1 cup Coconut Milk (page 19)
1 one-inch piece ginger, peeled and minced
10 cloves garlic, peeled
1 small green papaya, peeled, seeds removed, and diced
1/2 teaspoon ground nutmeg
1/2 teaspoon ground mace
1 tablespoon ground coriander
1 tablespoon ground cumin
6 fresh red chiles, such as serranos, seeds and stems removed
2 cups plain yogurt
Salt to taste
4 pounds lamb shanks, cut into 1-inch-long sections
4 teaspoons Ghee (page 17) or vegetable oil
2 large onions, finely chopped

🌸 *Kashmiri Gosht*

KASHMIRI MEAT

One of the simplest meat curries, this dish is popular in the entire Kashmir region.

Place the spareribs, milk, ginger, anise, cardamom, and black pepper in a saucepan and cook, covered, for about 30 minutes over low heat. If there is some liquid left, increase the heat and continue to cook until the spareribs are dry.

Beat the eggs with the salt and pour them over the spareribs, coating them on all sides.

Heat the oil in a frying pan over medium heat for 2 minutes, add the bay or curry leaves, and then add the spareribs and fry on all sides for about 3 minutes. Remove the bay or curry leaves before serving.

Serves: 4

1 pound lamb or beef spareribs,
  cut into 1-inch-long pieces
1 cup milk
1 teaspoon ground ginger
1/2 teaspoon ground anise
1 teaspoon ground cardamom
1 teaspoon freshly ground black
  pepper
3 eggs
Salt to taste
6 tablespoons vegetable or olive oil
6 bay or curry leaves

🌸 *Yakhni*

RIBS WITH ROSE PETALS

Here is another popular dish from the Kashmir region, full of nutty flavor and the fragrance of roses.

In a food processor or blender, grind the onions, ginger, and garlic to a paste. Reserve.

Soak the saffron in the hot milk for 5 minutes and then puree to a fine paste in a blender. Reserve.

Combine the cold milk and yogurt in a blender and make a smooth paste. Reserve.

Combine the tomatoes with the spareribs in a large skillet and cook over medium heat, covered, for 20 minutes.

Meanwhile, in another skillet, heat the Ghee over low heat for 1 minute, add the onion paste, and cook over high heat until it turns golden, about 2 minutes. Add the cumin, corian-

---

Serves: 4

2 medium onions, chopped
1 two-inch piece ginger, peeled
6 cloves garlic, peeled
1 teaspoon saffron
1/4 cup hot milk
1/2 cup cold milk
1 cup plain yogurt
6 large tomatoes, chopped
2 pounds lamb or beef spareribs,
  cut into 1-inch-long serving
  pieces
1/4 cup Ghee (page 17)
1 teaspoon ground cumin
1 teaspoon ground coriander
1/4 teaspoon each ground nutmeg,
  cloves, and cardamom
1 teaspoon red chile powder, such
  as New Mexican
1/4 cup almonds
1/4 cup raisins
Salt to taste

der, nutmeg, cloves, cardamom, and chile powder, and fry for 2 minutes.

Add this spice mixture and the saffron paste to the spareribs and mix well. Add the milk-yogurt paste, almonds, raisins, and salt, and stir well. Cook, half-covered, for about 10 minutes or until the gravy becomes thick.

Garnish with the rose petals and the edible silver foil.

1 cup fresh rose petals
Few pieces edible silver foil (available at Asian markets)

 # *Kichida*

LAMB WITH GRAINS

Serves: 4

This dish is a specialty of the Bohra Muslim community in Pakistan and India and is served at the end of the fasting day during the Muharram season. The recipe was graciously contributed by Maria Ghadiali, a New York–based journalist.

Drain the water from the soaked wheat, rice, and *dals*. In a large skillet, combine them with the ginger, chiles, cloves, peppercorns, aniseed, cayenne, and water, and bring to a boil. Reduce the heat and cook, covered, over medium heat for 35 to 40 minutes, stirring occasionally.

Remove from the heat and, when cooled, place in a food processor or blender and make a smooth paste.

Heat the oil in a skillet for 1 minute, add the onion, and cook until it wilts, about 1 minute. Add the lamb, water, and wheat-spice paste, and cook over low heat, covered, for 1 hour or until the lamb is tender. Add more water if required.

Garnish with the lemon wedges, mint or cilantro leaves, and ginger.

1 cup whole-grain wheat, soaked in 2 cups water overnight
1 tablespoon each uncooked rice, chana dal (dried split chickpeas), toovar dal (yellow split peas), and moong dal (greengram) (all available in Asian markets), soaked together in 1 cup water overnight
1 two-inch piece ginger, peeled and finely minced
4 green chiles, such as serranos, seeds and stems removed, finely chopped
6 whole cloves
6 whole peppercorns
1 teaspoon aniseed
1 teaspoon cayenne
4 cups water
2 tablespoons vegetable or olive oil
1 large onion, finely chopped
1 pound lamb, cubed
1 cup water
6 lemon wedges
1/4 cup mint or cilantro leaves for garnish
1 one-inch piece ginger, peeled and chopped, for garnish

1 teaspoon white vinegar
1 tablespoon cayenne
2 pounds lean boneless pork, cut
  into 1-inch cubes
2 cups plain yogurt
1 two-inch piece ginger, peeled and
  minced
1 teaspoon vegetable oil
1/4 cup Ghee (page 17)
1 teaspoon freshly ground black
  pepper
1 teaspoon ground turmeric
1 cup water
Salt to taste
1/2 cup cilantro leaves
1 teaspoon ground cumin
1 teaspoon ground nutmeg
1/2 teaspoon ground cloves
1/2 teaspoon ground cardamom

🌰 Gurkha Pork Curry

Gurkhas, the sturdy soldiers from Nepal, took this curry formula wherever they went, whether it was Malaya or the Falkland Islands. The use of yogurt in this curry tempers the cayenne.

Combine the vinegar and the cayenne and toss the pork in the mixture. Add the yogurt and the ginger and marinate the pork, covered, for about 3 hours at room temperature.

Heat the oil in a large skillet over low heat for 1 minute; add the Ghee, the pork with its marinade, black pepper, turmeric, water, and salt, and bring to a rapid boil. Lower the heat, cover the skillet, and simmer for 40 minutes.

Add the cilantro leaves, cumin, nutmeg, cloves, and cardamom, stir well, and serve hot.

❀ Stendhal's Aru Murgh

CHICKEN WITH APRICOTS

The well-known food writer and radio talk-show host Stendhal came across a mom-and-pop Indian kitchen in Los Angeles about sixty years ago. "In fact, I ran into the place when it was closed but the aroma of curries was everywhere around the place," he told Arthur during an interview. So he began investigating, became a curry buff, and ended up writing scores of articles about curries. During the interview, Stendhal gave the following recipe to Arthur.

Toss the chicken pieces with the vinegar and the turmeric; set aside.

Grind the chiles, garlic, and cumin and coriander seeds together in a food processor or blender; set aside.

In a heavy skillet, heat the oil, add the Ghee or butter, then add the onions and cook over medium heat for 1 minute. Add the chicken pieces and fry over medium heat until the chicken is brown on all sides, about 10 minutes, stirring often.

Add the paste from the food processor or blender, tomatoes, apricots, salt, and water, and simmer, covered, for 25 minutes, stirring occasionally.

Garnish with the cilantro or mint leaves just before serving.

1 three-pound chicken, cut into
 serving pieces
1 teaspoon white vinegar
1/4 teaspoon ground turmeric
3 small green chiles, such as serranos, seeds and stems removed
3 cloves garlic, peeled
1 teaspoon cumin seeds
1 teaspoon coriander seeds
1 tablespoon vegetable or olive oil
1 tablespoon Ghee (page 17) or
 butter
3 onions, sliced thin
3 tomatoes, quartered
6 dried apricots, chopped
Salt to taste
1/2 cup water
1/4 cup cilantro or mint leaves for
 garnish

Nimbu Masala Murgh

2 large onions, chopped
1 two-inch piece ginger, peeled
10 cloves garlic, peeled
2 cups plain yogurt
Salt to taste
1 teaspoon cayenne
1 tablespoon ground cumin
1 tablespoon ground coriander
1 tablespoon commercial garam
    masala
2 pounds boneless skinned chicken
    breast, cut into small pieces
1/4 cup Ghee (page 17) or vege-
    table oil
1 teaspoon mustard seeds
4 green chiles, such as serranos,
    seeds and stems removed, finely
    minced
1/4 cup freshly squeezed lime juice

For Garnish:

1 lime, cut into small pieces
1/2 cup cashews, preferably raw
1 large tomato, diced
1 large onion, cut into rings
1/4 cup cilantro or mint leaves

SPICY LIME CHICKEN

The Moghlai dishes, popular across India but particularly around Delhi and the neighboring state of Uttar Pradesh, owe their ancestry to sixteenth- and seventeenth-century Moghul rulers, Akbar and Shah Jahan, who were connoisseurs of music, literature, architecture, and food. Unlike their immediate ancestors, who had invaded India and who were too busy consolidating their empire to pay much attention to cuisine, Akbar and Shah Jahan recruited the best chefs in northern India and encouraged them to create dishes that carried the influence of the ingredients of Central Asia and India.

In a food processor or blender, grind the onions, ginger, and garlic into a smooth paste. Combine the paste with the yogurt, salt, cayenne, and half each of the cumin, coriander, and *garam masala*. Add the chicken pieces, mix well, and marinate, covered, at room temperature for 6 hours.

Place the chicken in a large skillet and cook, covered, for about 12 minutes over low heat.

In another skillet, heat the Ghee or oil over medium heat for 2 minutes. Add the mustard seeds, and when they begin to pop, add the chiles. Pour the contents of the skillet over the chicken, and continue cooking for 15 to 18 minutes over medium heat or until the moisture evaporates.

Place the chicken in a serving dish. Pour the lime juice over the meat and sprinkle with the remaining cumin, coriander, and *garam masala*. Garnish with the lime pieces, cashews, tomato, onion rings, and cilantro or mint leaves.

 **Biryani**

One of the most aromatic, rich, colorful, and tasty of Indian dishes, biryani *is prepared across India. But the best* biryani — *whether made from beef, lamb, chicken, fish, or vegetables — is found in the regions around Delhi and in the southern city of Hyderabad. These regions were ruled by Muslims for several centuries, and their hearty love for rich food has left behind a culinary legacy. Arthur serves this version with Baingan Burtha (page 98), a smoked eggplant dish that can be enjoyed by itself.* Biryani *is a time-consuming exercise, but it has rich rewards.*

Soak the saffron in the warm milk for 5 minutes and then puree in a blender. Add the chiles, onions, ginger, garlic, cloves, peppercorns, cardamom seeds, cinnamon, coriander and cumin seeds, poppy seeds, nutmeg, mace, cilantro or mint leaves, and lemon juice. Blend into a smooth paste. Put the paste into a large bowl, add the yogurt, and mix well.

Marinate the chicken in the yogurt mixture with salt to taste, covered, for at least 2 hours in the refrigerator. For the best results, marinate for 6 hours.

In a skillet, heat the oil over medium heat for 1 minute. Add the Ghee and 15 seconds later add the onion and fry for about 8 minutes. Reserve for garnishing.

In the same skillet, cook the chicken with its marinade with the tomatoes for about 10 minutes over medium heat, uncovered. Remove the chicken pieces from the sauce and set aside.

Add the rice to the sauce, bring to a boil, and cook, covered, over low heat for 15 minutes. Return the chicken and add the raisins, cashews, and almonds; mix well. Simmer, covered, for 5 minutes.

Place the chicken, eggs, and rice in a large serving dish in such a way that the yellow of the eggs, the saffron-colored rice, the nuts, and the chicken make a colorful display. Add the reserved onion as a garnish.

1 tablespoon saffron
4 teaspoons warm milk
2 green chiles, such as serranos, seeds and stems removed
2 fresh red chiles, such as serranos, seeds and stems removed
2 large onions, chopped
1 two-inch piece ginger, peeled
8 cloves garlic, peeled
1/4 teaspoon ground cloves
8 whole peppercorns
1/2 teaspoon cardamom seeds
1 one-inch piece cinnamon, crushed
1 teaspoon coriander seeds
1 teaspoon cumin seeds
1/4 teaspoon poppy seeds
1/4 teaspoon ground nutmeg
1/4 teaspoon ground mace
1/2 cup cilantro or mint leves
1/4 cup freshly squeezed lemon juice
2 cups plain yogurt
3 pounds boneless chicken, cut into 1-inch cubes
Salt to taste
2 tablespoons vegetable or olive oil
1 tablespoon Ghee (page 17)
1 onion, finely chopped
8 large tomatoes, chopped
2 cups uncooked basmati or other long-grain rice
1/3 cup each raisins, cashews (preferably raw), and almonds
6 hard-boiled eggs, halved

1/4 cup vegetable oil
3 pounds boneless skinned chicken
 breast, cut into small pieces
2 medium onions, chopped
2 cloves garlic, peeled and chopped
1 one-inch piece cinnamon,
 crushed
1 two-inch piece ginger, peeled and
 grated
Pinch saffron, stirred into 1/2 cup
 hot water
2 teaspoons freshly ground black
 pepper
6 tomatoes, halved
2 teaspoons white vinegar
Salt to taste

Ismail Merchant's Ginger Chicken for Anthony Hopkins

Ismail Mercant has been currying favor with writers, technicians, actors, and financiers for more than three decades, serving them his delicious home-cooked Indian meals. The producer of such acclaimed movies as Howards End *and* A Room with a View, *which have won six Academy Awards, shared two of his recipes with us. Sir Anthony Hopkins worked with Ismail Merchant for the first time in* Howards End. *"He loved the ginger chicken I cooked for him," Merchant told Arthur. Merchant made it in well under an hour. "It must have been good, otherwise Tony would not have been so pleased," he said. "See, Tony has been in love with Indian food long before he worked in my film."*

Heat the oil in a large frying pan over medium-high heat and add the chicken pieces in 3 batches. When they turn brown on all sides, remove them and drain on paper towels.

Add the onions, garlic, cinnamon, and ginger to the pan and cook over medium heat until the onions turn golden, stirring occasionally.

Return the chicken to the pan, add the saffron water, black pepper, tomatoes, vinegar, and salt, and cook, uncovered, for 20 to 25 minutes or until the curry is thick.

🏵 *Banik's Nehru Chicken*

This was one of the favorite dishes of Jawaharlal Nehru, free India's first prime minister. Sambhu Banik, a psychologist in Washington, D.C., came across the recipe when he was studying psychology in Britain, and over the years he has perfected it.

In a blender, puree the papaya with the salt. Coat the chicken with the papaya puree.

In a bowl, combine half the onions with the eggs, ginger, garlic, chiles, and the 2 tablespoons Ghee. Stuff the chicken with this mixture and sew the chicken shut.

In a food processor or blender, puree the almonds, cashews, pistachios, poppy seeds, cardamom, cinnamon, and cloves with 2 tablespoons warm water. Rub this paste on the outer surface of the chicken.

In a large skillet, heat the 6 tablespoons Ghee and fry the remaining onions until they are soft. Place the stuffed chicken in a casserole dish and surround it with the onions.

Combine the tomatoes, yogurt, cayenne, saffron, and salt to taste, and mix well. Pour this mixture over the chicken.

Cover tightly and bake in a preheated 325-degree oven for 1 hour.

1 medium green papaya, peeled, seeds removed, and diced
Salt to taste
1 four-pound broiler chicken
4 onions, chopped
3 hard-boiled eggs, mashed
1 two-inch piece ginger, peeled and minced
6 cloves garlic, peeled and minced
2 small green chiles, such as serranos, seeds and stems removed, chopped fine
2 tablespoons Ghee (page 17)
1/4 cup almonds, roasted and crushed
1/4 cup cashews, preferably raw, roasted and crushed
1/4 cup pistachios
2 tablespoons poppy seeds
1 teaspoon ground cardamom
1 teaspoon ground cinnamon
6 whole cloves, crushed
2 tablespoons warm water
6 tablespoons Ghee (page 17)
2 large tomatoes, chopped
1 cup plain yogurt
2 teaspoons cayenne
1/2 teaspoon saffron
Salt to taste

Serves: 6

1 tablespoon ground turmeric
1 teaspoon red chile powder, such
  as New Mexican
1 teaspoon ground coriander
1 teaspoon ground cumin
2 teaspoons dry mustard (or substitute Dijon mustard)
2 green chiles, such as serranos,
  seeds and stems removed, finely
  minced
Salt to taste
1 cup olive or corn oil
6 one-inch-thick swordfish, tilefish,
  or salmon steaks
6 banana leaves, cut into 6 sections, each 10 inches square

🌸 *Elish Macher Paturi*

FISH COOKED IN BANANA LEAVES

The use of banana leaves adds fragrance and unusual flavor to this easy-to-prepare dish popular throughout the coastal regions of Bangladesh and India's West Bengal state. Banana leaves are available in Asian and Latin American markets.

Combine the turmeric, chile powder, coriander, cumin, mustard, chiles, salt, and 1/4 cup of the oil in a bowl. Coat the fish with the mixture and marinate, covered, at room temperature for 20 minutes.

On each banana leaf, spread 1 tablespoon oil. Place a steak on each leaf, spread another 1 tablespoon oil on each steak, and wrap the steaks in the leaves. Tie the wrapped steaks with string to secure.

In a large skillet over medium heat, cook the wrapped steaks for 5 minutes. Turn over and cook for an additional 5 minutes. Serve hot.

Serves: 8

1 two-inch piece ginger, peeled
1 large onion, chopped
2 medium potatoes, peeled and
  thinly sliced
8 one-inch-thick salmon steaks (or
  substitute swordfish)
1 tablespoon ground turmeric
Salt to taste
6 cups vegetable or olive oil
4 bay or curry leaves
2 fresh red chiles, such as serranos, seeds and stems removed,
  chopped
1 large tomato, chopped
1 teaspoon ground cumin
1 teaspoon ground coriander
1/4 teaspoon ground cloves
1/4 teaspoon ground cardamom

🌸 *Macher Jhol*

BENGALI-STYLE FISH

This dish reportedly originated in the Cox Bazaar region of Bangladesh. Bengali families in India and Bangladesh take pride in preparing it.

In a food processor or blender, grind the ginger and the onion into a smooth paste. Set aside.

Sprinkle the potatoes and the fish with the turmeric and the salt.

In a deep skillet, heat the oil for about 2 minutes over medium heat. Add the potatoes, lower the heat, and fry for about 5 minutes.

Remove the fried potatoes and drain on paper towels.

A WORLD OF CURRIES

Lightly fry the fish in the same skillet for about 3 minutes, turning once halfway through the cooking time. Remove and drain on paper towels.

Remove all but 1/2 cup of the oil from the skillet. Add the ginger-onion paste, bay or curry leaves, chiles, tomato, cumin, coriander, cloves, cardamom, cayenne, sugar (if using), and water, and simmer for 2 minutes.

Increase the heat. When the sauce boils, gently add the fish and potatoes, lower the heat, and cook, covered, for 5 minutes. Remove the bay or curry leaves before serving.

1/2 teaspoon cayenne
1 teaspoon sugar (optional)
1/2 cup water

❀ Masala Dum Machchi

SPICED AND BAKED FISH

This popular Bengali fish recipe is usually prepared with hilsa, *a native fish with very firm flesh. Swordfish and tuna are good substitutes. The method of cleaning the fish described in the recipe — rubbing the fish with turmeric and then washing it — is part of Indian culinary tradition.*

Rub the turmeric on the fish, particularly on the bone, and wash in cold water. Dry the fish on paper towels.

In a large skillet, heat 4 tablespoons of the oil over medium heat for 3 minutes and add the mustard seeds; when they begin to pop, reduce the heat, add the ginger, garlic, and chile, and fry for 2 minutes. Add the cumin, coriander, and cloves. Fry for 1 minute. Remove the skillet from the heat and combine its contents with the yogurt in a large bowl. Add the salt.

Grease a large baking dish with the remaining 2 tablespoons oil, place the fish steaks in the dish, and pour the yogurt marinade over them. Marinate at room temperature, covered, for 30 minutes.

Heat the oven to 350 degrees. Bake the fish, uncovered, for 5 minutes. Gently flip the fish, reduce the heat to 250 degrees, and cook for 20 minutes.

Garnish with the cilantro or mint leaves just before serving.

Serves: 6

2 tablespoons ground turmeric
6 one-inch-thick swordfish, tuna, or kingfish steaks
6 tablespoons mustard or vegetable oil
1 teaspoon mustard seeds
1 two-inch piece ginger, peeled and finely minced
6 cloves garlic, peeled and minced
1 fresh red chile, such as serrano, seeds and stems removed, halved
1 teaspoon ground cumin
1 teaspoon ground coriander
1/2 teaspoon ground cloves
1 cup plain yogurt
Salt to taste
1/2 cup cilantro or mint leaves for garnish

Serves: 6

2 cups freshly shredded coconut
1 1/2 cups cilantro leaves
1/2 cup mint leaves
4 fresh red chiles, such as serranos, seeds and stems removed
1 green chile, such as serrano,
   seeds and stem removed
4 cloves garlic, peeled
1 teaspoon cumin seeds
1/4 cup cold water
Salt to taste
6 one-inch-thick tuna or swordfish
   steaks
1 teaspoon ground turmeric
3 tablespoons vegetable or olive oil

❦ Chutney Machi

FISH BAKED IN CHUTNEY

The Parsis are relative newcomers to India; they arrived between the eighth and eleventh centuries, following the conquest of their territory in Persia by the Arabs. They settled in western India and became prosperous merchants and industrialists. Although they came from a landlocked region, the Parsis fell in love with India's abundant fish supply, and some of their best dishes are made with fish today.

In a food processor or blender, grind the coconut, cilantro and mint leaves, chiles, garlic, cumin seeds, water, and salt, and make a smooth paste — this is the chutney.

Heat the oven to 350 degrees. Meanwhile, wash the fish and dry on paper towels. Sprinkle the steaks with the turmeric and coat them with the chutney.

Line a baking dish with aluminum foil brushed with the oil. Place the fish steaks in the dish and pour the remaining chutney over them. Bake for 12 to 15 minutes, turning the fish halfway through the process.

 # Fish Kalia

AROMATIC FISH

Sambhu Banik, psychologist and one of the more prominent Indian community leaders in Washington, D.C., is an award-winning chef, too. He recently published Sampling the Cuisine of India. *The following recipe, which he gave to Arthur during an interview, is a dish popular in India's northeast region, particularly Bengal.*

In a food processor or blender, puree the onion, ginger, cayenne, turmeric, yogurt, and coriander. Set aside.

In a large skillet, heat 4 tablespoons of the Ghee or oil for 1 minute, then lower the heat and add the potatoes. Brown for about 5 minutes. Remove the potatoes from the pan and set aside.

In another skillet, heat 2 tablespoons of the Ghee or oil. When the oil begins to smoke, lower the heat, add the fish steaks, and fry for about 2 minutes, turning once. Remove the fish from the skillet and reserve.

Add the bay or curry leaves to the skillet; simmer for 1 minute. Add the spice-yogurt puree and simmer for 5 minutes. Return the potatoes and the fish to the pan and add the tomatoes, nuts, and salt. Stir gently and cook, covered, over medium heat for 5 minutes.

In a small frying pan, heat the remaining 1 tablespoon Ghee or oil, fry the cardamom seeds and cinnamon for a few seconds, and pour over the fish curry just before serving. Remove the bay or curry leaves before serving.

Serves: 8

1 large onion, finely chopped
1 two-inch piece ginger, peeled and chopped
1 teaspoon cayenne
1 teaspoon ground turmeric
1/2 cup plain yogurt
1 teaspoon ground coriander
7 tablespoons Ghee (page 17) or vegetable oil
2 potatoes, peeled and diced
8 one-inch-thick tuna steaks (or substitute swordfish)
4 bay or curry leaves
4 large tomatoes, quartered
1/4 cup finely chopped almonds
1/4 cup pistachios
Salt to taste
6 cardamom seeds, crushed
1 one-inch piece cinnamon, crushed

🌸 *Bhinda Gharbano Patio*

FISH ROE WITH OKRA

2 pounds shad roe
6 cups water
2 tablespoons vegetable or olive oil
3 large onions, finely chopped
1 teaspoon cayenne
1 teaspoon ground turmeric
2 teaspoons ground cumin
3 cloves garlic, peeled and finely
  minced
1 one-inch piece ginger, peeled and
  finely minced
2 medium ripe tomatoes, chopped
1 tablespoon sugar (optional)
1/2 cup freshly squeezed lemon
  juice
4 cups okra, stems removed,
  halved
Salt to taste
1/4 cup cilantro or mint leaves for
  garnish

This simple but colorful dish is prepared by the Parsi people in Bombay and Surat. It can be made with any roe, but Arthur prefers shad or mackerel.

Place the roe in a saucepan in the 6 cups water and cook over medium heat for 5 minutes. Drain and cut each roe into 3 pieces. Set aside.

In a skillet, heat the oil over medium heat for 1 minute, add the onions, and fry until they wilt, about 1 minute. Add the cayenne, turmeric, cumin, garlic, and ginger, and continue cooking over medium heat for about 2 minutes.

Add the tomatoes, sugar (if using), lemon juice, and okra, and cook for 20 minutes over medium heat.

Add the roe and cook for another 5 minutes. Add salt to taste and garnish with the cilantro or mint leaves just before serving.

Ismail Merchant's Baked Salmon for Paul Newman

Serves: 6 or more

3/4 cup olive oil
4 tablespoons Dijon mustard
6 cloves garlic, peeled and minced
1 tablespoon cayenne
1 teaspoon ground coriander
4 tablespoons freshly squeezed lemon juice
Salt to taste
5 pounds salmon (or any firm-fleshed fish), cut into steaks 1 inch thick (or fillets)
1/4 cup fresh dill for garnish

"While shooting for Mr. and Mrs. Bridge in Kansas City, a friend of Paul Newman brought him a ten-pound Alaskan salmon," Ismail Merchant recalled in an interview with Arthur. "Paul asked me if I could cook it. I had a simple formula and suggested that we cut the salmon into halves, and using the same masala, one half of the salmon could be baked and the other half could be grilled, and we would see which one tasted better. Paul grilled his, and I baked my portion. We ended up saying each other's salmon tasted better." An exuberant Paul Newman said: "Let's start a restaurant." Has Merchant thought of it? "The idea has crossed my mind several times," he said. "But I will not. There is too much work there." Merchant said the mildly flavored dish below is inspired by Bengali cooking. "Don't the Bengalis love mustard," he said.

Combine 1/2 cup of the olive oil and all the remaining ingredients except the dill in a bowl and marinate, covered for 30 minutes at room temperature.

Heat the oven to 350 degrees. Use the remaining oil to grease the surface of a large baking dish. Place the salmon in the dish and bake for about 12 to 15 minutes, turning after 6 minutes.

Garnish with the dill.

Serve with white rice, a vegetable dish, chutney, and pickle.

Serves: 4

2 teaspoons salt
20 jumbo uncooked shrimp,
  shelled and deveined
1 teaspoon mustard or vegetable
  oil
1 teaspoon mustard seeds
4 tablespoons Ghee (page 17)
1 teaspoon ground cardamom
1/2 teaspoon ground cinnamon
4 bay or curry leaves
1 medium onion, finely chopped
1 two-inch piece ginger, peeled and
  finely minced
1 tablespoon raisins
1 tablespoon almonds
2 green chiles, such as serranos,
  seeds and stems removed, finely
  minced
1 cup plain yogurt
1 cup water
1 teaspoon sugar (optional)

🌸 *Dahi Chingree*

SHRIMP IN YOGURT SAUCE

Bengalis are among the biggest fish eaters in the Indian subcontinent. This tangy dish is popular chiefly among upper-middle-class Bengalis, since shrimp is very, very expensive in Bangladesh and India.

Sprinkle 1/2 teaspoon of the salt over the shrimp.

Heat the oil in a large saucepan over medium heat for 2 minutes. Add the mustard seeds, and when they begin to pop, reduce the heat and add the Ghee. Cook for 1 minute.

Add the shrimp and gently fry, uncovered, for about 3 minutes. Remove the shrimp and set aside.

In the same oil, simmer the cardamom and cinnamon along with the bay or curry leaves for 30 seconds.

Add the onion, ginger, raisins, and almonds, and fry for about 2 minutes. Add the chiles, yogurt, water, sugar (if using), and remaining salt, and bring the mixture to a boil. Lower the heat, add the shrimp, and cook, covered, over low heat for 5 minutes. Remove the bay or curry leaves before serving.

Peshawari Biryani

BIRYANI FROM PESHAWAR

The foods from the region of Pakistan bordering Afghanistan are heavily influenced by Afghan cuisine; they are less spicy than the cuisine of the rest of Pakistan and India and contain plenty of dried fruits and nuts. This biryani is one of the tastiest rice preparations from the Indian subcontinent.

Combine the soaked and drained *kabuli chana* with the 1 cup water and boil for about 12 minutes.

Melt the butter in a large skillet, add the cayenne, turmeric, ginger, and tomatoes, and cook, uncovered, over medium heat until the tomatoes turn into thick pulp, about 12 to 15 minutes. Add the cream, yogurt, cilantro and mint leaves, and *kabuli chana* with their water, and cook, covered, for about 5 minutes over low heat. Set aside.

Heat the Ghee in a large skillet for 1 minute, then add the cloves, cardamom, and cinnamon, and cook for 1 minute more. Add the rice and fry for 5 minutes over low heat. Add the milk, mix well, and bring to a boil; lower the heat and cook, covered, for 15 minutes or until the rice is tender and dry.

Add the reserved tomato mixture, salt, raisins, cashews, and almonds; stir well. Cook for 3 minutes. Stir in the rose essence. Sprinkle with the rose petals and the edible foil.

1 *cup* kabuli chana *(whole chickpeas, available in Asian markets), soaked overnight in 1 cup water and drained*
1 *cup* water
1 tablespoon butter
1 teaspoon cayenne
1 teaspoon ground turmeric
1 two-inch piece ginger, peeled and minced
4 large tomatoes, chopped
1 cup heavy cream
1 cup plain yogurt
1/4 cup cilantro leaves
1/4 cup mint leaves
2 tablespoons Ghee *(page 17)*
1 teaspoon ground cloves
1 teaspoon ground cardamom
1/2 teaspoon ground cinnamon
1 cup uncooked basmati or other long-grain rice
2 cups milk
Salt to taste
1/4 cup each *raisins, cashews (preferably raw), and almonds*
1 teaspoon rose essence
1 cup fresh rose petals for garnish
Handful edible silver or gold foil *(available in Asian markets) for garnish*

Serves: 4

1 large eggplant
1/2 cup plain yogurt
1 large onion, chopped
1 two-inch piece ginger, peeled
4 green chiles, such as serranos,
  seeds and stems removed,
  chopped
6 cloves garlic, peeled
4 tablespoons vegetable or olive oil
1 tablespoon Ghee (page 17)
  (optional)
1 teaspoon ground coriander
1/4 teaspoon ground mace
1/4 teaspoon ground turmeric
1 teaspoon ground cumin
4 large tomatoes, chopped
Salt to taste
1 teaspoon freshly squeezed lime
  juice
1/4 cup cilantro leaves for garnish

🌸 *Baingan Burtha*

SMOKED EGGPLANT

Created in northwestern India, this dish is considered one of India's most famous and is found in restaurants throughout the country. Originally it was cooked over an open wood flame; hence the term "smoked."

Hold the eggplant with tongs and, using a pot holder to grasp the tongs, place the eggplant over a gas flame on medium heat and sear the skin while cooking the flesh. When one side is seared, turn to the other side. The searing process should not take more than 20 minutes.

Hold the eggplant under cold running water for about 3 minutes. Remove the blackened skin and chop the flesh coarsely.

In a food processor or blender, combine the eggplant, yogurt, onion, ginger, chiles, and garlic, and make a smooth paste.

Heat the oil over medium heat in a skillet for 1 minute, add the Ghee (if using), and lower the heat. After 1 minute, add the eggplant paste, coriander, mace, turmeric, and cumin. Simmer for 3 minutes. Add the tomatoes. Mix well and cook over low heat for 5 minutes.

Add the salt, lime juice, and cilantro leaves just before serving.

Serves: 4

2 tablespoons sesame seeds
1 tablespoon coriander seeds
1 cup freshly shredded coconut
1 tablespoon cumin seeds
2 large onions, 1 whole and 1
  sliced
1 lemon-size ball tamarind pulp
1 cup warm water
1/4 cup sugar
1/4 cup each almonds, cashews
  (preferably raw), raisins, and
  peanuts
6 cloves garlic, peeled

🌸 *Baingan Mewaa Ke Saath*

EGGPLANT WITH NUTS

In Pakistan, unlike the southern region of India, coconut is sparingly used in curries. This is an atypical dish from the Punjab region.

Roast together in a skillet the sesame and coriander seeds, coconut, and cumin seeds over a low flame, making sure they don't burn, for 3 minutes. Set aside.

Hold the whole onion with tongs and, using a pot holder to

grasp the tongs, place the onion over a medium flame until its peel turns black. Let cool and remove the peel. Slice and set aside.

Soak the tamarind in the 1 cup warm water for 15 minutes, then strain the pulp, discard, and reserve the liquid (see Note). Add the sugar to the liquid and set aside.

In a food processor or blender, grind the nuts and the raisins with the roasted sesame mixture and the garlic, ginger, chiles, cilantro or mint leaves, turmeric, and salt until a smooth paste forms. Set aside.

Make 2 slits in each eggplant, cutting only halfway through. Stuff the paste from the blender into both eggplants.

Heat the oil in a large skillet for 1 minute. Add the Ghee; when it melts, add the sliced unroasted onion and the eggplants to the skillet and cook, covered, for about 10 minutes over medium heat. Turn the eggplants, lower the heat, and cook for another 10 minutes. Add the sweetened tamarind liquid. Garnish with the roasted onion slices.

Note: 2 teaspoons freshly squeezed lime juice can be substituted for the tamarind liquid.

1 two-inch piece ginger, peeled
2 fresh red chiles, such as serranos, seeds and stems removed
2 green chiles, such as serranos, seeds and stems removed
1/4 cup cilantro or mint leaves
1/2 teaspoon ground turmeric
Salt to taste
8 long, thin eggplants
2 teaspoons vegetable oil
1 cup Ghee (page 17)

🌼 Shukto

BITTER GOURD CURRY

This is a mixed-vegetable curry extremely popular in both Bangladesh and West Bengal, India, the predominant vegetable in it being bitter gourd (Chinese winter melon), which is available in Asian markets.

Heat the oil in a large saucepan over medium heat for 2 minutes. Add the mustard seeds; when they begin to pop, reduce the heat, add the ginger, and fry for half a minute.

Add the vegetables, salt, and sugar (if using), and stir-fry for 5 minutes.

Add the water, bring the dish to a boil, lower the heat, cover, and cook for 10 minutes.

Serves: 4

2 tablespoons olive oil
1/2 teaspoon mustard seeds
1 two-inch piece ginger, peeled and finely minced
2 bitter gourds, cut into 1/2-inch rounds
1 white radish, scraped and cut into 1/2-inch pieces
1 green banana, skin on, cut into 1-inch rounds
2 potatoes, peeled and cut into 1/2-inch dice
2 carrots, peeled and cut into 1/2-inch rounds
1 teaspoon salt
1 teaspoon sugar (optional)
2 cups water

Serves: 4

4 tablespoons butter
2 onions, sliced
1 two-inch piece ginger, peeled and
    minced
3 green chiles, such as serranos,
    seeds and stems removed,
    minced
2 bay or curry leaves
1/4 cup each diced carrots,
    chopped green beans, and lima
    beans
1 1/2 cups uncooked long-grain
    rice
Salt to taste
2 teaspoons ground coriander
1 teaspoon ground cumin
1 teaspoon commercial garam
    masala
1 teaspoon cayenne
1/2 teaspoon ground turmeric
3 cups chicken stock
6 hard-boiled eggs, halved, for gar-
    nish
1/4 cup cilantro or mint leaves for
    garnish

🌸 Sant's Korma Chawal

CURRIED RICE

Sant Chatwal, the owner of the Bombay Palace restaurants, is arguably the best-known Indian restaurateur in North America. His restaurants in nearly a dozen cities serve mostly Punjabi recipes and have introduced thousands to the delights of Indian cuisine. He has also published The Bombay Palace Cookbook. *He gave this recipe to Arthur during an interview.*

In a heavy skillet, heat the butter for 1 minute, add the onions, and stir-fry until they are brown, about 8 minutes. Add the ginger, chiles, bay or curry leaves, and vegetables, and stir-fry for 3 minutes.

Add the rice and continue cooking, stirring constantly, for 2 minutes.

Add the salt, coriander, cumin, *garam masala*, cayenne, turmeric, and chicken stock. Mix well, bring to a boil, and then lower the heat and simmer, covered, for 15 minutes.

Remove the skillet from the heat and let stand, covered, for 10 minutes.

Garnish the rice with the egg halves and the cilantro or mint leaves. Remove the bay or curry leaves before serving.

 # Bhatura

---

DEEP-FRIED BREAD

This bread is a delicious addition to any meat or vegetable dish. It originated in the Punjab region but has traveled across the Indian subcontinent and appears wherever Indian and Pakistani restaurants have prospered.

Warm the flour in an oven preheated to 300 degrees for 1 minute. Mix the baking soda and salt into the flour and sift into a bowl. Add the egg, sugar, yogurt, and warm water; mix well. Knead the dough until it stops sticking to the fingers.

Melt the 1 teaspoon of Ghee and add it to the dough; knead for about 10 minutes. Cover the dough with a wet towel and let it rise in a warm place for 4 hours.

Divide the dough into 8 balls. Roll out each ball so that it is 4 inches in diameter and about 1/2 inch thick. These are the *bhaturas*. Keep them covered on a tray.

Heat the 5 cups oil in a skillet; when it begins to smoke, add the 1 tablespoon Ghee and start frying the *bhaturas*, one at a time. Fry them until they puff up and turn golden.

Drain on paper towels and serve immediately.

Serves: 4

1 1/2 cups all-purpose flour
1/2 teaspoon baking soda
1/2 teaspoon salt
1 egg, beaten
1 teaspoon sugar
4 tablespoons plain yogurt
1/2 cup warm water
1 teaspoon + 1 tablespoon Ghee (page 17)
5 cups vegetable or olive oil

Yield: 8

1/2 cup milk
1 egg, beaten
2 teaspoons sugar
1 teaspoon baking powder
1/2 packet active dry yeast
3 tablespoons vegetable or olive oil
1/4 cup plain yogurt
Salt to taste
3 cups all-purpose flour
1 tablespoon milk
1 tablespoon vegetable oil for the
   kneaded flour
1 tablespoon vegetable oil for the
   baking sheets
1 tablespoon Ghee (page 17) or
   vegetable oil for the naan
1/4 teaspoon poppy seeds

🌸 Naan

FLAT BREAD

Although most South Indians eat their curries with rice, and northerners use more than two dozen varieties of unleavened breads, there is hardly a big city in India where varieties of unleavened breads are not eaten. In the southern region, the unleavened breads are often used in the first half of the meal, and the rice in the second.

Heat the milk over low heat for 3 minutes. Remove from the heat and set aside.

In a medium bowl, place the egg, sugar, baking powder, yeast, 3 tablespoons oil, yogurt, and salt. Mix well and combine the mixture with the flour in another bowl.

Add the 1 tablespoon milk and begin kneading. Continue adding the milk that has been heated as the kneading continues. Knead well for at least 8 minutes.

Brush the kneaded flour with 1 tablespoon oil, cover with a damp cloth, and set aside at room temperature for 2 hours. The flour should begin to rise by this time; if it has not, wait for another 30 minutes.

Heat the oven to 350 degrees. Cover 4 baking sheets with aluminum foil and brush with a total of 1 tablespoon oil.

Knead the dough for 3 minutes and then form 8 balls. Flatten each ball to form a tear-shaped bread (*naan*) that is about 9 inches long and 4 inches wide. Meanwhile, keep the rest of the flour balls covered with moistened cloth.

Place 2 *naan*s on each baking sheet; cover with moistened cloth for 12 minutes.

Remove the cloth; brush the center of each *naan* with water and a bit of the 1 tablespoon Ghee or oil. Sprinkle the center of each *naan* with some of the poppy seeds.

Place the baking sheets under the broiler and broil the *naan*s for about 2 minutes on each side or until lightly browned.

Serve hot with any curry that has plenty of gravy.

 **Chapatti**

Yield: 12

2 cups whole wheat flour
1 cup cold water
1/2 teaspoon salt
4 tablespoons all-purpose flour
2 tablespoons olive oil

The simplest of Indian breads, chapatti *is eaten at breakfast with curried potatoes and at lunch or dinner with curried meats and vegetable dishes.*

Place the flour in a bowl, slowly pour in the water, add the salt, mix well, and knead for about 6 minutes. Cover the flour with a damp cloth and let rest for an hour.

Divide the dough into 12 balls. Dip each ball into the all-purpose flour and roll out flat until it is about 6 inches in diameter. The *chapatti*s are ready to be fried.

Heat the *tawa* or griddle over high heat for 2 minutes, lower the heat, sprinkle on a bit of olive oil, and place 1 *chapatti* on it. Using a piece of cloth, press the *chapatti* against the surface of the griddle for about 1 minute. Flip it with a spatula and fry for 1 more minute. Repeat the procedure until all the *chapatti*s are ready.

Yield: 12

1/2 package (5 ounces) frozen
  chopped spinach
2 cups whole wheat flour
1/4 cup split pea flour (see Note)
Pinch baking soda
1 teaspoon cayenne
1 teaspoon salt
1 teaspoon fennel seeds
1 teaspoon ground cumin
1 cup cold water
4 tablespoons olive oil
1/2 cup vegetable oil for frying

🌿 *Palak Paratha*

HOT SPINACH BREAD

*Here is an unusual, spicy bread that goes well with curries from
any country.*

Thaw the spinach, drain, and set aside.

In a bowl, combine the flours, baking soda, and spices. Mix
well. Add the spinach and the water, mix thoroughly, and
knead for 15 minutes.

Divide the dough into about 12 lemon-size balls. Flatten
and roll out each ball into a 4-inch-broad *paratha*. Sprinkle a
little olive oil on each *paratha* and roll them out again until
they are 8 inches in diameter.

Heat the *tawa* or griddle over medium heat. Coat its surface with a little oil and fry each *paratha* for 1 1/2 minutes,
then add a little more oil, flip it with a spatula, and fry the
other side for 1 minute. Repeat the procedure until all the
*paratha*s are ready.

Note: If split pea flour is not available at the local health food
store or natural foods supermarket, buy dried split peas and soak
them overnight in water. Drain off the liquid and grind the peas
in a blender, adding some water if necessary. Then add the
remaining ingredients and proceed. The peas can also be boiled
in water until barely soft and then ground in the blender.

FOUR

Golden Triangle Curries

All curries do not taste

alike; they have as many

distinctive bouquets as

wine. You can develop

into a connoisseur of

curries just as you can

of the other good things

of life.

HARVEY DAY

*T*he region we call Southeast Asia is also known as Indochina, so named by the west because the countries ringing the Golden Triangle — an area encompassing parts of Burma, Laos, and Thailand — displayed the influences of both India and China.

"*The Return of the Oil*"

Burma has more than a hundred distinct ethnic groups, but Burmese cuisine has mostly been influenced by the cooking styles of India, Thailand, Cambodia, and China — the homes of most of the original immigrants. Tibetan people arrived in Burma in the ninth century A.D. The region was conquered by the Mongol dynasty from China in 1272, so the Chinese influence on cooking is significant. However, since the very first settlers of Burma were the Sakya warriors who migrated from India and settled at Tagung about 250 B.C., it is not surprising that curries play an important role in the cuisine.

Burmese cuisine is a culinary treasure; the dishes are easy to prepare and offer delightful challenges to adventurous cooks. The Burmese often quote a proverb to explain their love of good food: "You cannot meditate on an empty stomach." The cooking of the country, like that of any other nation, has regional varieties. The Shan people, from the area near China, use the least amount of spices and season with soy sauce instead of fish sauce. The people who live near the border with Thailand make their curries more soupy, and those in the southern region enjoy spicier curries.

According to Richard Sterling, who has reported on Cambodia, Vietnam, and Laos as a contributing editor of *Chile Pepper* magazine, "The Burmese cook approaches curry in a way as constant as the ancient past or the monsoon cycle." During his extensive visits to Burma, Richard watched many curries being prepared. First the Burmese make a curry paste out of their five basic ingredients: onion, garlic, chile, ginger, and turmeric. Some Burmese cooks use other spices as well, including an occasional prepared curry powder. But the hallmark of the Burmese curry

Merchant Street, Mandalay, Burma, 1880s. Note the tiffin (curry lunch) establishment.

is its oiliness. Cooks use a combination of peanut oil and sesame oil, about a cup of each in a wok, and heat it until it smokes — this is called cooking the oil. The curry paste is added, the heat is reduced, and the paste is cooked for 15 minutes. Then meat is added and cooked, and eventually the oil rises to the top. This state is called *see byan*, the return of the oil. When the oil floats on top, the dish is done. The oil is not skimmed off but rather is absorbed by the side dish of rice when it is served. Surprisingly, the curries, such as Swimming Chicken Curry (page 123), do not taste greasy, probably as a result of the light oil used. However, western cooks usually use less oil than Burmese cooks. Another Burmese chicken curry, quick to prepare, is *Kyethar Peinathar Hin* (page 125), which is heavily flavored with fenugreek. Sometimes chicken is curried with tomatoes, as in *Kyethar Sipyan* (page 124). Duck is also popular in Burma, as indicated by *Bairather Sepiyan* (page 125), which uses the technique of the return of the oil.

Arthur, who grew up thinking that curries were uniquely Indian, began to discover the world of Burmese curries more than twenty years ago in the southern Indian city of Madras. He didn't find the curries in Burmese restaurants — for there were none — but he ate them on the streets of the Burma Bazaar, where the wives of Indian merchants from Burma sold the mildly spicy (compared with the Madras curries, of course) Burmese curries to supplement their income.

Many of these Indian merchants in Burma had belonged to a trading community called Chettiar (see Chettiar Curry, page 133). They were expelled by the Burmese government in a nationalist fervor. When they returned to India, they brought with them many Burmese recipes, such as *Buthi-Kyetha Hin* (page 126), which features chicken and the Burmese long gourd. Arthur discovered the flavor of Burmese curries on the streets but has long wondered why the repatriates did not open restaurants in Madras. Indeed, he is still puzzled by the lack of Burmese restaurants outside of Burma.

The answer probably comes from Burmese political history. After being freed from British rule in 1948, Burma faced communist insurgency and ethnic unrest. It came under military control, and the chauvinistic military rulers sealed the country's borders, thus isolating Burma from the rest of the world. Few Burmese got out of the country — the exception being those Indian merchants in Madras.

Today, Burma is known as Myanmar. The military government renamed the country in 1989 as an effort to appease different warring ethnic factions that resented the dominance of people of Burman heritage.

Like the Buddhists in Sri Lanka, Tibet, Thailand, and elsewhere, the Burmese make hundreds of delicious dishes with quite a variety of meats and poultry. An example of a typical Burmese meat dish is Pork Curry (page 121), where the meat is combined with green mangoes or a mango pickle.

Fish is extremely important in Burmese cooking, both as a main ingredient to be curried and also in the form of fish sauces. The Burmese use a fish sauce that is identical to the *nam pla* that the Thais, Laotians, and Khmers use. But they also love a much stronger one, *Ngapi Ye* (page 117), which is made of anchovies. Cooks may use either in these curries. Aung Aung

Taik, author of *Under the Golden Pagoda: The Best of Burmese Cooking*, quotes a popular saying: "If one hasn't eaten *ngapi ye*, one is not a true-blooded Burmese." Traditionally, it is made with sun-dried anchovies that are fermented. "Some say it smells worse than Limburger cheese," notes Taik. Rudyard Kipling refers to it as "fish pickled when it ought to be buried."

One signature Burmese fish dish is *Mohinga* (page 130), a curried catfish soup. Interestingly enough, it is served over rice noodles. Some people believe that the Burmese habit of eating some curries with noodles shows the influence of Chinese cuisine, but in parts of southern India, rice noodles accompany some curried meat and fish dishes, too. Another popular Burmese fish dish is *Nga Baung Doke* (page 128), in which a lightly curried fish is steamed in banana leaves. An unusual vegetarian curry is *Shwephayonethee Hin* (page 134), featuring pumpkin and tamarind.

To accompany the Golden Triangle curries in this chapter, we recommend the Burmese-Style Rice (page 134) and *Ghin Thoke* (page 120), a Burmese pickled ginger salad.

Fiery Pastes and Carved Fruits

In neighboring Thailand, people believe that they had more time to evolve their unique cooking because they were smart enough to keep would-be foreign invaders at bay. Thailand is the only Southeast Asian country that was not subjected to European rulers; it has rarely been overrun by its Asian neighbors, and it has seen relatively few wars. These unique conditions gave the Thai kings time to dally with their queens and mistresses, to hire the best cooks, and to encourage the cooks to create new dishes and improve the traditional ones.

Thai curries are extensively spiced with chiles. Contrary to popular belief, there is not just one "Thai chile," but rather dozens of varieties used in cooking. When Dave toured the wholesale market in Bangkok in 1991, he found literally tons of both fresh and dried chiles in baskets and in huge bales five feet high. They ranged in size from piquinlike thin pods barely an inch long to yellow and red pods about four inches long. When making substitutions, cooks should remember that, generally speaking, the smaller a chile, the hotter it is.

It is the fresh chiles that are ground up with other ingredients to make the famous Thai curry pastes, but rehydrated dried chile can be substituted in a pinch. Two key curry pastes are the heart of Thai cooking: *Nam Prik Gaeng Ped* (page 116), a red paste, uses red chiles, lemongrass, galangal, and herbs; *Kreung Gaeng Kiow Wahn* (page 115), a green paste, is traditionally made with green Thai chiles, but serranos are a good substitute. This green curry paste looks deceptively mild, like a Mediterranean pesto, but it is very hot indeed.

These pastes, which are easily made fresh, keep well for at least a month in the refrigerator and add a terrific zing to curries, but some very tasty commercial curry pastes are available in Asian markets. A yellow curry paste, colored with ground turmeric, is perhaps the mildest among all Thai pastes.

The Muslim Curry Paste (page 116) is so named after Muslim traders (or perhaps Muslim harbor officials in the port of Bangkok), who first imported it from India. It is unique in that it uses curry spices most Thai dishes avoid, such as coriander, cloves, and cinnamon. It was first prepared in the court of King Rama I in the early nineteenth century. Another ruler who loved good food was Chulalongkorn, who reportedly had thirty-two wives. Each new year he required all his wives to prepare one new dish, and the wife who created the dish enjoyed most would receive special gifts and elevated status.

We have assembled quite a repertoire of Thai curries. Pannang Beef Curry (page 121) was probably influenced by trade with the island of Penang, off the coast of Malaysia. Another curry featuring beef is *Gaeng Bah* (page 122), highly spiced with extra red chiles, which are combined with fresh basil, eggplant, and green beans. *Gaeng Kiow Wahn Gai* (page 124) is a unique green chicken curry with eggplant and lime leaves. Seafood is a basic part of Thai cuisine, so fish sauce is used even in meat dishes. One interesting Thai fish curry is *Gaeng Leuang Pahk Dai* (page 130), which combines catfish with bamboo shoots and pineapple. *Haw Moke Phuket* (page 128) is another fish steamed in banana leaves, but with an entirely different taste from the Burmese version.

A visitor to a Thai home or restaurant is won over not only

by the aromatic food but also by the elegant way in which it is served. Commonly accompanying Thai curries are elaborately carved fruits and vegetables, which often resemble large flowers. Rosemary Brissenden, author of *Joys and Subtleties: South East Asian Cooking*, describes the art: "Fruit and vegetable carving is traditionally a highly cultivated art. Anyone who has watched the infinite calm of a Thai woman carving a piece of young ginger into the likeness of a crab with its pincers at the ready will bear witness to this."

Thai salads are also artistically arranged, and food historians believe that such elaboration dates back to the days of royal culinary competitions, when the dishes had to look as spectacular as they tasted. Among the many excellent Thai salads to accompany curries, the papaya salad *Som Tum* (page 119) vies for a top position. "Pungent chile, tart lime juice, and refreshing fruit combine to create the best salad I've ever tasted," says celebrity chef and restaurant owner Tommy Tang, author of *Tommy Tang's Modern Thai Cooking*. This salad is found on every Thai street corner and in most restaurants and homes at all times of the year. It is, notes Tang, "by far the most popular one in Thailand." Incidentally, the Burmese love their green papaya salad, too, as do the Laotians, who add crushed garlic and dry chiles to it. Tommy was also kind enough to furnish his recipe for Spicy Chile Shrimp (page 131), which calls for bell pepper and green beans.

When preparing Thai food (and, for that matter, any other recipe in this book), cooks should not be inhibited if they cannot find a particular ingredient. They should be adventurous and creative. And this is one of the secrets of Tommy Tang's cooking. For example, he uses rosemary, arugula, and pine nuts — ingredients not commonly available in Thailand — to enhance his Thai creations. "Traditional Thai cooking does not use olive oil," he says. "But I do."

While the Thais add sugar to many of their dishes, they are not very fond of desserts. "I guess that's because Thai food is so good, so satisfying, that there is no quarrel between the tongue and the brain," says Tommy. "When the food is not very good, the unsatisfied tongue quarrels with the brain, demanding to be satisfied, and desserts help settle that fight."

The Thais may not be great at desserts, but they love their

fruits. A meal often ends with a sweet syrup made from coconut milk, tapioca, bananas, rice, and flowers. Thai restaurants also serve an excellent pumpkin custard, and some serve what is popularly known as Siamese crullers, or *khanom sai*.

Of Lemongrass and Frog Legs

Although the foods of Thailand have been examined with increasing frequency in books and magazine articles, and articles and books about Burmese and Vietnamese cuisines appear occasionally, hardly any information is available about Cambodian and Laotian foods. This is one of the unfortunate results of recent warfare and unstable political situations in these two countries. We depended on Richard Sterling for most of our information about Cambodian and Laotian curries. He was brave enough to travel there in the early nineties, and he collected some curry recipes for us.

In Cambodia, which is now called Kampuchea, the Khmer cooks rely on chiles, lemongrass, galangal, and fish sauces in most of their curries. "The Cambodians are great eaters," Richard says. "Their calendar is full of historical feasts, and any gaps are filled by weddings, births, funerals, and auspicious alignments of the stars. Theirs is a land of abundance. They enjoy regular harvests of rice, wild and cultivated fruits, fresh and saltwater fish, domesticated animals, and fowl and game. They love to eat meat. Pork is the most popular, and it is excellent, as are all the meats. An English journalist we dined with said of her beefsteak that it was the best she ever had. We didn't tell her it was *luc lac*, or water buffalo.

"In Cambodia, as in India, there are as many curries as there are cooks. But all true Khmer curries have five constants: lemongrass, garlic, galangal, and coconut milk; the fifth constant is the cooking technique, dictated by the texture of lemongrass and the consistency of coconut milk."

Richard provided us with recipes for his basic Lemongrass Curry (page 117), which is an easy-to-prepare, coconut-based dish using the cook's choice of meat, and for Red Curry *Cambogee* (page 120), featuring potatoes and bean sprouts. We have

Rice fields, Mekong Delta, c. 1880.

included one curried venison recipe, *Phan Sin Fahn* (page 122), which was reported to be the favorite of the early Cambodian kings. Our version is very simple compared with the traditional palace recipe, which we believe took at least half a day to prepare. It was served with huge mounds of vegetables and garnishments, including watercress, indigenous fruits, and pickled garlic. Cooks can, of course, substitute rabbit, beef, or pork for the venison.

In nearby Laos, two distinctive cooking styles have emerged. One is that of the Laotians, whose cuisine is very similar to that of the Thais except that lemongrass and galangal are only rarely used in curries. The other is that of the Hmong, a tribal people of southern Chinese origin. The Hmong cuisine, naturally, drew its inspiration from the Chinese, so soy sauce replaces fish sauce. Laotian Beef *Laab* (page 118) is a typical tasty salad to accompany curries of the region.

Shallots, ginger, and chiles are common in Laotian curries. All of the ingredients are pounded together in a mortar until they are very smooth and then are cooked in coconut milk until a silky sauce is formed. "A good Laotian curry sauce is similar to the consistency of hollandaise," says Richard. Meats are commonly curried in Laos, but not vegetables, which are eaten on the side. Richard sent us his recipe for Laotian Catfish Curry

Ginger, a common ingredient in Southeast Asian curries.

(page 129), featuring the fish combined with eggplant and coconut milk.

We should point out that there are some eighty thousand Laotians in the United States, and most of them arrived on the West Coast when the communists tightened their grip on this small country sandwiched between Thailand and Vietnam. The majority of the Laotians settled in the San Joaquin Valley of central California.

Laos represents a culinary division between Cambodia and Vietnam — the people of the latter two countries have little in common. Northern Vietnam was more influenced by China than by India, and heavy curry sauces are not common. However, other types of curries appear in the cuisine of Vietnam, especially in the south, where Indian traders and merchants made an impression.

One of the most interesting Vietnamese curries Arthur has eaten, *Saigon Echnau Cari* (page 132), combines frog legs and cellophane noodles; this was understandably one of the curries beloved by the French, who occupied Vietnam between 1858 and 1954, except for the Japanese conquest during World War II. Our other Vietnamese curries include *Saigon Cari* (page 126), a chicken curry combined with sweet potatoes and coconut milk, and *Cari Ga* (page 127), in which chicken is combined with taro root. We have also included two Vietnamese salads to accompany the curries in this chapter: Hanoi Pork Salad (page 118) and Papaya Salad (page 119). Another favorite salad from the region is also one of Arthur's favorites, Golden Triangle Beef Salad (page 119).

The following recipes are fun to try, but the cook should not limit the meal to the cuisine of just one region. Try a menu made up of a curry from one country, a pickle from another, a chutney from a third country, and a bread from a fourth. We should note that since chicken curries and salads are so commonly served in the region, we have included quite a variety of both of them.

While the curries are cooking, think of this Burmese saying: "Eat hot curry, drink hot soup, burn your lips, and remember my dinner."

A WORLD OF CURRIES

Kreung Gaeng Kiow Wahn

GREEN CURRY PASTE

This standard Thai green curry paste has dozens of uses. It is a must for such curries as Gaeng Kiow Wahn Gai, Green Chicken Curry (page 124), and it can be added to any other curry preparation, be it Indian, Vietnamese, or Cambodian. Just 1 teaspoon of this paste will make other curry concoctions more flavorsome, zesty, and pungent. Marinate a dozen shrimp in this paste, stir-fry them quickly in olive oil, and the result is an instant lunch or dinner.

Roast the coriander and cumin seeds for about 2 minutes in a dry skillet. When they have cooled, grind to a fine powder in a spice mill.

Combine the roasted ground spices with all the remaining ingredients in a food processor or blender and puree until a fine paste is formed.

Pour the paste into an airtight jar and refrigerate. It will keep in the refrigerator for about a month.

Yield: About 1 1/4 cups

1 tablespoon coriander seeds
1 tablespoon cumin seeds
6 whole peppercorns
3 two-inch stalks lemongrass, including the bulbs, chopped
1/2 cup cilantro leaves
1 two-inch piece fresh galangal (or substitute ginger), peeled
1 teaspoon lime zest
8 cloves garlic, peeled
4 shallots, peeled and coarsely chopped
12 green chiles, such as serranos, seeds and stems removed, halved
1/4 cup water
1 teaspoon salt
1 teaspoon shrimp paste (available in Asian markets)

Yield: About 1 cup

10 small dried red chiles, such as
  piquins, seeds and stems removed
1 cup warm water
2 teaspoons cumin seeds
2 teaspoons coriander seeds
2 small onions
1 teaspoon whole black peppercorns
1/2 cup cilantro leaves
1/4 cup basil or mint leaves
1 teaspoon salt
3 two-inch stalks lemongrass, including the bulbs
1 one-inch piece fresh galangal (or
  substitute ginger), peeled
1 tablespoon chopped garlic
1 tablespoon shrimp paste (available in Asian markets)
1 tablespoon corn or peanut oil
1 tablespoon lime zest
1/4 cup water

🌸 Nam Prik Gaeng Ped

RED CURRY PASTE

*A popular ingredient in Thailand, this curry paste can be added
to any dish to enhance its flavor. It is, of course, a primary ingredient in many of the famous Thai curries. Traditionally, it is pa-
tiently pounded by hand with a heavy mortar and pestle, but a
food processor does the job quickly and efficiently. The paste will
keep in the refrigerator for about a month.*

Soak the chiles in the warm water for 20 minutes to soften,
then remove and drain.

Roast the cumin and coriander seeds for about 2 minutes in
a dry skillet, and when they are cooled, grind to a fine powder
in a spice mill.

Combine the drained chiles and the roasted ground spices
with all the remaining ingredients in a food processor or
blender and puree into a fine paste. Store in a tightly sealed
jar in the refrigerator.

Yield: About 1 1/4 cups

12 dried red chiles, such as piquins, seeds and stems removed
1 cup warm water
2 tablespoons cumin seeds
1 teaspoon coriander seeds
1 teaspoon whole black peppercorns
1 teaspoon whole cloves
1 teaspoon each ground cinnamon,
  mace, nutmeg, and cardamom
3 two-inch stalks lemongrass, including the bulbs
1 two-inch piece fresh galangal (or
  substitute ginger), peeled
2 teaspoons salt
6 shallots, peeled and finely
  chopped
1 tablespoon shrimp paste (available in Asian markets)

🌸 Gaeng Mussaman

MUSLIM CURRY PASTE

*This is a relatively recent curry for Thailand — it is only about
two hundred years old. Food historians say that Muslim traders
from India introduced it to King Rama I, and the royal cooks
perfected it. Initially, the story goes, the cooks were not keen on
using cinnamon, but once they tasted their preparation, they fell
in love with the new curry. It is commonly combined with beef,
potatoes, tamarind, and coconut milk to make a curry served at
wedding feasts.*

Soak the chiles in the warm water for 20 minutes, then remove and drain.

Meanwhile, in a frying pan, roast the cumin and coriander
seeds, peppercorns, and cloves in a dry skillet for 2 minutes,

then remove from the heat. Roast the cinnamon, mace, nutmeg, and cardamom in the skillet for 1 minute, then remove from the heat. Grind the cumin, coriander, peppercorns, and cloves in a spice mill and then combine with the other roasted spices. Set aside.

In a food processor or blender, combine the drained chiles and the roasted spices with all the remaining ingredients and puree into a fine paste.

Transfer to a clean airtight jar and refrigerate. The paste keeps for about 1 month in the refrigerator.

🌸 𝒩gapi 𝒰e

ANCHOVY SAUCE

This highly aromatic sauce is commonly used in Southeast Asian curries. The fermented dried fish, found in Asian markets, can be replaced by canned anchovy fillets or by shrimp or prawn paste.

In a saucepan, bring the fish and the water to a boil, then reduce the heat, simmer for 5 minutes, and mash the fish. Remove from the heat. When the mixture has cooled, add the remaining ingredients and stir well.

Yield: 3/4 cup

2 cups fermented dried fish
1/2 cup water
1/4 cup dried shrimp powder
   (available in Asian markets)
1 teaspoon cayenne
2 tablespoons freshly squeezed lime
   juice
6 cloves garlic, peeled and minced

🌸 𝐿emongrass 𝒞urry

This recipe was collected in Cambodia in 1992 by Richard Sterling, a contributing editor of Chile Pepper *magazine. Richard comments: "This is my personal all-purpose 4-cup curry, which is based on extensive observation and many trials. To prepare a meal for one, pour 1/2 cup of this curry sauce into a shallow vessel or a wok. Add 1/2 cup of meat or vegetables, bring to a medium boil, and cook to the desired degree. Try it with frog legs, as the Cambodians do."*

In a food processor or blender, puree together the lemongrass, garlic, galangal, turmeric, jalapeño, and shallots.

Yield: 4 cups

1/3 cup sliced lemongrass, including the bulbs
4 cloves garlic, peeled
1 teaspoon dried ground galangal
   (or substitute ginger)
1 teaspoon ground turmeric
1 jalapeño, seeds and stem removed
3 shallots, peeled
3 1/2 cups Coconut Milk (page 19)
3 fresh lime or lemon leaves
Pinch salt or shrimp paste (available in Asian markets)

GOLDEN TRIANGLE CURRIES

117

Bring the Coconut Milk to a boil and add the pureed ingredients, lime or lemon leaves, and salt or shrimp paste, and boil gently, stirring constantly, for about 5 minutes. Reduce the heat to low and simmer, stirring often, for about 30 minutes or until the lime or lemon leaves are tender and the sauce is creamy. Remove the leaves before serving.

✿ Laotian Beef Laab

TANGY BEEF SALAD

One of the most popular of Laotian recipes, this salad is also one of the easiest Southeast Asian dishes to prepare. Chicken may be substituted for the beef.

Heat the oil in a heavy skillet or wok, add the beef slices, and stir-fry for about 2 minutes. Finely chop the beef.

Transfer the beef to a large bowl, add the rice powder, cayenne, garlic, fish sauce, *Ngapi Ye*, and lime juice; mix well. Add the green onions, cilantro leaves, cucumber, and tomato, and mix well.

Serves: 4

2 teaspoons vegetable oil
1 pound lean beef, thinly sliced (or substitute chicken)
4 teaspoons uncooked rice, roasted 1 minute in a dry skillet, then ground to a powder in a mortar
1/2 teaspoon cayenne
2 cloves garlic, peeled and minced
2 teaspoons fish sauce (nam pla)
2 teaspoons Ngapi Ye (page 117)
1 tablespoon freshly squeezed lime juice
2 green onions, chopped
1/4 cup cilantro leaves
1 small cucumber, peeled and diced
1 tomato, diced

✿ Hanoi Pork Salad

This delicious Vietnamese salad is easy to prepare and is a great accompaniment to the curries in this chapter — or any of the curries in this book, for that matter.

Place the pork in the water in a large saucepan, add the cayenne, and bring to a boil. Lower the heat, cover the pan, and cook over low heat for 40 minutes.

Let the pork cool; cut into 1-inch cubes.

In a large bowl, combine the pork with all the remaining ingredients. Toss before serving.

Serves: 4

2 pounds pork butt
4 cups water
1 teaspoon cayenne
2 cucumbers, peeled and cut into 1-inch sections
1 large onion, sliced into rings
3 tablespoons freshly squeezed lime juice
1/2 cup cilantro leaves
6 cloves garlic, peeled and finely minced
1 two-inch piece ginger, peeled and finely chopped
2 tablespoons fish sauce (nam pla)
1 teaspoon Ngapi Ye (page 117)
Salt to taste

 # Som Tum

PAPAYA SALAD

This crunchy and tangy salad is very similar to the papaya salad Arthur has tasted on the southwest coast of India except that the Thai and Vietnamese use fish sauce and dried shrimp powder. Since the sauce and shrimp have salt in them, there is no need to add salt to the salad. The Vietnamese version of this salad, thinnabawathe thoke, uses a large onion and a pinch of ground turmeric. Laotians also love this dish; they add crushed garlic and dried chile to it.

In a bowl combine the lime juice, fish sauce, shrimp powder, sugar, garlic, and chile, and mix well. Add the papaya, tomato, and cilantro or basil leaves. Sprinkle the peanuts on top and serve.

1/4 cup freshly squeezed lime juice
1/4 cup fish sauce (nam pla)
2 tablespoons dried shrimp powder (available in Asian markets)
1 teaspoon sugar or honey
4 cloves garlic, peeled and finely minced
1 green chile, such as serrano, seeds and stem removed, finely chopped
1 medium green papaya, peeled, seeded, and chopped
1 large tomato, diced
1 tablespoon cilantro or basil leaves
3 tablespoons peanuts, roasted and ground to a powder

Golden Triangle Beef Salad

Serves: 4

Arthur and Betty serve this beef salad with curries on summer evenings. A combination of Indian and Thai elements, it can also be eaten as a main dish. This salad is an onion lover's dream.

In a large saucepan, combine the beef, Coconut Milk, bouillon cube, tomatoes, ginger, cumin, and coriander. Cook over low heat, uncovered, for about 40 minutes. The liquid should be nearly evaporated. Remove from the heat.

Meanwhile, boil the potatoes, with their skins on, for 10 minutes. Remove, cool, peel, and dice.

Combine the meat and potatoes with the Green and Red curry pastes and the fish sauce and mix well. Add the onions and the mint leaves and cool, covered, in the refrigerator for 30 minutes.

1 pound sirloin steak, cut into thin strips
2 cups Coconut Milk (page 19)
1 beef bouillon cube
2 tomatoes, chopped
1 two-inch piece ginger, peeled and chopped
2 teaspoons ground cumin
2 teaspoons ground coriander
4 potatoes
4 tablespoons Green Curry Paste (page 115)
1 teaspoon Red Curry Paste (page 116)
2 tablespoons fish sauce (nam pla)
6 red onions, chopped
1/4 cup mint leaves

Serves: 3 to 4

2 tablespoons olive or corn oil
2 tablespoons sesame seeds
1 onion, chopped
1 cup kizami shoga (pickled ginger)
1 cup cooked chana dal (dried split chickpeas, available in Asian markets)
1/2 cup roasted peanuts, coarsely chopped
Salt to taste
2 tablespoons dried shrimp powder (available in Asian markets)
4 cloves garlic, peeled and minced
1 green chile, such as serrano, seeds and stem removed, minced

🌸 Ghin Thoke

BURMESE PICKLED GINGER SALAD

It is difficult to imagine a Burmese meal without this salad. Every Burmese restaurant we have dined in serves it. The main ingredient — kizami shoga, or pickled ginger — is available in Asian markets.

Heat the oil in a skillet over medium heat for 1 minute. Add the sesame seeds, lower the heat, and cook for 2 minutes. Add the onion and fry until it wilts, about 1 minute. Remove from the heat.

Squeeze the water out of the *kizami shoga*, combine it with the onion–sesame seed mixture and all the remaining ingredients, and mix well.

Serves: 4

4 dried red New Mexican chiles, seeds and stems removed
1 cup boiling water
4 tablespoons paprika
2 to 3 tablespoons vegetable oil
4 cups Lemongrass Curry (page 117)
3/4 pound diced beef
2 potatoes, peeled and diced
1/2 cup chopped peanuts
2 cups bean sprouts

🌸 Red Curry Cambogee

Here is a variation on Cambodian curries from Richard Sterling. Chicken may be substituted for the beef.

Break the chiles into small pieces. Pour the boiling water over them to cover and let steep until they are soft, about 15 minutes. Combine the chiles, chile water, and paprika in a blender to make a paste.

Heat the oil in a wok or skillet, add the chile paste, and stir-fry until it begins to darken. Reduce the heat, if necessary, to prevent burning.

Stir enough of the paste into the Lemongrass Curry to give it a good red color. Bring to a boil, reduce the heat, and simmer for 5 minutes.

Add the meat and potatoes to the curry sauce. Simmer for 20 to 30 minutes or until the meat and potatoes are done.

Garnish with the peanuts and serve over the bean sprouts.

❀ *Gaeng Pannang Nua*

PANNANG BEEF CURRY

This signature Thai dish can also be prepared with chicken or lamb. Note the name, which shows the influence of Malaysia's Penang Island. By substituting Muslim Curry Paste (page 116) for the Red Curry Paste and adding some tamarind paste, onions, and peanuts, a Mussaman curry is made.

Soak the kaffir leaves in the hot water for 10 minutes, then drain.

In a large saucepan, heat 1 cup of the Coconut Milk over low heat, stir in the Red Curry Paste and the kaffir lime leaves, and simmer for 2 minutes.

Add the beef, stir, and cook, covered, for about 30 minutes over low heat. Add the sugar (if using), fish sauce, remaining Coconut Milk, water, potatoes, and salt. Cook, covered, over low heat for 30 minutes. Remove the kaffir lime leaves before serving.

Serves: 4

3 dried kaffir lime leaves
1/2 cup hot water
3 cups Coconut Milk (page 19)
4 tablespoons Red Curry Paste (page 116)
2 pounds stew beef, diced
1 teaspoon sugar (optional)
1 teaspoon fish sauce (nam pla)
1 cup water
5 large potatoes, peeled and diced
Salt to taste

❀ *Whethar Thayathee Thanut Hin*

PORK CURRY

This Burmese curry is delicious made with a mild Indian mango pickle. The pickle can usually be found in Asian markets, but if it is not available, green mango slices make a good substitute.

Combine the pork with the onions, mango pickle or mangoes, salt, turmeric, fish sauce, lemongrass, garlic, ginger, and cayenne, and marinate, covered, in a large bowl in 2 tablespoons of the oil for 1 hour at room temperature.

In a skillet, heat the rest of the oil, pour in the pork with its marinade, and stir-fry for 7 minutes over medium heat. Sprinkle with some of the water from time to time to keep the curry from getting too thick.

Add the rest of the water, lower the heat, and cook, covered, for 20 minutes.

Serves: 4

2 pounds boneless pork, cut into 1-inch cubes
2 large onions, finely chopped
1 cup mango pickle or 2 green mangoes, skins and seeds removed, sliced
Salt to taste
1 teaspoon ground turmeric
3 teaspoons fish sauce (nam pla)
3 two-inch stalks lemongrass, including the bulbs, minced
6 cloves garlic, peeled and minced
1 two-inch piece ginger, peeled and minced
2 teaspoons cayenne
1/4 cup corn or peanut oil
1 cup water

Serves: 4

3 tablespoons vegetable or olive oil
3 tablespoons Red Curry Paste
  (page 116)
1 pound boneless pork, beef, or
  chicken, cut into thin strips
1 cup Coconut Milk (page 19)
2 beef or chicken bouillon cubes
3 tablespoons fish sauce (nam pla)
1 tablespoon sugar (optional)
1/3 cup bamboo shoots
1 eggplant, skin on, diced
1/4 cup green beans, halved
1 cup water
1/4 cup basil or mint leaves,
  chopped
6 fresh red chiles, such as serranos, seeds and stems removed,
  halved

🌸 Gaeng Bah

COUNTRYSIDE CURRY

*This robustly flavorsome Thai dish can be prepared with any
meat. It is usually served with Thai rice, better known as jasmine
rice. Since this dish uses bouillon cubes and fish sauce, which
have plenty of salt in them, no additional salt is needed. This
curry is quite spicy, so cooks may want to adjust the number of
chiles added.*

In a large skillet or wok, heat the oil for 1 minute over moderate heat, add the Red Curry Paste, lower the heat, and simmer for 3 minutes.

Add the meat, mix well, increase the heat, and stir-fry for 3
minutes. Add the Coconut Milk, bouillon cubes, fish sauce,
sugar (if using), bamboo shoots, eggplant, and green beans.
Mix well. Add the water and bring to a boil. Reduce the heat
to medium and cook, covered, for 10 minutes.

Add the basil or mint leaves and the chiles and simmer, uncovered, for 3 minutes. Serve hot.

Serves: 4

3 pounds venison, cut into 1-inch
  cubes
1 teaspoon ground turmeric
1/4 cup fish sauce (nam pla)
Salt to taste
2 tablespoons vegetable or olive oil
2 tablespoons butter
4 tablespoons corn or peanut oil
1 tablespoon unsalted butter
6 shallots, peeled and finely
  chopped
6 cloves garlic, peeled and minced
1 two-inch piece ginger, peeled and
  minced
1 teaspoon freshly ground black
  pepper

🌸 Phan Sin Fahn

CAMBODIAN CURRIED VENISON

*Venison, dried shrimp, fish sauce, watercress, tomatoes, and the
usual Southeast Asian spices make for a heady, aromatic curry
combination. Try this dish with other game, too.*

Combine the venison with the turmeric, fish sauce, and salt,
and marinate, covered, at room temperature for 15 minutes.

In a large skillet, heat the 2 tablespoons of vegetable or
olive oil. When it begins to smoke, add the butter and reduce
the heat. Add the venison and fry for about 10 minutes, stirring constantly. Drain the oil.

In another skillet, heat the corn or peanut oil for 1 minute over high heat, add the unsalted butter, lower the heat, add the shallots, and fry for 2 minutes. Add the garlic, ginger, black pepper, cayenne, dried shrimp, and tomatoes, and fry for 2 minutes.

Add the venison and the water and cook, covered, for 40 minutes or until the venison is tender. Add the banana pieces and the watercress leaves and cook for 5 minutes before serving.

1 teaspoon cayenne
1 cup dried shrimp (available in Asian markets), pounded
4 large tomatoes, cut into small pieces
2 cups water
1 unripe banana, cut into 1-inch-thick pieces
1 cup watercress leaves (or substitute cilantro leaves)

🌼 *Swimming Chicken Curry*

Here is a curry done in the Burmese style from a recipe collected by Richard Sterling. He comments: "This is a wet curry, or curry with gravy; it cries out for rice, or even mashed potatoes, to sop up the delicious sauce." The eggplants are the small Asian variety.

Combine the oils in a wok, heat, and quickly brown the eggplant, stirring often, for about 6 minutes. Remove the eggplant with a slotted spoon and drain on paper towels.

Combine the chile, onions, garlic, ginger, turmeric, and lemongrass in a food processor or blender and puree to a fine paste. Add the paste to the oil in the wok and cook, stirring often, for about 10 minutes, adding a little water if the paste begins to stick to the wok.

Add the chicken pieces, stir to coat with the paste, cover, and simmer for 20 minutes. Add the beer, wine, eggplant, and fish sauce; stir, cover, and simmer for another 20 minutes. Just before serving, stir in the cardamom and the cilantro leaves, cover, and let sit for a minute or two.

Serves: 4

3 tablespoons sesame oil
3 tablespoons peanut oil
4 Japanese eggplants, peeled and diced
1 small green chile, such as serrano, seeds and stem removed, chopped
2 onions, coarsely chopped
4 cloves garlic, peeled
2 teaspoons chopped ginger
1 teaspoon ground turmeric
1 two-inch stalk lemongrass, including the bulb
1 chicken, cut into serving pieces
1 cup beer (or substitute water)
1/4 cup dry white wine
1 tablespoon fish sauce (nam pla) (or substitute light soy sauce)
1/4 teaspoon ground cardamom
1/8 cup chopped cilantro leaves

Serves: 4 to 6

2 pounds boneless chicken,
   chopped
1/2 teaspoon ground turmeric
3 tablespoons fish sauce (nam pla)
3 large onions, chopped
6 cloves garlic, peeled
1 one-inch piece ginger, peeled
1 teaspoon paprika
1 one-inch piece fresh galangal (or
   substitute ginger), peeled and
   minced
2 fresh red chiles, such as serranos, seeds and stems removed,
   chopped
1/4 cup corn or peanut oil
2 large tomatoes, chopped
1 cup water

🌺 *Kyethar Sipyan*

BURMESE CHICKEN CURRY

*Here is a simple but robustly flavored curry popular across
Burma.*

Combine the chicken with the turmeric and the fish sauce
and marinate, covered, for 1 hour at room temperature.

In a food processor or blender, grind together the onions,
garlic, ginger, paprika, galangal, and chiles.

Heat the oil in a skillet over medium heat, add the ground
ingredients from the food processor or blender, and stir-fry
over medium heat for 2 minutes.

Add the chicken and stir-fry for 12 minutes. Add the tomatoes and the water, mix well, and simmer, covered, for about
15 minutes.

Serves: 4 to 6

2 pounds boneless skinned chicken
   breast, cut into 1-inch cubes
6 chicken drumsticks, skinned
1 teaspoon ground turmeric
4 cups Coconut Milk (page 19)
4 tablespoons Green Curry Paste
   (page 115)
2 large tomatoes, quartered
1 large eggplant, peeled and diced
2 tablespoons fish sauce (nam pla)
1 tablespoon sugar
2 cups water
Salt to taste
12 fresh lime leaves or 1/2 cup
   cilantro leaves
3 fresh red chiles, such as serranos, seeds and stems removed,
   halved

🌺 *Gaeng Kiow Wahn Gai*

GREEN CHICKEN CURRY

*Like most Thai dishes, this curry is aromatic and pleasing to the
eye. The green curry paste, a key ingredient, can be homemade or
purchased at Asian markets.*

In a large bowl, toss all the chicken — the breast cubes and
the drumsticks — with the turmeric and set aside.

In a large skillet, heat the Coconut Milk over low heat for 5
minutes. Add the Green Curry Paste and the tomatoes and
continue cooking over low heat for 5 minutes.

Add the chicken drumsticks and cook, covered, over medium heat for 5 minutes. Add the breast cubes, stir well, and
cook for 5 minutes.

Add all the remaining ingredients, stir well, cover, and cook
over low heat for 15 minutes. Remove the lime leaves before
serving.

𝒦yethar 𝒫einathar ℋin

CHICKEN WITH FENUGREEK AND CHICKPEAS

This is one of Burma's curries in a hurry. It is a relatively simple preparation and is ideal for cooks who want something different but not too spicy.

Combine the chicken with the onions, garlic, vinegar, cumin, fenugreek, coriander, cayenne, and cardamom, and marinate, covered, in a large bowl at room temperature for 1 hour.

Heat the oil in a skillet, and when it begins to smoke, lower the heat and add the chicken with its marinade. Stir-fry for 5 minutes, then add the water. Cover and cook over low heat for 20 minutes. Add the chickpeas and simmer, uncovered, for 5 minutes.

1 three-pound chicken, skinned, boned, and chopped (1 1/2 to 2 pounds meat)
3 onions, finely chopped
6 cloves garlic, peeled and minced
1 teaspoon vinegar
1 tablespoon ground cumin
2 teaspoons ground fenugreek
1 teaspoon ground coriander
1 teaspoon cayenne
1/4 teaspoon ground cardamom
1/3 cup corn or peanut oil
1 cup water (or more as needed)
2 cups canned chickpeas (garbanzo beans)

𝐵airather 𝒮epiyan

DUCK CURRY

George Orwell, who lived and worked in Burma for several years, is said to have loved this curry. However, like much of Burma's delightful cuisine, it did not become famous across the Raj because few Burmese were allowed to emigrate from their closed society.

In a large bowl, combine the duck with the onions, garlic, ginger, paprika, salt, vinegar, cayenne, fish sauce, tomatoes, and 2 tablespoons of the oil. Marinate, covered, at room temperature for 1 hour.

In a skillet or wok, heat the rest of the oil for 2 minutes, add the duck with its marinade, and stir-fry for 3 minutes over medium heat.

Add the water, lower the heat, and cook, covered, for 40 minutes. Skim off any fat that rises to the surface. Add the cumin and the coriander and mix well just before serving.

1 three-pound duck, skinned, fat removed, boned, and chopped
3 large onions, chopped
6 cloves garlic, peeled and chopped
1 two-inch piece ginger, peeled and minced
1 teaspoon paprika
1/4 teaspoon salt
1 teaspoon vinegar
1 teaspoon cayenne
2 tablespoons fish sauce (nam pla)
3 large tomatoes, diced
2 cups corn or peanut oil
1 cup water
2 tablespoons ground cumin
1 teaspoon ground coriander

Serves: 4 to 6

1 teaspoon cayenne
1 teaspoon ground cumin
1 teaspoon ground coriander
1/4 teaspoon ground cardamom
1/4 teaspoon ground cloves
1 teaspoon freshly ground black pepper
1 teaspoon sugar
1/4 teaspoon salt
1 three-pound chicken, skinned, boned, and coarsely chopped (1 1/2 to 2 pounds meat)
1/3 cup peanut or vegetable oil
2 cups sweet potatoes, peeled and cut into 1-inch cubes
6 cloves garlic, peeled and chopped
1 large onion, finely chopped
4 bay or curry leaves
1 two-inch stalk lemongrass, including the bulb
2 cups Coconut Milk (page 19)
1 cup carrots, cut into 1-inch-long pieces
1 cup milk

🌸 Saigon Cari

VIETNAMESE CHICKEN CURRY

According to tradition, Indian merchants brought this curry to Vietnam more than ten centuries ago. The Vietnamese have made it their own, adding lemongrass and sweet potatoes.

Combine all the dry spices, sugar, and salt, and toss with the chicken. Marinate, covered, for 1 hour at room temperature.

In a large skillet or wok, heat the oil for 1 minute over medium heat, add the sweet potatoes, and fry for about 10 minutes. Remove the sweet potatoes with a slotted spoon and set aside.

Using the same oil, fry the garlic and the onion for 3 minutes over low heat. Add the bay or curry leaves and the lemongrass. Stir and cook for 1 minute.

Add the chicken with its marinade, mix well, and cook over high heat for 2 minutes, stirring occasionally. Add the Coconut Milk, mix well, and cook, covered, for 10 minutes. Add the carrots and the milk and cook, covered, for 10 minutes.

Serves: 4 to 6

1 three-pound chicken, skinned, boned, and coarsely chopped
1 long gourd, peeled and cut into 1/2-inch-thick sections
3 tablespoons fish sauce (nam pla)
1/2 teaspoon ground turmeric
2 large onions, finely chopped
1 teaspoon paprika
1 two-inch piece ginger, peeled and minced
6 cloves garlic, peeled and minced
4 two-inch stalks lemongrass, including the bulbs, minced
1 teaspoon ground cumin
1 teaspoon ground coriander
1/4 cup corn or peanut oil
1 cup water (or more as needed)

🌸 Buthi-Kyetha Hin

CHICKEN AND LONG GOURD CURRY

This traditional Burmese curry has traveled well; Indian merchants expelled from Burma by the military government introduced it into Madras City more than thirty years ago — and with great success! Long gourds are available in Asian markets.

Combine all the ingredients except the water in a large bowl and marinate, covered, at room temperature for 30 minutes.

In a large skillet or wok, cook the mixture, covered, over medium heat for 10 minutes.

Add the water, mix well, and bring to a boil. Lower the heat and simmer, covered, for 30 minutes.

126

 **Cari Ga**

CHICKEN CURRY WITH TARO ROOT

Another popular dish from the southern region of Vietnam, this chicken curry with taro is gaining popularity in Vietnamese restaurants abroad.

In a food processor or blender, combine the onion, ginger, sliced lemongrass, garlic, salt, black pepper, chiles, and Red Curry Paste, and puree.

In a large bowl, combine the puree with the chicken and marinate, covered, for 2 hours at room temperature.

Heat half of the oil in a large skillet or wok for 2 minutes, then add the taro root and fry for about 3 minutes. Drain on paper towels.

Add the remaining oil to the skillet, heat, and add the chicken with its marinade. Stir-fry for 5 minutes. Add the minced lemongrass, bay or curry leaves, fried taro, thin Coconut Milk, and water, and mix well. Bring to a boil, lower the heat, cover, and simmer for 20 minutes.

Gently add the eggs, thick Coconut Milk, and sugar (if using), and simmer, uncovered, for 3 minutes.

Garnish with the green onion or cilantro leaves. Remove the bay or curry leaves before serving.

1 large onion, chopped
1 two-inch piece ginger, peeled
8 two-inch stalks lemongrass, including the bulbs, 4 very thinly sliced, 4 minced
6 cloves garlic, peeled and minced
1/4 teaspoon salt
1 teaspoon freshly ground black pepper
2 fresh red chiles, such as serranos, seeds and stems removed
2 teaspoons Red Curry Paste (page 116)
1 three-pound chicken, skinned, boned, and coarsely chopped
1/2 cup corn or peanut oil
2 pounds taro root (or substitute potatoes or yams), peeled and diced
2 bay or curry leaves
1/2 cup thin Coconut Milk (page 19)
1/2 cup water
4 hard-boiled eggs, halved
1 cup thick Coconut Milk (page 19)
1 teaspoon sugar (optional)
1/2 cup chopped green onion or cilantro leaves for garnish

Serves: 4 to 6

2 pounds firm whitefish fillets
1 teaspoon salt
1 teaspoon ground turmeric
1 teaspoon cayenne
4 cloves garlic, peeled and minced
1 two-inch piece ginger, peeled and
   minced
4 large onions, sliced
1 tablespoon all-purpose flour
1 cup Coconut Milk (page 19)
Cabbage or lettuce leaves
Banana leaves, cut into 6-inch
   squares

🌺 Nga Baung Doke

STEAMED FISH IN BANANA LEAVES

Here is a traditional Burmese delicacy. The banana leaves can be found in Asian or Latin American markets. If they are unavailable, you can substitute aluminum foil, but the taste will not be the same.

Cut the fillets into finger-size pieces and toss them with the salt and the turmeric. Set aside.

In a food processor or blender, combine the cayenne, garlic, ginger, and half the sliced onions, and process. Stop after 2 minutes, add the flour and the Coconut Milk, and continue processing for 2 more minutes. Combine this mixture with the remaining sliced onions and mix well.

Place a cabbage or lettuce leaf on top of a banana leaf. Add some of the onion mixture from the food processor or blender, some of the fish, and cover with another cabbage or lettuce leaf. Fold into a neat bundle and close it, using a toothpick. Repeat the process until all the fish is packaged.

Place the banana leaf packages in a steamer and steam for 15 minutes.

Serves: 4

8 dried red chiles, such as piquins,
   seeds and stems removed
1 cup warm water
2 two-inch stalks lemongrass, including the bulbs, chopped
6 cloves garlic, peeled and minced
6 shallots, peeled and chopped
1/2 teaspoon ground turmeric
10 whole black peppercorns
1 teaspoon Red Curry Paste (page
   116)
1 cup Coconut Milk (page 19)

🌺 Haw Moke Phuket

BANANA LEAF FISH

This is another banana-wrapped delicacy, from the southern region of Phuket, in Thailand. It is one of the finest — and most interesting — curries that Thailand has to offer.

Soak the chiles in the warm water for 10 minutes, then drain. In a food processor or blender, puree the chiles, lemongrass, garlic, shallots, turmeric, and peppercorns into a smooth paste.

Combine this paste with the Red Curry Paste and the Coconut Milk and mix well. Pour this mixture over the fish and marinate, covered, at room temperature for 10 minutes.

Take a banana leaf and smear it with some Ghee or oil. Top with a spinach leaf, then with about 3 or 4 pieces of the fish, and cover with another spinach leaf. Fold up the banana leaf and make a neat packet, sealing it with toothpicks. Repeat the process with the rest of the fish, spinach, and banana leaves.

Place the packets in a steamer and steam for 15 minutes.

2 pounds whitefish fillets, cut into 1-inch-thick finger-size pieces
3 tablespoons Ghee (page 17) or olive oil
About 4 full banana leaves, cut into 8- × 11-inch pieces
1/4 pound fresh spinach leaves

 *ℒaotian 𝒞atfish 𝒞urry*

Serves: 4

This curry recipe, collected by Richard Sterling in Laos, features the silky smooth paste typical of that cuisine. "Maceration of the curry paste ingredients is critical," he observes. The ginger, he says, "is used for both its culinary and mystical value; in the currency of the spirit world it represents gold."

In a food processor or blender, combine the shallots, ginger, chiles, garlic, and galangal, and puree to a smooth paste.

Bring the Coconut Milk to a boil in a wok, add the paste, reduce the heat slightly, and cook, stirring occasionally, for about 5 minutes. Add the tomato and the eggplant and cook for 5 more minutes.

Add the catfish, beans, cilantro leaves, and fish sauce, and cook over medium heat for 10 minutes or until the beans are tender. The curry should be quite liquid, so add some water or fish stock if necessary.

Serve garnished with the green onion.

6 shallots, peeled
1 two-inch-piece ginger, peeled
3 small fresh red chiles, such as serranos, seeds and stems removed
5 cloves garlic, peeled
1 two-inch piece fresh galangal (or substitute ginger), peeled
2 cups thick Coconut Milk (page 19)
1 tomato, peeled and chopped
1 small eggplant, peeled and diced
1 pound catfish (or other whitefish), cut into bite-size pieces
1/2 pound green beans, cut into 1-inch sections
2 tablespoons minced cilantro leaves
1 teaspoon fish sauce (nam pla)
Water or fish stock as needed
1 green onion, sliced, for garnish

Serves: 4

10 dried red chiles, such as piquins, seeds and stems removed
1 cup warm water
1 teaspoon salt
4 green chiles, such as serranos, seeds and stems removed, minced
3 large onions, chopped
6 cloves garlic, peeled and chopped
1 teaspoon ground turmeric
1 tablespoon shrimp paste (available in Asian markets)
3 cups water
2 teaspoons Red Curry Paste (page 116)
1 cup bamboo shoots
10 green beans, halved
1/2 pineapple, peeled, cored, and cut into 1-inch-thick pieces
2 tablespoons fish sauce (nam pla)
1 tablespoon tamarind paste
1 teaspoon sugar (optional)
2 pounds catfish (or other whitefish), cut into 1-inch pieces
2 tablespoons freshly squeezed lime juice
1/4 cup cilantro leaves for garnish

❧ *Gaeng Leuang Pahk Dai*

FISH CURRY WITH BAMBOO

Not many curries use bamboo shoots, a Chinese influence, but this zesty fish curry from Thailand does. It is also one of the most colorful dishes from that country. The green beans, pineapple, and bamboo shoots add to its visual appeal — and enrich its taste.

Place the red chiles in the warm water for 10 minutes, then drain.

In a food processor or blender, combine the red chiles, salt, green chiles, onions, garlic, turmeric, and shrimp paste, and puree.

Bring the 3 cups water to a boil in a large saucepan. Add the puree, Red Curry Paste, bamboo shoots, and green beans, and cook, covered, over medium heat for 5 minutes.

Add the pineapple, fish sauce, tamarind paste, and sugar (if using), and cook, covered, for 3 minutes. Add the fish, stir gently, and cook, covered, for 7 minutes. Stir in the lime juice just before serving. Garnish the curry with cilantro leaves.

Serves: 4 to 6

1 cup moong dal (greengram, available in Asian markets)
2 cups water
3 pounds catfish (or other whitefish), cut into bite-size pieces
1 teaspoon salt
1 teaspoon ground turmeric
3 two-inch stalks lemongrass, including the bulbs
1/2 cup roasted peanuts
1/2 cup uncooked long-grain rice
1 cup corn or peanut oil
5 medium onions, finely chopped
6 cloves garlic, peeled and chopped

❧ *Mohinga*

CURRIED FISH WITH NOODLES

This is one of Burma's classic dishes. Tourists who visited Burma before the country closed its doors to the outside world in the 1960s remember how the Rangoon streets used to swarm with mohinga sellers. The dish, cooked the previous night, was available in the streets in the early mornings. The hawkers carried it on their shoulders on a long bamboo pole that held two evenly balanced containers. True mohinga contains the outer bark of the banana tree — which is difficult to find in the United States. It still tastes great even without the bark.

Boil the *moong dal* in the 2 cups of water for 12 minutes over low heat. Set aside.

Toss the fish with the salt and the turmeric and marinate, covered, at room temperature for 15 minutes.

Pound the lemongrass lightly. Put the peanuts in a spice mill and pulverize for a minute; set aside. In a dry skillet, heat the rice, stirring continuously for about 5 minutes. Place the rice in a mortar and grind to a powder.

Heat the oil in a large skillet for 1 minute. Add the onions and fry over low heat until they turn golden, about 5 minutes. Add the marinated fish, garlic, pounded lemongrass, ginger, paprika, black pepper, and fish sauce, and cook, uncovered, over medium heat for 5 minutes.

Add the Coconut Milk, water, pulverized peanuts, rice powder, shallots, and bamboo shoots, and stir well. Bring to a boil, lower the heat, cover, and simmer for 12 minutes.

Meanwhile, heat the other 4 cups water in a large pot; add the salt and the oil as the water starts boiling. Add the noodles and cook, covered, for about 5 minutes. Drain and set aside.

To serve, place the curry, rice noodles, and garnishes in separate bowls in the center of the table. Guests should fill their soup bowls first with noodles, next with the fish curry, and then with whatever garnishes they wish.

1 two-inch piece ginger, peeled and minced
1 tablespoon paprika
1 teaspoon freshly ground black pepper
1/4 cup fish sauce (nam pla)
2 cups Coconut Milk (page 19)
4 cups water
12 shallots, peeled and chopped
1 cup bamboo shoots
4 cups water
1/2 teaspoon salt
1 tablespoon olive oil
1 pound rice noodles

For Garnish:
6 hard-boiled eggs, halved
1 cup cilantro leaves
1 large green onion, finely chopped
6 limes, quartered
2 tablespoons fish sauce (nam pla)
1 teaspoon cayenne

✿ Prik King Shrimp

SPICY CHILE SHRIMP

Tommy Tang, the celebrated Thai chef, passed on this recipe to us, which we have modified slightly. Prik in Thai means chile.

Heat the oil in a large skillet over high heat. Add the garlic and the ginger and sauté for 1 minute. Add the Coconut Milk, Red Curry Paste, and paprika, and cook over medium heat for 2 minutes. Add all the remaining ingredients except the basil leaves and cook, uncovered, for 5 minutes over

Serves: 4

1/3 cup olive oil
6 cloves garlic, peeled and minced
1 two-inch piece ginger, peeled and minced
1 cup Coconut Milk (page 19)
1 tablespoon Red Curry Paste (page 116)
2 teaspoons paprika
24 large uncooked shrimp, shelled and deveined
2 cups green beans, cut into julienne

1 bell pepper, seeds and stem removed, diced
1 tablespoon ground unsalted peanuts
1 tablespoon Thai fish sauce (nam
pla)
1 tablespoon dried shrimp powder
(available in Asian markets)
2 dried kaffir lime or fresh lemon
leaves
1 teaspoon sugar (optional)
Basil leaves for garnish

medium heat, stirring gently from time to time. Garnish with
the basil leaves. Remove the kaffir lime or lemon leaves before serving.

Serves: 4

2 pounds frog legs (or substitute
chicken), boned and cut into
bite-size pieces
1 two-inch stalk lemongrass, including the bulb
3 fresh red chiles, such as serranos, seeds and stems removed
3 shallots, peeled and chopped
6 cloves garlic, peeled and chopped
1 teaspoon sugar
1 teaspoon ground cumin
1 teaspoon ground coriander
1 teaspoon Red Curry Paste (page
116)
Salt to taste
1 tablespoon fish sauce (nam pla)
2 cups cellophane noodles
4 cups warm water
2 tablespoons peanut or vegetable
oil
3 large onions, finely chopped
1 cup chicken or beef broth
1 cup Coconut Milk (page 19)
1 teaspoon cornstarch mixed with
1 tablespoon cold water
1/4 cup cilantro or mint leaves for
garnish

❀ *Saigon Echnau Cari*

CURRIED FROG LEGS

*Here is a mild, aromatic curry immensely popular in southern
Vietnam, particularly in Saigon. This dish has been influenced by
the cuisines of India, Thailand, and China.*

Rinse the frog legs in cold water, pat dry, and refrigerate, covered, for 15 minutes.

Meanwhile, in a food processor or blender, combine the lemongrass, chiles, shallots, garlic, sugar, cumin, coriander, Red
Curry Paste, salt, and fish sauce, and puree to a silky paste.
Toss the frog legs in this paste and refrigerate, covered, for 30
minutes.

Soak the noodles in the warm water for 30 minutes; drain
and cut them into 1-inch lengths.

Heat the oil in a skillet or wok over medium heat, add the
onions, and fry for 2 minutes. Reduce the heat and add the
frog legs with their marinade; fry for 4 minutes. Add the
chicken or beef broth, bring to a boil, and reduce the heat.
Cover the skillet and cook for 12 minutes.

Uncover the pan, add the Coconut Milk and the cornstarch
mixture, stir gently, and cook, uncovered, for 3 minutes.

Add the noodles, bring to a boil, and remove from the heat.
Garnish with the cilantro or mint leaves. Serve immediately.

Chettiar Curry

MIXED-VEGETABLE CURRY

This dish is also called monsoon curry. The Chettiars, originally from Madras, owned large estates in colonial Burma, and the Burmese farmers who worked for them used to joke that their low wages could not buy them anything but the Chettiar vegetable curry. Nevertheless, this is one of the most highly treasured Burmese curries.

In a saucepan, combine the *toovar dal* and the 1 cup water and boil for 20 minutes. Set aside.

Combine the tamarind and the warm water for 10 minutes; strain the pulp, discard, and save the liquid (see Note).

In a large skillet, heat the oil over medium heat. Add the onions and sauté for 2 minutes. Add the ginger, turmeric, salt, cumin, coriander, paprika, and bay or curry leaves, and sauté for 2 minutes. Add the *toovar dal* along with the water in the saucepan. Cover and cook for 2 minutes. Add the tamarind liquid, eggplant, pumpkin, daikon, potatoes, carrots, and tomatoes. Add the water and the Coconut Milk, cover, and simmer for about 20 minutes.

Garnish with the cilantro leaves just before serving.

Note: 1 teaspoon freshly squeezed lime juice can be substituted for the tamarind liquid.

1 cup toovar dal *(yellow split peas, available in Asian markets)*
1 cup water
1 lime-size ball tamarind pulp
1/2 cup warm water
1 cup corn or peanut oil
2 onions, chopped
1 two-inch piece ginger, peeled and minced
1/2 teaspoon ground turmeric
Salt to taste
2 teaspoons ground cumin
1 teaspoon ground coriander
1 teaspoon paprika
4 bay or curry leaves
1 large eggplant, cubed
1/2 pumpkin, skinned, seeded, and diced
1 large daikon (Asian radish), peeled and diced
4 large potatoes, diced
6 carrots, peeled and cut into 1/2-inch sections
4 large tomatoes, quartered
4 cups water
1 cup Coconut Milk *(page 19)*
1/2 cup cilantro leaves for garnish

🌸 *Shwephayonethee Hin*

PUMPKIN CURRY

Serves: 4

1 lime-size ball tamarind pulp
1/2 cup warm water
1 three-pound pumpkin
1/2 cup olive or corn oil
2 large onions, finely chopped
6 cloves garlic, peeled and finely
minced
1 green chile, such as serrano,
seeds and stem removed, minced
1 teaspoon ground turmeric
1 teaspoon paprika
1 cup water
Salt to taste
1/4 cup cilantro leaves for garnish

This Burmese curry is very similar to ones found in the southern states of India. For an Indian variation, add 1 cup Coconut Milk along with the water.

Soak the tamarind in the warm water for 10 minutes; strain the pulp, discard, and save the liquid (see Note).

Meanwhile, with a sharp knife, remove the skin of the pumpkin and remove the seeds, but keep the fiber. Cut into 1-inch cubes.

Heat the oil in a large frying pan and add the onions; when they turn golden, add the garlic, chile, turmeric, and paprika. Simmer for 2 minutes. Add the pumpkin, water, and salt, and mix well. Cook, covered, for 20 minutes over medium heat, and then add the tamarind liquid.

Garnish with the cilantro leaves just before serving.

Note: 1 teaspoon freshly squeezed lime juice can be substituted for the tamarind liquid.

🌸 *Burmese-Style Rice*

Serves: 4

2 cups glutinous rice
3 onions
1 1/2 teaspoons ground turmeric
1/4 cup vegetable oil
4 cups water
1/2 teaspoon salt

Although the Burmese usually prepare plain rice to accompany curries, this recipe from Richard Sterling gives the rice a richer taste and a texture that is almost velvety.

Wash the rice and drain it.

Slice the onions and sprinkle them with the turmeric. Heat the oil in a saucepan and fry the onions until they are brown, but don't let them burn.

Remove the onions with a slotted spoon and serve them alongside the rice.

Add the rice to the pan and stir well to mix it with the oil. Add the water and the salt and bring to a boil. Reduce the heat, cover, and simmer for 20 minutes.

A WORLD OF CURRIES

FIVE

Spice Island Curries

Spices had a considerable

place in life; men were

prepared to die in search

of them, and many did;

no gift was more

acceptable, and to be well

supplied was a mark of

status; wealth could be

measured in spices.

BRIAN GARDNER

he original Spice Islands were the Moluccas, those remote isles of cloves and nutmeg that lie some fifteen hundred miles east of Djakarta, Indonesia. But throughout history, the location of the Spice Islands gradually broadened to include all of the East Indies — now the countries of Malaysia, Indonesia, and Singapore. There was a simple reason for the wider definition: the spice-growing locations expanded as the region was conquered by one spice-seeking world power after another.

Spice Wars

During the Roman empire, the spice trade was dominated by the Arabs. Their ships sailed from the Red Sea to India, where they bought spices carried by Malay traders from the Spice Islands. The Arabs sailed back to the Mediterranean and sold the spices to the Romans, who had become so addicted to them that they paid the equivalent of forty dollars an ounce for black pepper!

But about A.D. 100, the Romans built ships large enough to sail to India and back, a trip that took roughly a year. Soon the Arab spice monopoly was broken and prices dropped. The Romans enjoyed only a slight break in prices, since the Indian merchants still wanted a good profit. But because of the increased availability of spices the Romans proceeded to spice their wines, write spice cookbooks, and bathe in spiced oils. However, the fall of the Roman empire (which cannot be blamed on spices alone!) ended such trade, and the Arabs gradually regained control of the spice routes from India.

While that was happening, the Indians themselves took quite an interest in the Spice Islands. Around the fifth century A.D. (some sources say as early as the eighth century B.C.), both Buddhist and Hindu traders arrived in what are now Malaysia and Indonesia, bringing spices like cumin and coriander and vegetables such as mangoes, eggplants, and onions. They were the first outside culinary influence on the region, but their primary interest was money, not cooking.

The Indians set up trading posts, which became city-states, each ruled by a local Malay chief who favored the interests of the Indian traders. These posts were midway between India and China, and they serviced the Indian traders plying the seas between the two great civilizations. By the ninth century, Indian traders, operating from the island of Java, held the first spice monopoly in the region.

But the Arabs were not far behind. The spread of Islam, combined with the continuing interest in spices, led Arab traders directly to the source — the Spice Islands. By the eleventh century, they had literally taken over the spice trade from the Indians, and Hinduism had been replaced by Islam as Muslim seafarers began colonizing many of the Indonesian Islands. The Arabs had barely won control of the spice monopoly when competition came from another source — Europe.

Nutmeg, native to the Moluccas.

Marco Polo was the first westerner to visit the Spice Islands, landing in Sumatra around 1292. It is said that he was the one who named the region the Spice Islands, because he found black pepper, nutmeg, and cloves growing there. Other spices are native to the region as well, including cinnamon, cassia, turmeric, and ginger, although some sources claim that ginger is native to India and was brought to the Spice Islands by the early Indian traders.

The European desire to take advantage of the region was delayed, however, by the daunting distances, and the Arabs controlled the spice trade until the late fifteenth century. They shipped the highly valued spices from the Spice Islands to Alexandria, Egypt, and from there Venetian ships carried them to Europe. The spices were so valuable that black pepper was used to pay taxes in England, and European female slaves were traded for cinnamon and cloves. In Germany, a pound of nutmeg could purchase seven oxen.

But Vasco da Gama's circumnavigation of Africa in 1497–99 changed the spice trade forever. After landing at Calicut, India, he soon learned that although the Indian traders would not sign a formal treaty with the king of Portugal, they would gladly sell the Portuguese all the spices they wanted — in return for gold and silver. The Portuguese moved quickly to end the Arab and Venetian monopolies through both trade and war.

Lisbon soon became the new spice capital of Europe, eclipsing Venice completely. As the Portuguese historian Tomé Pires notes, "Whoever is lord of Malacca has his hand on the throat

of Venice." (Malacca, far from the Moluccas, was an important port on the west coast of Malaya.) Portuguese warships attacked Muslim ports in India and Ceylon, thereby successfully interrupting the Arab spice trade. In 1509, the combined Arab fleet from Egypt and Calicut was defeated by Francisco de Almeida off Diu, in western India. It was one of the most important naval battles in history, and soon the Portuguese expanded their raids to the Spice Islands themselves.

After the Portuguese conquered Malacca in 1511, they expanded their territory to include parts of what is now Indonesia. Portuguese and Spanish traders introduced beans, chiles, tomatoes, corn, and potatoes to the region. The Portuguese also introduced the peanut, via Africa, and it became one of the dominant tastes in Indonesian cookery.

The Portuguese controlled the Spice Islands for about seventy years, until they came under attack by Dutch forces. The Dutch forced a Portuguese retreat to the city of Ambon in 1580, decisively defeated the Portuguese fleet, and captured Java in 1602. They finally captured Malacca in 1641, effectively removing the Portuguese from the region.

The Dutch formed the Dutch East India Company in 1602 to control the spice trade. The company announced that the entire region was to be known as the Netherlands East Indies. The Dutch introduced cauliflower, cabbage, and turnips and worked hard to maintain their monopoly of the spice trade, putting into action the supply-and-demand theory. By cutting down three quarters of the spice trees in the Moluccas, including the valuable cloves, they reduced supplies, raised spice prices, and did not have to defend the Moluccas. They imposed the death penalty on anyone who possessed or sold nutmeg and cloves illegally. The domination of the spice market by the Dutch so upset the British that they founded the East India Company in India in order to compete in the spice trade; however, the Dutch managed to control the Spice Islands (with the exception of a brief period of British rule from 1811 to 1816) until they were occupied by the Japanese, in 1942.

Today, Malaysia, Singapore, and Indonesia are separate, independent countries, and these "spice islands" still live up to their name. Indonesia produces about 70 percent of the world's

Borneo women collecting fruits for curries, c. 1875.

nutmeg and mace, plus large amounts of cassia, turmeric, black pepper, and cloves. Most of the cloves consumed in Indonesia, incidentally, are not eaten but rather are smoked in cigarettes. Other curry ingredients grown in the region include chile, ginger, galangal, lemongrass, kaffir lime leaves, and coconut, the last perhaps the most important single ingredient in Spice Island curries. These culinary components, combined with the many ethnic influences on the area, have created a fascinating and complex gastronomic stew.

In addition to the original Malays, now mostly Muslims, and all the other peoples who have inhabited the Spice Islands, one other group also immigrated there — the Chinese. Although the region had been visited by traders from China for centuries, the first main influx came in the 1820s, as Chinese construction workers contributed to the building of Singapore. The second wave of laborers came in the 1840s, to work the tin mines.

The influence of the Chinese, who now compose about three quarters of the population of Singapore, has been vast. The major Chinese immigrants were Hokkiens (from Fujian province), Teochews, Cantonese, and Hainanese. All brought their own regional cultures and food traditions and settled in their own enclaves in Singapore and Malaysia. Most of the earliest Chinese settlers were men, and because of the lack of Chinese women, they married Malay women. Thus a distinct subculture was born, known in Malay as *peranakan* (meaning to be born here) and in English as Straits Chinese. The women of that subculture were known as *nonya*s, Malay for ladies.

The intermarriage of Chinese men and Malay women ended once the population of Singapore grew large enough to include Chinese women, and Nonyas eventually became part of the mainstream of Singapore culture. Their influence lives on in Nonya cooking, a blend of Chinese subtlety and techniques and spicy Malay ingredients. It has been said that in one meal, the diner receives a perfect balance of opposing flavors, textures, and colors. Three favorite Nonya dishes are our Indonesian Curried Mutton Soup (page 151), Singapore Fish-Head Curry (page 158), and Mixed-Vegetable and Soy Curry (page 161).

The British, of course, also had an influence on the culture of the region. After Sir Stamford Raffles of the East India Company gained possession of Singapore for the British in 1819, the small fishing village became the leading port east of the Suez Canal. The British influence accounts for the fact that the principal language of Singapore is English (other official languages are Tamil, Malay, and Mandarin), but the British had a much smaller impact on the food. Nowadays, about the only surviving British culinary heritage involves drinking; the hotels and restaurants serve high tea in the afternoon, excellent Singapore-brewed beers and stouts, and plenty of gin drinks.

The expansion of Singapore as a major trading center led to settlement by other ethnic groups. The main Indian immigration came during the nineteenth century, when indentured Indian laborers came to work on the rubber plantations, and now the population of Singapore is about 6 1/2 percent Indian. Under British control, the settlers were kept in their own ethnic enclaves, so they could not easily unite and rebel. These communities (such as Chinatown, Arab Street, and Little India), though unofficial now, still exist to this day, and each area has its own markets, spice shops, and restaurants.

In Singapore and the rest of the region, the words for rice *(nasi)*, chicken *(ayam)*, hot sauce *(sambal)*, and many other food terms are identical, so it is difficult — if not impossible — to separate the Malaysian and Indonesian influences on the food of the Spice Islands. The famous *satay*s, barbecued meats and seafood, occur in both countries and are very popular in Singapore. Interestingly enough, the *satay*s are thought to have originated with the early Arab spice traders, who introduced the concept of *kebab*s to the region. *Kebab*s are small chunks of spiced meat that are grilled on skewers. As we have seen in chapter 3, the concept was expanded in India to include meatballs and renamed *kabab*s.

Beyond a doubt, the two principal foods of Malaysia, Indonesia, and Singapore are rice and seafood. Rice was introduced by Indian traders about A.D. 1000, and dozens of varieties are grown and consumed in the region. *Nasi Lemak* (page 163), the most popular rice dish on the west coast of Malaysia, is flavored with cloves and *pandan* (screw pine) leaves. Another rice favorite, particularly in Singapore, is *Nasi Kunyit* (page 163), a dish flavored with turmeric and other curry spices.

Because of the proximity to the sea, the Spice Islands have a great variety and abundance of seafood. Three very popular items are red snapper, prawns, and clams. Our sampling of the seafood of the region includes *Bia Kare* (page 159), a clam curry; a classic Penang Fish Curry (page 157); and *Gulai Malabar*, Curried Fish Balls (page 158). In addition to all the fresh seafood, an important Malaysian curry ingredient known as *blacan*, a fermented prawn paste, is made from seafood.

The most popular cooking style of the Spice Islands is currying. "Curries, easily the most common dish eaten with rice, are a definite mark of the Indian influence in Malay cooking," notes Singapore restaurateur Fawziah Amin. "For almost every meal, a dish of fish, prawn, or chicken curry has to be on the menu. While Indian curry is hot, rich, and fiery, with yogurt added, the Malays opt for a milder, delicate taste, with the creamy flavor of coconut milk in generous portions."

Harvey Day notes: "No one with a discriminating palate would mistake a Malayan curry for an Indian curry." A quick glance at two of our recipes reveals the differences. Singapore Curry Powder (page 148) is typically Indian, and while Malaysian Curry Paste (page 148) contains some Indian curry spices, it also shows the influence of Malay ingredients such as galangal, lemongrass, coconut, and candlenuts.

In Malaysia, the curry concept is taken a step further with an impressive array of currylike sauces. For example, *lemak kuning* is a coconut-based sauce made with most of the regional curry ingredients; *kerabu kerisik* is made with fried, pounded coconut, lime juice, dried shrimp, shallots, and chiles; and *kacang* blends together the flavors of peanuts, lemongrass, galangal, chiles, and coconut milk.

Similarly, the famous *sambal*s range from simple chile sauces to currylike pastes and are primarily used to spice up other dishes, such as mild curries. The basis for most *sambal*s is chiles, onions (or shallots or garlic), and citrus, but many other ingredients are used, including lemongrass, *blacan*, ginger, galangal, candlenuts, kaffir lime leaves, and coconut milk. Thus the *sambal*s resemble a curry paste, but with a much greater amount of chiles. Some of the *sambal*s, such as *buah tomat*, incorporate a western ingredient — tomatoes. Our recipe for *Sambal Badjak* (page 149) is one of the more complex *sambal*s, being both hot and sweet at the same time. Other interesting uses of curry spices include the Penang dish *enche kay bin*, in which chicken pieces are seasoned with curry powder and salt, marinated in coconut cream for a couple of hours, and then deep-fried until crisp.

Indonesian cookery is similar to Malaysian because the two share many ingredients: coconut, chiles, ginger, galangal, and, in particular, tamarind. The Indonesian version of prawn paste is called *trasi* and is commonly used, as are a bewildering number of Indonesian *sambals*. One word in particular frequently comes up in discussions of Indonesian food, and that is rijsttafel, which means rice table in Dutch. It is not a dish, but rather a feast of many dishes, including curries. The term derives from the Dutch settlers, who gave elaborate dinner parties in an attempt to upstage one another. It was up to the creative chef never to duplicate flavors, types of meat, or cooking styles, and for every dish that was spicy-hot, there had to be a bland one to offset it. Likewise, sweet dishes were offset by sour dishes, warm dishes by cold dishes, wet by dry, and firm-textured by soft-textured. Often, as many as fifty or sixty dishes were served, but despite such attention to detail, the food was not as important as the spectacle in a rijsttafel, and the quality of the party was judged by the number of servants it took to produce the affair. If fifty servants were required, the party was known as a "fifty-boy rijsttafel," a phrase the Indonesians naturally found offensive. Today the term is considered a degrading holdover from colonial times; however, scaled-down rijsttafels are still staged for tourists — but without all the servants.

Some of the curry dishes included in early rijsttafels were *gulai*s and *rendang*s (sometimes spelled *randang*), which are meat dishes cooked in coconut milk and spices. A popular *rendang* is one from Sumatra, which features either water buffalo or beef (beef is a minor meat in Indonesia), and we have re-created it in our Sumatran *Rendang* (page 153). Other favorite meat curries are *Gulai Kambing* (page 154), a classic goat curry from Sumatra; the very spicy Devil's Pork Curry (page 154); a liver curry called *Rendang Limpa* (page 157); and the popular chicken curry *Gulai Putih* (page 156), a Singapore favorite.

A wonderful description of the effects of Indonesian curries appeared in a nineteenth-century travel book, *The Boy Travellers in the Far East*, by Thomas Knox:

> This is the famous Java curry; and if you have taken plenty of the pepper and chutney, and other hot things, your mouth will burn for half an hour as though you had drunk from a kettle of boiling water. And when you have eaten freely of curry, you don't want any other breakfast. Everybody eats curry here daily, because it is said to be good for the health by keeping the liver active, and preventing fevers.

Vegetables and fruits are important in the curries of the Spice Islands. Okra, called lady fingers in Malaysia and Singapore, is commonly used as a thickening agent in curries with a gumbolike consistency. Potatoes are combined with coconut in *Ubi Kentang Kari* (page 161), and eggplant is the star of *Terong Kari* (page 162). Bananas, called *pisang* in Malay, appear in a curry recipe, *Pisang Kari* (page 160).

Hawkers, Chefs, and Tiffin Curries

In 1991, Dave and his wife, Mary Jane, traveled to Singapore to experience the foods of the Spice Islands and to collect curry recipes. The night they arrived, friends immediately drove them to the Newton Food Centre for dinner. Newton is one of the famous hawker centers — so named because in the past the cooks would hawk their food to customers. The center consisted of perhaps fifty open-air stalls and a hundred tables and was jam-packed with hungry diners.

Intense and exotic aromas wafted from the food stall, which sported an intriguing array of signs, such as "Juriah Nasi Padang" and "Rojak Tow Kua Pow Cuttlefish." The hawkers specialized in a bewildering selection of quick and inexpensive foods from many cuisines. Among the delicacies Dave and Mary Jane tasted their first night in Singapore were Chinese thousand-year-old eggs, the famous Singapore chile crab, Indonesian *satays*, Indian curried dishes, and a barbecued Malayan stingray. A favorite hawker recipe is *Laksa Kari* (page 152), Curried Noodle Soup with Prawns.

Then it was off to the markets. In Little India, they first visited the "dry" markets selling the various spices that compose the curries: chiles, cloves, turmeric, star anise, peppercorns, cinnamon, coriander — and more. It was a vivid sensory assault on the eyes and nose. As Mary Jane puts it, "I've never been any place that smelled so wonderful and exotic." They watched Indian cooks prepare *chapatti* flat bread and tasted a wide variety of "chips" made from numerous flours.

The Little India "wet" market, so named because there was water on the floor from the cleaning of seafood and meats, was a huge warehouselike affair with the sides open to the air. It was neatly divided into sections: fruits, vegetables, meats, seafood, groceries, and food vendors. Despite the noise and crowded conditions, the market was very clean. All vendors touching meats or seafood wore plastic gloves, and everyone was low-key and very friendly, encouraging Dave on occasion to photograph them in action, such as the fishmonger cleaving the heads off fish. They found out later what the fish heads were used for.

There was a profusion of food in the wet market. "Lamb" and "mutton," probably goat, were hanging to age, every type of tropical fruit was available for sale except the notorious durian, which was out of season, and there were tiger prawns seven to eight inches long. There was a good variety of fresh chiles for sale but, typical of chile nomenclature around the world, the kinds available were "bird chiles," green or red piquinlike fiery little devils less than an inch long; "yellow chiles," about three inches long; and "red chiles," which looked like a cross between cayenne and New Mexican varieties and which were also sold in the green form.

At the wet market in Chinatown, Dave and Mary Jane were surprised by the number of live animals for sale. There were large fish swimming in aquariums — the freshest imaginable — and huge crabs crawling around in cages. There was one memorable transaction in which the vendor removed several frogs from a cage to show a customer how fresh they were. The woman chose the one that jumped the farthest, and the vendor quickly killed and skinned it on the spot.

After seeing the markets, it was time to interview two of Singapore's noted cooking authorities. Dave and Mary Jane's first visit was to the Thomson Cooking Studio, where Mrs. Devagi Shanmugam was preparing dishes that were being photographed for a brochure for McCormick Spice Company. Mrs. Shanmugam is of Indian heritage but has mastered all of Singapore's numerous cuisines. They tasted her green beans with spicy prawn paste, which were excellent, and Mrs. Shanmugam showed them her huge recipe collection and let them choose several recipes that they had tasted and enjoyed at restaurants and at the hawker center.

Next they interviewed Violet Oon, the cooking star of Singapore. She not only has a cooking school and her own line of products, she publishes the *Food Paper*, a fascinating monthly publication devoted to the cuisines of the Spice Islands. Mrs. Oon conducted her own culinary tour, taking Dave and Mary Jane to the Madras New Woodlands Restaurant for vegetarian curries and to the Banana Leaf Apolo, where banana leaves are used for plates. There they dined on a variety of curried dishes, including fish-roe curry cakes, and learned the purpose of the fish heads in the market when they ate the delicious Singapore Fish-Head Curry (page 158). Mrs. Oon was also gracious enough to provide some of her Singapore recipes.

Later, at the famous Raffles Hotel, Dave and Mary Jane learned about the evolution of another curry style in Singapore and parts of Malaysia. The "tiffin curry lunches," still served at Raffles and other hotels, actually originated in India, where men went to work carrying a tiffin carrier, a stacked series of containers (enamel or stainless steel) held together by a metal frame. The concept was brought to Singapore by the British, because they were loath to dine in local establishments for fear of tropical diseases such as typhoid, cholera, and dysentery.

One of the main ingredients of a tiffin lunch was a tiffin curry, which went easy on the chiles and spices so as not to offend British tastes. Tiffin curries were served by the best hotels, such as Raffles, and a famous tiffin room was Emerson's Tiffin, Billiards, and Reading Room, which opened in 1866 near Cavenagh Bridge. Tiffin curries became popular partly because the moderately spicy curries were believed to aid in curing hangovers, a typical affliction of the British, who dearly loved to carouse. Early tiffins usually featured curried eggs, chicken, prawns, or eggplants accompanied by rice, *sambals*, and a mango chutney. A typical later tiffin curry lunch, as served by the Europe Hotel in 1932, consisted of curried fish and rice accompanied by iced consommé, veal, ham, fruits, and a watercress salad. Our recipe for Curry Puffs (page 150) is a classic tiffin curry lunch.

Incidentally, Sir Stamford Raffles, founder of the Raffles Hotel, modeled his hotel after the Indonesian concept of *bojo kromo*, or good hospitality. "By the customs of the country," he wrote in 1917 in his *History of Java*,

> good food and good lodging are ordered to be provided for all strangers and travellers arriving at a village. "It is not sufficient,"

say the Javan institutions, "that a man should place good food before his guest; he is bound to do more: he should render the meal palatable by kind words and treatment, to soothe him after his journey, and to make his heart glad while he partakes of the refreshment."

Interestingly enough, in Noel Coward's play *Pretty Polly Barlow*, the death of Mrs. Innes Hook is blamed on her having "stuffed herself with curry at the Raffles . . . three gin slings before lunch and an enormous plate of prawn curry at lunch." We have included a not-so-dangerous prawn curry, *Gulai Udang* (page 160).

Speaking of danger, we should warn cooks that the recipes in this chapter contain coconut in various forms. See chapter 1 for substitutions.

Popular condiments to serve with Spice Island curries include sliced raw bananas, fried bananas, sliced pineapple, chopped peanuts, grated coconut (either raw or roasted), fried eggplant, and even deep-fried anchovies topped with chile powder. Additionally, our recipes for a classic regional bread, *Roti Djala* (page 164), and the famous Indonesian pickle, *Acar* (page 149), make splendid accompaniments.

The Malaysians have a saying, "Good food and happiness go hand in hand." We hope our fellow cooks will find happiness with the Spice Island curries that follow.

Yield: 3 1/2 cups

1 cup coriander seeds
1 cup cumin seeds
2/3 cup whole star anise
1/3 cup dried red chiles, seeds and
   stems removed
1/4 cup ground turmeric
1 one-inch piece cinnamon
4 whole cloves
2 tablespoons whole black peppercorns

🪷 Singapore Curry Powder

Here is a basic curry powder, obviously of Indian origin, that is used to flavor the more traditional Indian curry dishes found in the region. Cardamom and nutmeg can be added — use about 2 tablespoons of each if desired. Adjust the heat level by using piquin or Thai chiles for extra heat or New Mexican chiles for less heat.

Roast each of the spices separately in a dry skillet over low heat, stirring constantly, until they are lightly browned and quite aromatic. Take care that they do not burn.

Grind the spices together in a mortar and pestle or food processor until they form a fine powder. Store in a small airtight bottle.

Yield: About 1 cup

2 tablespoons coriander seeds
1 tablespoon cumin seeds
1 tablespoon fennel seeds
5 dried red chiles, such as piquins,
   seeds and stems removed
2 tablespoons dried shredded coconut
1 teaspoon shrimp or prawn paste
   (available in Asian markets)
1 one-inch piece cinnamon
1 one-inch piece fresh galangal (or
   substitute ginger), peeled and
   chopped
5 candlenuts (or substitute macadamia nuts or cashews), chopped
1 two-inch piece ginger, peeled and
   chopped
3 three-inch stalks lemongrass, including the bulbs, chopped
1 teaspoon ground turmeric
3 cloves garlic, peeled and chopped
1/2 small onion, chopped
1 teaspoon salt
1/4 to 1/2 cup water for blending

🪷 Malaysian Curry Paste

Although some Indian curry spices are used in this paste, it has a flavor all its own because of the addition of such Malaysian ingredients as shrimp paste, coconut, and lemongrass. This basic paste can be substituted for the spice mixtures in many of the recipes in this chapter.

In a mortar or spice mill, grind the coriander, cumin, and fennel seeds into a powder. Place the powder and all the remaining ingredients in a food processor or blender and puree to a fine paste. Store in the smallest possible screw-top glass jar and refrigerate. To prevent oxidation, cover the paste with a thin layer of vegetable oil. It will keep for a couple of months.

🏵 *Sambal Badjak*

Yield: About 1 1/2 cups

INDONESIAN CHILE PASTE

This currylike paste is used to add heat to curries or other dishes. There are many types of sambals *in Indonesia, ranging from simple blends of chiles and shallots to the more complicated pastes, such as this one.*

In a food processor or blender, combine the chiles, onions, garlic, shrimp or prawn paste, candlenuts, tamarind, and galangal, and puree to a fine paste.

Heat the oil in a skillet. Add the paste and sauté until aromatic, about 3 to 4 minutes. Add the remaining ingredients and simmer for about 15 minutes or until the mixture thickens.

8 to 10 fresh red chiles, such as
  serranos or jalapeños, seeds and
  stems removed
2 medium onions, chopped
4 cloves garlic, peeled and chopped
1 teaspoon shrimp or prawn paste
  (available in Asian markets)
5 candlenuts (or substitute macadamia nuts or cashews)
1 teaspoon tamarind concentrate
1 one-inch piece fresh galangal (or
  substitute ginger), peeled and
  chopped
3 tablespoons vegetable oil
1 teaspoon salt
1 teaspoon brown sugar
2 dried kaffir lime leaves, crushed
1 cup thick Coconut Milk (page 19)

🏵 *Acar*

Yield: About 3 or 4 cups

MALAYSIAN VEGETABLE PICKLE

Also spelled achar, *this pickle is a traditional accompaniment to Malaysian entrées, including curries. It tastes best after it has marinated overnight in the refrigerator. Indonesian versions contain — what else? — coconut milk!*

In a saucepan, bring the vinegar to a boil and parboil, separately, for 1 minute each, the cucumber, carrots, cauliflower, cabbage, and red and green chiles. Remove each vegetable with a slotted spoon. Place the vegetables in a large bowl and reserve the vinegar. Add the sugar, peanuts, and sesame seeds to the vegetables and mix well.

Heat the oil in a pan and fry the garlic for 3 minutes. Add the turmeric, Malaysian Curry Paste or chile powder, and salt, and fry for an additional 5 minutes.

Add the fried paste to the vegetables along with 3 tablespoons of the reserved vinegar. Mix well and allow to marinate for at least 1 hour to blend the flavors.

2 cups cider vinegar
1 cucumber, peeled and diced
3 carrots, peeled and diced
1 cauliflower, separated into florets
1/2 pound cabbage, coarsely
  chopped
3 fresh hot red chiles, such as serranos, seeds and stems removed,
  halved
3 hot green chiles, such as serranos, seeds and stems removed,
  halved
1/2 cup sugar
1/2 cup ground salted peanuts
1/2 cup sesame seeds, roasted
1/2 cup vegetable oil
6 cloves garlic, peeled and minced
1 teaspoon ground turmeric
1 teaspoon Malaysian Curry
  Paste (page 148) or 2 teaspoons
  hot red chile powder, such as
  cayenne
1/2 teaspoon salt

Yield: About 20 puffs

For the Filling:
1/2 pound lean ground beef, lamb, or pork
1 onion, minced
2 medium potatoes, peeled, boiled, and diced
1 teaspoon Singapore Curry Powder (page 148)
1/2 teaspoon Malaysian Curry Paste (page 148)
1/2 cup Coconut Milk (page 19)

For the Pastry:
2 cups flour
Pinch salt
1/2 teaspoon baking powder
1 tablespoon butter
1 egg, beaten slightly
Water
Vegetable oil for deep-frying

🌿 Curry Puffs

Here is a curried accompaniment that differs greatly from the other curried dishes from the Spice Islands. Curry puffs are commonly sold as a snack by street vendors, served as tiffin curry lunches, and sampled at afternoon teas. They make a superb appetizer.

For the filling, fry the meat and the onion together in a pan until the meat is browned.

Add all the remaining ingredients and cook over medium heat, uncovered, until all the liquid has evaporated, about 10 minutes. Drain the mixture through a sieve to remove all the remaining oil and set aside.

For the pastry, sift the flour, salt, and baking powder together. Cut the butter into the mixture until it resembles bread crumbs. Add the egg and enough water to make a dough and knead for 5 minutes. Separate the dough into balls about the size of a walnut; there should be about 20. Roll out the balls on a floured board into thin rounds about 4 inches across.

Place about 1 tablespoon filling on each round and spread it over half the round. Fold the other half of the round over, wet the edges with a little water, and crimp with a fork.

Deep-fry the rounds in hot oil, turning until both sides are brown. Drain on paper towels and keep in a 325-degree oven until ready to serve. The puffs should be served hot with a *sambal* or hot sauce on the side.

🌺 *Indonesian Curried Mutton Soup*

Indonesians raise goats rather than sheep, yet "mutton" is the meat of choice in the wet market of Little India in Singapore, right across the Strait of Malacca. We assume that this delicious curried soup can be made from either goat or lamb. The recipe is from Mrs. Devagi Shanmugam of the Thomson Cooking Studio in Singapore.

Place the meat and the water in a stockpot.

In a food processor or blender, coarsely grind together the chiles, ginger, peppercorns, aniseed, cumin seeds, cardamom, cloves, coriander seeds, cinnamon, bay leaves, mint leaves, lemongrass, turmeric, curry leaves, and water. Using a strainer, strain this mixture into the stockpot containing the meat and the water. Save the residue, tie it up securely in a muslin or cotton cloth, and add it to the stockpot.

Heat the oil in a skillet. Fry the tomatoes, cinnamon, cardamom, and cloves until the tomatoes are soft. Add the mixture to the stockpot.

Bring the contents of the stockpot to a boil and continue to boil until the meat is tender and nearly falls apart, at least 1 hour. Remove the spice bundle and the cinnamon and thicken the soup with the rice flour if necessary. Garnish with the green onions before serving.

2 pounds goat meat or lamb, cut into 1-inch cubes
3 quarts water
5 small green chiles, such as serranos, seeds and stems removed
5 small fresh red chiles, such as serranos, seeds and stems removed
1 two-inch piece ginger, peeled
2 teaspoons whole black peppercorns
2 teaspoons aniseed
2 teaspoons cumin seeds
2 tablespoons ground cardamom
3 whole cloves
3 tablespoons coriander seeds
1 two-inch piece cinnamon
5 bay leaves
1 cup mint leaves
4 two-inch stalks lemongrass, including the bulbs
1 teaspoon ground turmeric
4 curry leaves
1 cup water
5 tablespoons vegetable oil
4 tomatoes, diced
2 two-inch pieces cinnamon
1 tablespoon ground cardamom
5 whole cloves, crushed in a mortar
3 teaspoons rice flour for thickening (optional)
Green onions for garnish

Laksa Kari

Serves: 6 or more

CURRIED NOODLE SOUP WITH PRAWNS

3 cups water
1/2 teaspoon salt
1/2 teaspoon sugar
1/2 pound uncooked prawns or
large shrimp
1/3 cup vegetable oil
1/4 cup Malaysian Curry Paste
(page 148)
2 two-inch stalks lemongrass, in-
cluding the bulbs, chopped
2 teaspoons shrimp or prawn paste
(available in Asian markets)
3 cups Coconut Milk (page 19)
1/2 pound bean sprouts, parboiled
for 2 minutes and drained
1 pound rice vermicelli (preferably
fresh), soaked in hot water until
soft, drained

For Garnish:
Sambal Badjak (page 149)
2 small cucumbers, peeled and
sliced lengthwise
Fish balls (see Gulai Malabar,
page 158) (optional)
Chopped cilantro leaves

A favorite at the hawker centers in Singapore, this rice noodle (laksa) dish is usually garnished with cooked prawns, fish balls or cakes, cucumbers, and polygonum, an herb that is difficult to find in the United States. We have substituted cilantro for it. In Johore Bahru, Malaysia, spaghetti is often used instead of the rice noodles.

Combine the water, salt, and sugar in a large pot and bring to a boil. Add the prawns or shimp and boil for 6 minutes. Remove the prawns or shrimp and reserve the stock. Peel the prawns or shrimp and save the shells. Remove the heads and tails and slice the prawns or shrimp lengthwise in half, reserving them for garnish.

Return the shells to the stock and boil for 10 minutes. Strain the stock to remove the shells and reserve the stock.

Heat the oil in a wok and fry the Malaysian Curry Paste, lemongrass, and shrimp or prawn paste together for 5 minutes. Add the Coconut Milk and the reserved stock and boil, uncovered, over medium heat for 15 minutes, until slightly thickened.

To assemble the dish, divide the bean sprouts among 6 soup bowls. Add the rice vermicelli on top of the sprouts and fill the bowls with the curry soup. Place some sliced prawns or shrimp, a small spoonful of the *Sambal Badjak*, cucumber slices, and cooked fish balls (if using) in the soup and sprinkle the cilantro leaves on top.

🌸 *Sumatran Rendang*

CURRIED COCONUT BEEF

This recipe, featuring beef simmered for hours in coconut milk and fresh curry spices, undoubtedly was prepared with water buffalo in its original form, since beef is uncommon in Malaysia and Indonesia.

Deep-fry the coconut in the oil until it is dark brown. Remove from the oil with a slotted spoon and drain on paper towels. Combine the coconut, beef, salt, sugar, and tamarind, and marinate in the refrigerator, covered, for at least 3 hours.

In a food processor or blender, combine the turmeric, kaffir lime leaves, lemongrass, galangal, shallots, chiles, garlic, brown sugar, salt, black pepper, and soy sauce, and puree to a fine paste.

Heat the 2 tablespoons oil in a large skillet. Sauté the paste for 2 minutes, add the beef with its marinade, and sauté for 5 minutes. Add the Coconut Milk, reduce the heat, and simmer, uncovered, for about 2 hours or until the beef starts to fall apart and the gravy thickens. Add more water if necessary.

4 ounces freshly grated coconut
Vegetable oil for deep-frying
2 pounds beef, cut into 1-inch cubes
1 teaspoon salt
2 teaspoons sugar
1 teaspoon tamarind concentrate
1/2 teaspoon ground turmeric
2 dried kaffir lime leaves, crushed
2 four-inch stalks lemongrass, including the bulb, chopped
2 three-inch pieces fresh galangal (or substitute ginger), peeled and chopped
10 shallots, peeled and chopped
5 fresh red chiles, such as serranos or jalapeños, seeds and stems removed
10 dried red chiles, such as piquins, seeds and stems removed
2 cloves garlic, peeled
1 tablespoon brown sugar
1/2 teaspoon salt
1/2 teaspoon freshly ground black pepper
2 teaspoons soy sauce
2 tablespoons vegetable oil
6 cups Coconut Milk (page 19)

Serves: 6

1/4 cup vegetable oil
1/2 cup Malaysian Curry Paste
  (page 148)
2 pounds lamb, cut into 1/2-inch
  cubes
1 large tomato, coarsely chopped
2 cups Coconut Milk (page 19)
1/4 teaspoon ground cloves
1 teaspoon ground cinnamon
2 two-inch stalks lemongrass, including the bulbs, chopped
Juice of 1 lime

🌸 Gulai Kambing

LAMB CURRY FROM SUMATRA

A gulai in Sumatra is a curry cooked with coconut milk. Although kambing means goat in Indonesia, lamb is more readily available in American supermarkets and can be substituted.

Heat the oil in a wok, add the Malaysian Curry Paste, and stir-fry until the paste darkens. Add the lamb and stir-fry for 5 minutes.

Add the tomato, Coconut Milk, cloves, cinnamon, and lemongrass, and bring to a boil. Reduce the heat, cover, and cook over low heat for 30 minutes. Stir in the lime juice just before serving.

Serves: 4 to 6

1 1/2 pounds pork, cut into 1/2-
  inch cubes
1 quart beef broth
4 tablespoons vegetable oil
2 onions, chopped
4 tablespoons Malaysian Curry
  Paste (page 148)
3 tablespoons malt vinegar
2 tablespoons hot red chile powder, such as cayenne (optional)
2 tablespoons tomato paste
2 tablespoons grated ginger
1 teaspoon sugar

🌸 The Devil's Pork Curry

This dish hails from Malacca, the city on the strait between Indonesia and Malaysia that was so crucial in the history of the spice trade. The curry is so named because of the intensity of the chiles used to prepare it, and according to most sources, it is one of the few local curries that reflect the influence of the Portuguese. In some versions of this dish, pork livers are combined with the pork.

Parboil the pork in the broth for 15 minutes. Remove the pork, set aside, and reserve the stock.

Heat the oil in a wok or large saucepan, add the onions, and sauté until soft and browned, about 10 minutes. Add all the remaining ingredients and fry for 5 minutes. Add at least 2 cups of the reserved stock and bring to a boil. Reduce the heat and simmer, uncovered, until the pork is tender and the sauce is thickened, about 40 minutes.

Variation: For a more Indonesian version of Devil's Pork Curry, add 1/4 cup Coconut Milk (page 19) and 1/4 cup freshly squeezed lime or lemon juice 15 minutes before serving and increase the heat to thicken the mixture.

🌸 *Rebong Masak Lemak*

Serves: 6 to 8

CHICKEN AND BAMBOO SHOOTS IN SPICY COCONUT GRAVY

A Singapore favorite, this curry dish from Violet Oon is best cooked in a wok. Serve it with Nasi Kunyit *(page 163) or another favorite rice dish.*

Add 1 cup of the water to the coconut, let sit for 30 minutes, and squeeze through cloth to make thick coconut milk. Reserve this milk. Add the rest of the water to the coconut, let sit for 30 minutes, and squeeze through cloth to make thin coconut milk. Reserve.

In a food processor or blender, puree together the chiles, candlenuts, galangal, lemongrass, turmeric, garlic, shrimp paste, and shallots to make a thick paste. Mix in the white pepper and the coriander.

Heat the oil in a wok and fry the paste for about 5 minutes until it is fragrant. Add the chicken, bamboo shoots, and thin coconut milk. Bring to a boil, reduce the heat slightly, and cook, uncovered, until the chicken is tender, about 20 minutes. Add the reserved thick coconut milk, soy sauce, sugar, and salt, and cook for another 10 minutes.

5 cups water
2 cups freshly grated coconut
10 small dried red chiles, such as piquins, seeds and stems removed, soaked in hot water for 30 minutes, then coarsely chopped
5 candlenuts (or substitute macadamia nuts or cashews)
1 three-inch piece fresh galangal (or substitute ginger), peeled
3 three-inch stalks lemongrass, including the bulbs
1 tablespoon ground turmeric
5 cloves garlic, peeled and chopped
1 tablespoon shrimp paste (available in Asian markets)
10 shallots, peeled and chopped
1 tablespoon ground white pepper
1 tablespoon ground coriander
1/2 cup vegetable oil
2 pounds chicken, cut into serving pieces
10 ounces cooked bamboo shoots, cut in half lengthwise
2 tablespoons soy sauce
3 teaspoons sugar
Salt to taste

Serves: 4 to 6

6 cloves garlic, peeled and minced
1/2 teaspoon ground turmeric
1 teaspoon salt
2 1/2 cups Coconut Milk (page
   19)
1 three-pound chicken, cut into
   serving pieces
5 small dried red chiles, such as
   piquins, seeds and stems removed (optional)
4 shallots, peeled and chopped
1 one-inch piece fresh galangal (or
   substitute ginger), peeled and
   chopped
1 whole clove
6 cashews
6 almonds
6 candlenuts (or substitute macadamia nuts or cashews)
1 teaspoon ground cumin
1 teaspoon ground coriander
1 curry leaf
3 tablespoons Ghee (page 17) or
   vegetable oil
3 salam leaves (or substitute bay
   leaves)
2 two-inch stalks lemongrass, including the bulbs, left whole
1 one-inch piece cinnamon

*Okra, a common thickening ingre-
dient in Spice Island curries.*

✿ Gulai Putih

WHITE CHICKEN CURRY

*This lovely dish from Sumatra is popular in Singapore, where
cashews and almonds are combined with the candlenuts. Some
versions of this dish omit the chiles, which is very unusual in
Spice Island curries.*

Combine the garlic, turmeric, salt, and 1 cup of the Coconut
Milk, and marinate the chicken in the mixture, covered, for at
least 1 hour.

In a food processor or blender, combine the chiles (if
using), shallots, galangal, clove, nuts, cumin, coriander, curry
leaf, and 1/2 cup of the Coconut Milk, and puree to a fine
paste.

Heat the Ghee or oil in a large saucepan or wok, add the
paste, and stir-fry for about 5 minutes. Add the chicken with
its marinade, the remaining 1 cup Coconut Milk, and all the
remaining ingredients and cook, uncovered, over low heat
until the chicken is tender, about 40 minutes. Add a little
water if the curry starts to dry out. Remove the *salam* leaves,
lemongrass, and cinnamon before serving.

Variation: After the chicken is done, cut all the meat off the
bones, return it to the curry, and heat through.

🏵️ *Rendang Limpa*

LIVER CURRY WITH ROASTED COCONUT

The choice of liver used in this Malaysian curry is up to the cook. We prefer chicken livers, but beef or pork liver is perfectly acceptable.

Roast the coconut in a dry pan, stirring constantly, until it turns dark brown. Remove from the pan and mince as fine as possible.

In a food processor or blender, combine the lemongrass, ginger, chiles, turmeric, coriander, five-spice powder, and salt, and puree to a fine paste.

Fry the shallots in the Ghee or oil until browned. Add the paste and fry for 5 minutes. Add the chicken livers and the Coconut Milk and cook, uncovered, over low heat until the livers are cooked and the curry is thick, 30 to 40 minutes. Stir in the roasted coconut and cook for 5 minutes. Sprinkle with the lime or lemon juice and serve.

Serves: 4

1 cup freshly shredded coconut
1 three-inch stalk lemongrass, including the bulb
1 one-inch piece ginger, peeled
3 dried mild red chiles, such as New Mexican, seeds and stems removed
1 teaspoon ground turmeric
1 teaspoon ground coriander
1 teaspoon five-spice powder
1/2 teaspoon salt
4 shallots, peeled and chopped
2 tablespoons Ghee (page 17) or vegetable oil
1 pound chicken livers, sliced
1/2 cup Coconut Milk (page 19)
2 teaspoons freshly squeezed lime or lemon juice

🏵️ *Penang Fish Curry*

Here is a classic Malaysian fish curry from Penang as prepared at the Equatorial Penang Hotel. It is interesting because it contains okra, which is called lady fingers in Malaysia and Singapore.

Heat the oil in a wok and sauté the garlic, shallots, and onions along with the curry leaves until they are slightly browned. Add the Malaysian Curry paste and cook for 1 minute. Add the Coconut Milk and the tamarind liquid and bring to a boil. Reduce the heat and add all the remaining ingredients. Simmer, uncovered, until the fillets are tender, about 25 minutes.

Serves: 6

4 tablespoons vegetable oil
10 cloves garlic, peeled and chopped
4 shallots, peeled and chopped
3 medium onions, chopped
5 curry leaves, crushed
1/4 cup Malaysian Curry Paste (page 148)
3 cups Coconut Milk (page 19)
2 teaspoons tamarind paste dissolved in 1 cup water
6 thick fillets of whitefish, such as snapper
1/2 pound okra, parboiled for 2 minutes, drained, stems removed, and chopped
3 medium tomatoes, chopped
3 green onions, chopped
Salt to taste

Serves: 2 to 4

1/4 cup vegetable oil
2 curry leaves, crushed
1 one-inch piece fresh galangal (or substitute ginger), peeled and grated
2 cloves garlic, peeled and chopped
2 medium onions, sliced
1 cup Coconut Milk (page 19)
1/4 cup Singapore Curry Powder (page 148), mixed with 1 cup water to make a paste
1 tablespoon Malaysian Curry Paste (page 148)
1 teaspoon salt
1 teaspoon sugar
3 tomatoes, coarsely chopped
2 teaspoons tamarind paste dissolved in 1 cup water
3 small hot green chiles, such as serranos, seeds and stems removed, halved
3 small fresh hot red chiles, such as serranos, seeds and stems removed, halved
1 large fish head (about 1 pound)
6 small okra, parboiled for 2 minutes, drained, stems removed, and sliced

Singapore Fish-Head Curry

Although it does not sound particularly appetizing, this South Indian curry, transformed a bit by Malaysian ingredients, is truly delicious — if guests can get accustomed to the fish's eyeball staring at them! A readily available fish that works well in this dish is red snapper. Diners pick the meat off the head with a fork, then dip the meat in the curry sauce.

Heat the oil in a wok and fry the curry leaves and galangal for 2 minutes. Add the garlic and the onions and fry until the onions are soft. Add the Coconut Milk, Singapore Curry Powder mixed with water, and Malaysian Curry Paste, and stir-fry for about 5 minutes.

Add the salt, sugar, tomatoes, and tamarind liquid, and cook for 5 minutes. Add the green and red chiles, fish head, and okra, and simmer, uncovered, until the meat starts to fall off the fish head, about 45 minutes.

Serves: 4

1 pound raw fish, such as snapper, finely minced
1/4 cup freshly grated coconut
2 tablespoons minced onion
3 cloves garlic, peeled and minced
4 candlenuts (or substitute macadamia nuts), minced
1 tablespoon minced galangal (or substitute ginger)
1 teaspoon ground coriander
1 teaspoon shrimp or prawn paste (available in Asian markets)
1 teaspoon ground turmeric

Gulai Malabar

CURRIED FISH BALLS

The Chinese influence on the region is revealed by these fish balls, which the Malays, of course, turned into a curry. Sometimes this dish is served over rice vermicelli in bowls, but a rice dish works equally well.

Combine the fish, coconut, onion, garlic, candlenuts, galangal, coriander, shrimp paste, turmeric, and cumin, and mix well. Fashion this mixture into 1-inch balls and set aside.

158   A WORLD OF CURRIES

Heat the oil in a wok or skillet and stir-fry the onions and the Malaysian Curry Paste until the onions are soft. Add the tomato paste, lemon juice, water, chiles, lemongrass, salt, and sugar, and bring to a boil. Reduce the heat, add the okra, and simmer for 3 minutes. Add the fish balls and simmer, uncovered, for 15 minutes. Serve over rice or vermicelli and garnish with the cilantro leaves.

1 teaspoon ground cumin
1/4 cup vegetable oil
2 medium onions, chopped
3 tablespoons Malaysian Curry Paste (page 148)
1 tablespoon tomato paste
Juice of 2 lemons
2 cups water
3 fresh hot red chiles, such as serranos, seeds and stems removed, halved
2 two-inch stalks lemongrass, including the bulbs, chopped
1 teaspoon salt
2 teaspoons sugar
4 whole okra
Cilantro leaves for garnish

❦ *Bia Kare*

INDONESIAN CLAM CURRY

This quick dish can be made with either clams or mussels, both of which are abundant in coastal areas of Indonesia. In Malaysia, a nearly identical dish, ketam kari, *is made with crabmeat and roe.*

In a food processor or blender, combine the chiles, candlenuts, shallots, garlic, lemongrass, galangal, coriander, cumin, shrimp paste, and 1/4 cup of the Coconut Milk, and puree to a fine paste.

Heat the Ghee or oil in a wok and stir-fry the paste for about 5 minutes. Add the clams, broth, and remaining 1 cup of Coconut Milk, and cook, uncovered, over medium heat for about 5 minutes to blend all the flavors.

Serves: 4

4 fresh red chiles, such as serranos, seeds and stems removed
8 candlenuts (or substitute macadamia nuts or cashews)
5 shallots, peeled and chopped
2 cloves garlic, peeled and chopped
2 two-inch stalks lemongrass, including the bulbs
1 three-inch piece fresh galangal (or substitute ginger), peeled and chopped
1 teaspoon ground coriander
1 teaspoon ground cumin
1/2 teaspoon shrimp paste (available in Asian markets)
1 1/4 cups Coconut Milk (page 19)
1 tablespoon Ghee (page 17) or vegetable oil
1 pound clams, steamed and removed from the shells
1/2 cup clam broth

Serves: 4

10 small dried hot red chiles, such as piquins, seeds and stems removed
5 candlenuts (or substitute macadamia nuts or cashews)
2 two-inch stalks lemongrass, including the bulbs
1/2 teaspoon ground turmeric
1 three-inch piece fresh galangal (or substitute ginger), peeled and chopped
1 small onion, chopped
1 teaspoon shrimp or prawn paste (available in Asian markets)
1 tablespoon Ghee (page 17) or vegetable oil
4 curry leaves
1 1/2 pounds uncooked prawns or large shrimp, peeled, heads and tails left on, deveined if desired
1 1/2 cups thick Coconut Milk (page 19)

Serves: 4 to 6

4 large unripe bananas
1 teaspoon salt
1/2 teaspoon ground turmeric
3 tablespoons Ghee (page 17) or vegetable oil
2 cups Coconut Milk (page 19)
2 small hot green chiles, such as serranos, seeds and stems removed, chopped
2 teaspoons pounded Bombay duck (available in Asian markets) (optional)
1/2 teaspoon ground fenugreek
1/2 teaspoon crushed fennel seeds
1 one-inch piece cinnamon
3 curry leaves, crushed
1/2 cup minced onion

Gulai Udang

PRAWN CURRY

In Malaysia, this dish is sometimes prepared with as many as forty small red-hot chiles, making it one of the hottest dishes in the Spice Islands. We have toned it down a bit, but it is still quite hot. In some versions of this gulai, tomatoes and/or tamarind paste are added.

In a food processor or blender, combine the chiles, candlenuts, lemongrass, turmeric, galangal, onion, and shrimp or prawn paste, and puree to a fine paste.

Heat the Ghee or oil in a skillet or wok and fry the paste and curry leaves for 5 minutes. Add the prawns or shrimp and the Coconut Milk and cook, uncovered, over medium heat until the prawns or shrimp are done, about 15 minutes.

Pisang Kari

MALAYSIAN BANANA CURRY

Malaysia is believed to be the original home of the banana, or pisang, *cultivated there for more than four thousand years. Banana leaves are often used as plates for curry — at the Banana Leaf Apolo Restaurant in Singapore, for example. Do not use ripe bananas in this recipe.*

Peel the bananas, cut them in half lengthwise, and sprinkle them with the salt and the turmeric. Fry the bananas in the Ghee or oil for 2 minutes on each side.

In another pan, combine the Coconut Milk, chiles, Bombay duck (if using), fenugreek, fennel seeds, cinnamon, curry leaves, and onion. Cook over medium heat for 30 minutes, then add the bananas and cook, uncovered, over low heat for 10 minutes.

Mixed-Vegetable and Soy Curry

Serves: 6

A vegetarian curry that shows some Chinese influence, this recipe is simple and quick to prepare. Cooks can vary the vegetables according to what is available from the garden or the market.

Heat the oil in a wok or large pan and fry the onion, garlic, and galangal until the onion is soft. Add the shrimp paste and stir-fry for 2 minutes.

Add the Singapore Curry Powder, Coconut Milk, salt, and sugar, and bring to a boil. Reduce the heat, add the vegetables and the tofu, and cook, uncovered, over medium heat until the vegetables are tender, about 30 to 40 minutes.

1/3 cup vegetable oil
1 large onion, chopped
3 cloves garlic, peeled and chopped
1 two-inch piece fresh galangal (or substitute ginger), peeled and chopped
2 teaspoons shrimp paste (available in Asian markets)
4 tablespoons Singapore Curry Powder (page 148)
3 cups Coconut Milk (page 19)
1 teaspoon salt
1 teaspoon sugar
1 pound cabbage, coarsely chopped
1/2 pound green beans, cut into 1-inch pieces
1 carrot, peeled and cut into 1-inch pieces
1/2 pound cauliflower, separated into florets
1/2 pound eggplant, peeled and cut into 1-inch cubes
1/2 pound soybean curd (tofu), cut into 1-inch cubes

Ubi Kentang Kari

Serves: 4

POTATO-COCONUT CURRY

This vegetarian curry from Malaysia is unusual because of the addition of fenugreek seeds, sesame seeds, and bell peppers. It is sometimes served with deep-fried anchovies sprinkled with chile powder as an accompaniment.

In a food processor or blender, combine the galangal, garlic, fenugreek and sesame seeds, salt, turmeric, and chile powder, and puree with enough water to make a thick paste.

Heat the oil in a wok or skillet and stir-fry the paste for 5 minutes. Add the Coconut Milk and the bell peppers and

1 two-inch piece fresh galangal (or substitute ginger), peeled and chopped
1 clove garlic, peeled and chopped
1 teaspoon fenugreek seeds, dry-roasted in a pan and ground
3 ounces sesame seeds, dry-roasted in a pan and ground
1 teaspoon salt
1/2 teaspoon ground turmeric
1 teaspoon red chile powder, such as New Mexican
Water
1/4 cup vegetable oil
1 cup Coconut Milk (page 19)

1 green bell pepper, seeds and stem
   removed, cut into 1/2-inch slices
1 red bell pepper, seeds and stem
   removed, cut into 1/2-inch slices
4 potatoes, peeled, boiled, and cut
   into 1-inch cubes
Chopped cilantro leaves for garnish

cook over medium heat for 3 minutes. Add the potatoes and
simmer for 5 minutes or until the sauce thickens. Serve garnished with the cilantro leaves.

Serves: 4

1 pound eggplant, peeled and cut
   lengthwise into slices about 1/2
   inch thick and then cut into 1-
   inch-wide strips
1/4 cup vegetable oil
1/2 small onion, chopped
2 cloves garlic, peeled and chopped
2 teaspoons Singapore Curry Powder (page 148)
1 teaspoon Sambal Badjak (page
   149)
1 cup Coconut Milk (page 19)
1 salam leaf (or substitute bay
   leaf), left whole
1 dried kaffir lime leaf, crushed
2 two-inch stalks lemongrass, including the bulbs, chopped
1 teaspoon shrimp paste (available
   in Asian markets)
1/2 teaspoon salt
1/2 teaspoon sugar

Terong Kari

EGGPLANT CURRY

*There are many variations on this Indonesian dish. Sometimes
curry powder is used as the main spicing ingredient, sometimes a
sambal, and often, as in this version, both are present to spice up
the bland eggplant. The eggplant should be just barely ripe —
some cooks even prefer green eggplant. Whichever is chosen, it
should not be overcooked.*

Soak the eggplant in salted water for 30 minutes. Remove,
dry, and fry the slices in half the oil until browned, about 3 to
4 minutes. Remove, drain on paper towels, and reserve.

Heat the remaining oil, add the onion and the garlic, and
fry until the onion is soft. Add all the remaining ingredients
except the eggplant and cook over medium heat for 5 to 6
minutes.

Add the eggplant and cook, uncovered, over medium heat
for 3 to 4 minutes or until the sauce has thickened and the
eggplant is tender but not falling apart.

 Nasi Lemak

COCONUT MILK RICE

Here is the most popular rice dish on the west coast of Malaysia. It is served in coffee shops and roadside stands, wrapped in banana leaf and garnished with a sambal, peanuts, egg, and cucumber slices. It makes a perfect side dish to the Spice Island curries in this chapter. For a less pronounced coconut flavor, use 1 1/2 cups Coconut Milk and 1 1/2 cups water in place of the 3 cups Coconut Milk.

Combine all the ingredients in a pot and bring to a boil. Reduce the heat to low, cover the pot, and cook until the rice is done and fluffy, about 35 to 40 minutes. Remove the cloves and *pandan* leaves before serving.

Serves: 6 to 8

2 cups long-grain rice, washed and drained
3 cups Coconut Milk (page 19)
1/2 teaspoon salt
1 teaspoon butter
2 whole cloves
2 pandan (screw pine) leaves, tied in a knot

 Nasi Kunyit

YELLOW FESTIVE RICE

This recipe, from the Thompson Cooking Studio of Mrs. Devagi Shanmugam in Singapore, makes a very colorful rice with curry spice fragrances. Kunyit is the Malay word for turmeric; nasi, of course, is rice.

In a food processor or blender, puree together the coriander, cumin, turmeric, ginger, garlic, shallots, and water. Fry this paste in the oil in a saucepan until fragrant, about 5 to 7 minutes. Add the Coconut Milk and bring to a boil.

Reduce the heat to a simmer, add the rice and the lemongrass, cover, and cook until the rice is done, about 40 to 45 minutes. Add salt to taste and garnish with the fried green onion rings.

Serves: 6

4 teaspoons ground coriander
2 teaspoons ground cumin
1 teaspoon ground turmeric
1 five-inch piece ginger, peeled
3 cloves garlic, peeled
20 shallots, peeled
1 cup water
6 tablespoons vegetable oil
6 cups Coconut Milk (page 19)
3 cups rice, washed and drained
4 three-inch stalks lemongrass, including the bulbs, chopped
Salt to taste
Fried green onion rings for garnish

Yield: About 20 to 25 three-inch roti

2 cups sifted flour
Pinch salt
2 eggs, slightly beaten
4 cups milk
2 tablespoons Ghee (page 17) or vegetable oil

❦ Roti Djala

LACE PANCAKES

The word djala *actually means a casting net, an allusion to the lacy look of this pancake with holes. It has obvious Indian origins and is a great accompaniment to Spice Island curries. Using a slotted spoon to drizzle the batter onto the skillet will create the lacy effect. The* roti *can be made with either coconut milk or cow's milk, but since coconut milk appears in so many Spice Island curry recipes, we have opted for the latter here.*

Combine the flour and the salt in a bowl, add the eggs, and gradually add 1 cup of the milk, stirring well. Beat the batter with a whisk to remove lumps, add the rest of the milk, and beat again.

Brush a skillet or omelette pan with the Ghee or oil. Using a slotted spoon, drizzle the batter onto the skillet to make 3-inch pancakes. Fry until set and lightly browned.

Variation: Turn the *roti* once and cook longer for a crispier pancake.

SIX

African Curries

There is reason to

assume that the ambrosia

of which the ancient poets

spoke so often was a kind

of ginger chile called

pinang *curry.*

C. L. LEIPOLDT,

AFRIKAANS POET

*A*frica has the most varied curries in the world — with the possible exception of India. They range from spice mixtures with aphrodisiac beetles to scaldingly hot chile pepper blends to elegant weekend curry lunches at the club. The contrasting curries reflect the ethnic diversity of Africa as well as the influence of the eight European countries that colonized the continent: Britain, the Netherlands, France, Germany, Italy, Portugal, Spain, and Belgium. In addition, there were strong culinary influences on African curries from unexpected places: the Middle East and the Spice Islands.

*A*mbrosia from the *C*ape

The Dutch colonized South Africa because of its ideal position halfway between the Netherlands and the Spice Islands. It was a perfect outpost for raising the vegetables and livestock necessary to replenish their ships. In 1652, the Dutch East India Company dispatched a party of officials to the Cape of Good Hope to establish a "revictualling station."

"Within fourteen days of their arrival," writes Renata Coetzee in *The South African Culinary Tradition*, "these early settlers had laid out a vegetable garden." They planted sweet potatoes, pineapples, watermelons, pumpkins, cucumbers, radishes, and lemon and orange trees.

Late in the seventeenth century, with the revictualing station in operation, commerce between the Dutch East India Company and the new Dutch colony of South Africa picked up considerably because of an important commodity: Malay slaves, referred to in South African literature as "the king of slaves." The men were put to work as farmers, carpenters, musicians, tailors, and fishermen, while the women were expert cooks who not only introduced exotic Spice Island dishes but also imported the spices necessary to prepare them.

Among the Malaysian spices transferred by the slaves to South Africa were aniseed, fennel, turmeric, ginger, cardamom, cumin, coriander, mustard seed, tamarind, and garlic. Chiles, of course, were introduced by the Portuguese traders and eventually were disseminated across Africa by birds. Curiously, coconuts — so

important in the Spice Islands — do not play a role in South African curries.

Cape Town, South Africa, c. 1885.

The Cape Malays, as the slaves' descendants became known, developed a unique cuisine called, by some, Old Cape Cookery. It evolved into a mixture of Dutch, English, and Malay styles and ingredients — with an emphasis on the Malay. Predominant among the numerous cooking styles were curries and their accompaniments. As early as 1740, "kerrie-kerrie" dishes were mentioned in South African literature. That terminology had changed by 1797, when Johanna Duminy of the Riviersonderend Valley wrote in her diary: "When the evening fell I had the candles lit, the children were given their supper and put to bed. At nine o'clock we are going to have a delicious curry."

Johanna's curry probably was milder than that of today in South Africa, because for a time the amounts of chiles and green ginger used in cooking were greatly reduced to accommodate the Dutch palate. But the Cape Malays relished the heat, and Harva Hachten, author of *Kitchen Safari*, points out: "Curries are as much a part of Malay cooking as they are of Indian."

AFRICAN CURRIES

Tamarind, used in pinang *curry.*

Generally speaking, Cape Malay curries contain meat and are not as highly spiced with chiles as their Asiatic cousins. Onions and tomatoes are added to achieve a truly thick mixture, and sometimes potatoes are placed in the curry for extra body. The Malay curries — usually eaten with the fingers — are a meal in themselves. They are eaten with rice and *roti* bread as accompaniments and are served with salads, *sambals*, pickles, and chutneys.

Perhaps the all-time favorite Cape Malay curry is *pinang* curry. It is this curry — flavored with curry spices, tamarind, and fresh orange leaves — that prompted the passionate quotation by C. L. Leipoldt that begins this chapter. Leipoldt also observes: "Do not suppose that *pinang* meat is just an ordinary curry." Our recipe for that dish, *Pinang-Kerrie*, appears on page 188, and we too think that it is extraordinary.

Other types of Cape Malay curries are denning curry — *dendeng* in Malay — flavored with mace and tamarind; a very popular *Frikkadel* Curry (page 185); and two interesting seafood curries, Cape Curried Fish Soup (page 184) and Capetown Curried Lobster Tail (page 193). Additional dishes flavored with curry spices enjoy great popularity in South Africa and include *Bobotie*, Raisin-Almond Curried Casserole (page 189); *Sosaties* (page 188), grilled curried lamb that has been twice marinated; *Kerrieboontjies Bredie*, Curried Kidney Beans (page 186); and Curry of Three Dried Fruits (page 186), apples being a commonly curried fruit in the country.

The curries are served with a number of accompaniments, of which chutneys, *sambals*, and *atjar*s (pickles) are the most popular. Renata Coetzee observes: "The Cape Malays are past masters at combining a variety of spices in one dish or at serving 'hot' dishes with a cool 'sambal' or, alternatively, hot chutney or pickles to add piquancy to bland foods." Our Cluster of Cape Chutneys (page 182) offers three favorite South African chutneys, with varying heat levels.

The Cape Malays, however, were but one of the curry influences on South Africa. The first shipment of indentured Indian laborers arrived in Natal, in the eastern part of the region, on November 16, 1860, to work on the sugar plantations. Within six years, about five thousand Indians were working in Natal, and of course, they brought their Indian curry traditions with them. It seems that the British taste for curries had waned somewhat as the pioneers ventured farther from Cape Town.

The Indian laborers "helped re-stimulate the flagging appetite for Far Eastern dishes," explains Laurens Van Der Post in his book *First Catch Your Eland*. "Curries again became a regular feature of life in the interior. No week would go by without at least one if not two main curry dishes appearing in the average household." Van Der Post notes that nearly everything edible was curried, including headcheese and sheep's heads, feet, and tripe. "The reappearance of curry in the fundamental and most conservative departments of the kitchen of the interior," he writes, "shows to what depth the Indian influence spread."

The indentured laborers used a spice mix called *mussala* (an obvious corruption of *masala*), which is the simplest form of curry powder in South Africa, but its basic ingredients vary considerably. One version contains only turmeric, cumin, and red chile powder, while another is composed of equal amounts of fennel, coriander, cinnamon, and cumin. We have opted for a more complex mixture, Cape Curry Powder (page 179), which reflects both the Malay and Indian influences.

There are numerous prepared curry blends available in South Africa; however, as Mary Phillips, author of *Passages from India*, points out: "It is authenticity with a difference — the spices for the curry powder are grown and processed in the fields and food factories of the local Indian community."

Curries are universally loved in South Africa and cross cultural and racial barriers. In describing the curries of Natal, Laurens Van Der Post makes a sort of culinary appeal to free South Africa:

Curry in all the forms in which it is done in India is served in hotels and homes and eaten with relish, however strong the colour prejudice of the household in which they are served. If only the heart in South Africa could be governed for a year or two by the national palate, there would be no apartheid or racial prejudice left in the land, because our cooking is the best advertisement the world could possibly offer for a multi-racial society, free of religious, racial, and other forms of discrimination.

On the Edge of the Sahara

Thousands of miles north of the Cape, and millennia earlier, North Africa had developed its own intriguing curry tradition. The Middle East and Rome were the two main influences on curries there, and it is likely that the first Asian spices were introduced into the region by the Phoenicians, who around the eighth century B.C. traveled from what is today northern Syria to establish colonies in North Africa at Carthage and modern-day Algiers. The Phoenicians invented a dried sausage to sustain them on long sea voyages, and they carried with them spices such as nutmeg, cumin, coriander, and cloves, which formed the basis of Middle Eastern spice blends such as *baharat*.

During this time North Africa was known (as it is today) as the Maghreb, and it was inhabited by nomadic Berbers. It is likely that the Phoenicians — or the Carthaginians, who followed them — introduced durum wheat to the region. The wheat became a favorite of the Berbers, who invented couscous, a granular semolina that is now a staple food in North Africa.

The Romans needed wheat to feed their growing empire and began trade with Carthage around the third century B.C. The Romans probably also introduced their beloved spices, such as black pepper and cinnamon, into North Africa as part of the trade in wheat and other foodstuffs.

During the seventh century A.D., North Africa was invaded by Arab armies, which brought additional spices to the region. However they arrived, spice mixtures became very important in the cuisines of North Africa, and they are some of the most unusual curry combinations we encountered during our globe-circling curry tour — a direct result of the availability of seasonings in the area.

"The North African housewife can choose from up to 200 different spices and herbs when she stops to replenish her supplies at a spice stall in the *souks* of the *medinas*," observes Harva Hachten. This diversity is reflected in the unique spice mixture *ras el hanout*, which is prepared with twenty to thirty spices ranging from the familiar to the downright weird.

Paula Wolfert, in her book *Couscous and Other Good Foods from Morocco*, states that "it is incorrect to think of *ras el hanout*

North African spice mixtures are found in spice stalls on streets like this one in Tangier.

as curry powder by another name," because it lacks sufficient amounts (or any, in some cases) of cumin, coriander, fenugreek, and mustard. However, most versions of *ras el hanout* contain other major curry spices, such as turmeric, ginger, cinnamon, nutmeg, black pepper, and chiles, so let's compromise and say that the mixture is a variation on curry powders.

If these spices are too tame for adventurous cooks, Moroccan spice makers will gladly revise their *ras el hanout* by throwing in some belladonna berries, iris leaves, and Spanish fly — the reputedly aphrodisiac cantharides beetles. *Ras el hanout* means top of the shop or shopkeepers' choice, indicating that the mixture is individually prepared by each spice seller. We have cleaned up our recipe (page 180), leaving out the aphrodisiacs.

If *ras el hanout* itself is too tame, then the ultimate high of North African curries is *el majoun*, a sweetmeat of almonds, honey, butter, and fruits, spiced with a dangerous dollop of the aphrodisiac *ras el hanout* and a heavy helping of hallucinogenic hashish. In 1846, the French poet, novelist, and dedicated hashish devotee Théophile Gautier described *majoun* in his book *Revue des deux mondes:*

> The doctor stood by the side of a buffet on which lay a platter filled with small Japanese saucers. He spooned a morsel of paste or greenish jam about as large as a thumb from a crystal vase, and placed it next to the silver spoon on each saucer. . . . "This will be deducted from your share in paradise," he said as he handed me my portion.

The effects of the *majoun* were strange indeed, especially in a culinary sense. "I had experienced a complete transformation in taste," wrote Gautier. "The water I drank seemed the most exquisite wine, the meat, once in my mouth, became strawberries, the strawberries, meat. I could not have distinguished a peach from a cutlet."

Incidentally, cannabis was introduced into Europe from North Africa in the form of a curried aromatic cake called *dawamesk*, which was composed of sinsemilla (seedless) cannabis flowers, sugar, orange juice, cinnamon, cloves, cardamom, nutmeg, pistachios, and pine nuts. One of the principal importers of *dawamesk* was the notorious Le Club de Hashischins, a group of hashish-loving Parisian intellectuals led by — who else? — Théophile Gautier. Among the club's other members were Victor Hugo, Honoré de Balzac, and Charles Baudelaire.

Less controversial curry mixtures found in North Africa include the basic Tunisian *tabil* mixture of coriander, caraway, garlic, and crushed red chile; *la kama*, a Moroccan blend of black pepper, turmeric, ginger, cumin, and nutmeg; *zahtar*, a combination of sesame seeds, ground sumac, and powdered thyme; and Tunisian Five-Spice Powder (page 180), which is another simple mixture — similar to a basic *masala* — of five curry spices, with cloves, black peppercorns, and nutmeg providing the dominant flavors.

Another, more complex and powerful curry compound is the chile-based *harissa*, which is of Tunisian origin but is found all over North Africa. Our recipe for this paste featuring red chiles for heat and color and curry spices such as cinnamon, coriander, and cumin for flavor is found on page 181. *Harissa* is used in the kitchen and at the table to fire up soups, stews, and less spicy curries.

The most famous North African curries, served from Morocco to Egypt, are called *tajines*, and they are named after the earthenware *tajine* pot in which they are cooked. Just about any meat — chicken, pigeon, mutton, beef, goat, and even camel — can be made into a *tajine*, with the exception of pork, proscribed by Islamic law. The meat is usually cubed, and, according to Harva Hachten, "the cooking liquid is the secret of a *tajine*'s tastiness. This is usually a combination of water and butter or oil (characteristically, olive oil) and seasonings to suit what's being cooked." The long cooking time allows the ingredients to become very tender and the cooking liquid to reduce to a thick, savory sauce. Our recipe for *Harira Kefta Tajine* (page 187) is slightly unusual in that it features ground instead of cubed lamb, which is made into curried meatballs.

In 1902, Budgett Meakin, a traveler in North Africa, described a recipe for the preparation of couscous that involved mutton curried with ginger, pepper, nutmeg, allspice, turmeric, and saffron. The mutton was sautéed in a *tajine* with butter and onions, the spices were added along with freshly chopped parsley, marjoram, and cilantro, and water was added to the mixture for stewing. When the meat was nearly done, a steamer filled with couscous was placed on top of the *tajine* and the rising steam finished the cooking. Meakin noted that raisins or quinces were added when the *tajine* was served with the couscous.

Over in West Africa, particularly the former British colony of Nigeria, the curries are distinguished by an extra infusion of hot chiles. As Ellen Wilson, author of *A West African Cookbook*, has observed: "Learning to eat West African food means learning to enjoy [chile] pepper." She adds: "West African dishes can be searing or simply warm, but it is noticeable that the [chile] pepper never conceals the other ingredients; in fact, it seems to enhance them."

Another distinguishing characteristic of Nigerian curries is that they are served with an inordinate number of accompaniments. In addition to the usual chutneys and raisins and shredded coconut, the Nigerians offer as many as twenty-five condiments,

including chopped dates, diced cucumber, diced citrus fruits, ground dried shrimp, diced mangoes and papayas, peanuts, grapes, fried onions, chopped fresh red chiles, and bananas.

"Nigerians and old African hands," notes Harva Hachten, "spoon out a portion of everything so their plates become a mound of curry and rice completely hidden by a patchwork of color and tastes." A typical Nigerian curry is our Chicken Curry with Yogurt (page 190), which can be served with white rice and any or all of the above condiments.

In some parts of West Africa where the British traditions are still apparent, the larger hotels serve a weekend curry lunch. The tradition came from colonial officers who had been assigned to Africa after their stints in India. We can imagine a tasty West African dish, Nigerian Coconut-Curry Soup (page 184), being served at just that sort of weekend curry lunch.

In East Africa, the curry influences came from many sources. The earliest date to the third century B.C., when the region was, for a brief time, one of the first colonies of the Indian kingdoms. Also, the region's proximity to the Middle East led to familiarity with spice mixtures such as *baharat* from the Arabian Gulf states and *zhug* from Yemen. Arab traders had virtual control of the region — especially the coast — for a thousand years, while trading in spices and slaves.

Around A.D. 1000, the island of Zanzibar, now part of Tanzania, was settled by African mainlanders, but it soon hosted traders from Persia (modern Iran), India, and Arabia. With these traders arrived spices — in particular, cloves, which grew very well on the island. Later visits by the Portuguese and Dutch to Zanzibar secured its place in spice-growing history. Because of the Dutch destruction of the clove trees in the Moluccas (see chapter 5), new clove-growing regions were needed, and Zanzibar was perfect. Today, the "Isle of Cloves" grows 80 percent of the world's supply, and the populace takes clove growing seriously indeed. As late as 1971, it was a capital offense to smuggle any cloves from Zanzibar out of the country. That year, fifteen smugglers were sentenced to death for possessing contraband cloves. Our clove-studded Curried Beef and Bananas (page 185) from Tanzania celebrates the spice from the Isle of Cloves.

However, the greatest influence upon the curries of East Africa was the British, who controlled present-day Kenya, Malawi, Zambia, and Uganda beginning in the nineteenth century. Laurens Van Der Post comments: "Already firmly entrenched in the highlands of Kenya, supported by a middle class of Indian artisans and civil servants, the British became all-powerful in East Africa, and British and Indian concepts of food took charge of the modern East African kitchen."

The large number of Indians, of course, resulted from the same influx of indentured laborers that flooded South Africa. Many of the Indians who settled in East Africa were Muslims from the Bombay area who arrived during the early days of British rule to build the railroad that runs from Mombasa, on the coast of

Kenya, to Kampala, Uganda. Christians from Goa also immigrated, to work as teachers and clerks.

Other people of Indian descent in East Africa are Ismaili Muslims, followers of the Aga Khan, and one of their favorite dishes is Eggplant and Potato Curry (page 193), from Tanzania. Tanzanians are fond of currying goat or chicken in a stew or simply charcoal broiling the meats after they have been marinated in a mixture of curry spices and chiles.

In Kenya, a stew called *kima* is served, combining chopped beef with red chile powder and curry spices. It is obviously derived from *keema*, the minced-meat curries of India. The weekend curry lunch, a holdover from British colonial days, was still observed in some parts of East Africa well into the 1970s.

Curries are also important in the cookery of Mozambique, despite its history as a Portuguese colony. Its proximity to Natal, in South Africa, is probably the reason. Sometimes cashews, a major crop in Mozambique, are added to curries, much as candlenuts are added to Malaysian curries. Mozambique cooks are known for a chile paste that's almost a curry paste. *Piripiri*, made with the narrow, fiery African chiles of the same name, contains garlic, herbs, and oil — but no curry spices. It is, however, analogous to curries in the native cuisine of East Africa, those foods not influenced by Arabs, Indians, or the British.

Curries abound in Malawi, which became the British protectorate of Nyasaland in 1891. Local cookbooks have recipes for specific curry powders for meats, fish, and vegetables, and a few universal powders containing — as is typical for East Africa — a large helping of chiles. Our Malawi Curry Powder (page 179) is characteristic of a universal powder in that it contains nine different spices; a fish curry powder, for example, usually contains four fewer spices, just chiles, coriander, cumin, turmeric, and mustard. Another interesting recipe from Malawi is the visually appealing Curried Prawns in Pineapple Boats (page 192).

Ethiopia, the last outpost of African curries, is also the part of East Africa least influenced by British and Indian versions of curry. Instead, it evolved its own unique curry tradition. According to Daniel Jote Mesfin, author of *Exotic Ethiopian Cooking*, "Marco Polo did not visit our country. And Ethiopia was never conquered. It came under brief Italian rule during Mussolini's time, but for the most part, we did not have direct and intimate dealings with foreign powers. And Ethiopian cuisine remained a secret."

Ethiopia was isolated from Europe, but not from the spice trade. "Since Ethiopia was located at the crossroads of the spice trade," observes Michael Winn, owner of New York's Blue Nile restaurant, "its people began to pay keen attention to blending spices. Fenugreek, cumin, red chiles, and varieties of herbs are used lovingly in creating meat, fish, and vegetable dishes."

Even the butter is curried in Ethiopia, with ginger, garlic, turmeric, basil, cardamom, and other spices combined to make a ghee-like concoction known as *nit'ir qibe* (see Ethiopian Curried Butter, page 182). But the most important spice mixture is a condiment called *berbere*, which is made with the hottest chiles available, plus other spices, and is served as a side dish with meat or used as a coating for drying meats or as a major ingredient of curried meats. Tribal custom dictated that *berbere* be served with *kifto*, a raw meat dish that is served warm. According to legend, the more delicious a woman's *berbere*, the better chance she had to win a husband. Recipes for *berbere* were closely guarded, since the marriageability of women was at stake.

Laurens Van Der Post philosophized on *berbere* in 1970:

Berbere gave me my first inkling of the essential role played by spices in the more complex forms of Ethiopian cooking. . . . It seemed to me related to that of India and of Indonesia, particularly Java; I suspect that there may have been far more contact between Ethiopia and the Far East than the history books indicate.

Our recipe for *Berbere* (page 181) contains twelve curry spices in addition to garlic; notable for its absence is turmeric, a popular ingredient in Indian-influenced curries but not in Ethiopian ones. Our recipe is not as hot as some versions, which require up to several cups of powdered cayennes or *piripiris*! Chile peppers are obviously extremely important in Ethiopian curries, and they have even inspired a derogatory expression, *ye wend alich'a*, meaning a man who has no pepper in him.

In Ethiopian cookery, *berbere* is an indispensable ingredient in the national dishes known as *wats* or *w'ets* (depending on the transliteration), currylike stews of lamb, beef, chicken, beans, or vegetables (never pork). Our *Doro W'et* (page 191), a chicken stew, contains curry spices in addition to those already in the *berbere*.

Nowadays, Ethiopian cuisine is no longer a secret, for about seventy Ethiopian restaurants have opened in a number of North American cities during the past decade. Since Africa was one of the few major curry regions we were unable to visit personally, we did the next best thing and dined at an Ethiopian restaurant in New York City, the Blue Nile, on West Seventy-seventh Street.

Arthur, Betty, Dave, and Mary Jane tried several variations on *w'et* at the Blue Nile that included such ingredients as fennel and cardamom seeds, ginger, garlic, red chiles, and cloves. The four *w'et*s were placed on a wide tray covered with *injera*, a sourdough pancakelike bread made from *t'ef*, a cereal grain also called love grass (it can also be made with barley, corn, wheat, or millet).

As is the tradition of communal eating with fingers rather than forks, we tore off a corner of *t'ef*, using the right hand only, and used the spongy bread to pinch some of the *w'et* and transfer it to the mouth. The eating experience reminded Arthur of some Indian Muslim communities that eat from the same platter — and expect their guests to join them, too.

The experience also opened our eyes to the breadth of curries around the world. Dave had dined the previous night at the Dawat restaurant, tasting a wide variety of Indian curries. What the Blue Nile had served was curries, too; they simply had a different selection and mixture of spices — and different names, of course.

Like other African curries, the Ethiopian *w'et*s were powerfully pungent in taste. And we remembered the Yoruba proverb: The man that eats no chile is weak; chile is the staff of life.

Cape Curry Powder

Yield: About 2 cups

This blend of spices, with its mix of Malay and Indian influences, can be used in South African recipes calling for curry powder or in recipes from other parts of the continent. It makes a medium-hot powder.

In a dry skillet, toast separately the cloves, peppercorns, and the coriander, cumin, fennel and mustard seeds over medium heat, taking care not to burn them.

Combine the toasted ingredients and the chiles in a spice mill and grind to a fine powder. Combine with the remaining ingredients and mix until a uniform color is achieved. Store in an airtight jar.

1 tablespoon whole cloves
2 tablespoons whole black peppercorns
1/2 cup coriander seeds
3 tablespoons cumin seeds
1 tablespoon fennel seeds
1 tablespoon mustard seeds
3 small dried hot red chiles, such as piquins or santakas, seeds and stems removed
1/4 cup ground cardamom
1/4 cup ground turmeric
3 tablespoons ground fenugreek
1 tablespoon ground ginger

Malawi Curry Powder

Yield: About 3/4 cup

This blend is the hottest curry powder we found in Africa, although some pastes like harissa *and* berbere *might top it on the heat scale. Traditionally in Malawi, the spices are sun-dried before being ground and are not toasted. Note the large amount of cloves in this recipe, a possible influence from nearby Madagascar, a clove-growing island.*

Combine all the ingredients in a spice mill and process to a fine powder. Store in an airtight jar.

10 small dried hot red chiles, such as piquins or santakas, seeds and stems removed
3 tablespoons coriander seeds
1 tablespoon whole black peppercorns
3 tablespoons poppy seeds
2 teaspoons mustard seeds
1 tablespoon cumin seeds
1 tablespoon ground turmeric
10 whole cloves
2 teaspoons ground cinnamon

Tunisian Five-Spice Powder

Yield: About 1/4 cup

1 tablespoon whole cloves
1 tablespoon whole black peppercorns
1 1/2 teaspoons malagueta pepper
1 1/2 tablespoons freshly grated nutmeg
1 teaspoon ground cinnamon

A simple blend of curry spices from North Africa, this powder is called qalat daqqa *in Arabic and contains the malagueta pepper, also known as the "grains of paradise" (available from mail order spice companies). The mixture is used to flavor lamb and vegetable dishes.*

Grind together the cloves, peppercorns, and malagueta pepper. Add the nutmeg and the cinnamon and blend well. Store in an airtight jar.

Ras el Hanout

Yield: About 3/4 cup

2 tablespoons whole black peppercorns, crushed
1 tablespoon ground cardamom
1 tablespoon ground mace
1 tablespoon ground ginger
1 teaspoon hot red chile powder, such as cayenne
1 teaspoon fennel seeds, crushed
1 teaspoon ground nutmeg
1 teaspoon ground allspice
1 teaspoon ground cinnamon
1 teaspoon crushed malagueta pepper
2 teaspoons dried ground galangal (or substitute ginger)
4 whole cloves, crushed
1 tablespoon ground turmeric
2 tablespoons crushed dried lavender
2 tablespoons crushed dried rosebuds

This blend is used to spice up tajines *(stews), rice, and couscous. It is the only curry powder we know of that uses dried flowers. A true Moroccan recipe would also include those shiny green cantharides beetles known as Spanish fly. Some other hard-to-find spices, such as nigella, orrisroot, and even the dangerous belladonna berries, would also be added, but this recipe is our drug-free approximation.*

Place all the ingredients in a food mill or spice mill and process to a fine powder. Store in an airtight jar.

 # Harissa

7 dried red New Mexican chiles, seeds and stems removed
5 small dried hot red chiles, such as piquins, seeds and stems removed
5 cloves garlic, peeled
1 tablespoon ground cumin
1 teaspoon ground caraway seeds
1 teaspoon ground cinnamon
1 teaspoon ground coriander
1 teaspoon dried mint
2 tablespoons olive oil
Water as needed

This fiery chile curry is found in Algeria, Tunisia, and Morocco. It is commonly added to vegetable and meat tangines, or stews, and is also served as a table condiment, much like the Indonesian and Malaysian sambals. Ready-made harissa is available in specialty markets and by mail order, but this recipe is easy to make and will keep for at least 6 weeks in the refrigerator. Place the harissa in a jar and cover it with a thin film of olive oil.

Soak the chiles in water until they are soft, at least 30 minutes. Place them in a food processor or blender with the rest of the ingredients and puree to a thick paste, adding water if necessary to avoid a mixture that is too dry.

Berbere

Yield: About 1 cup

1 teaspoon ground cardamom
2 teaspoons cumin seeds
1/2 teaspoon coriander seeds
1/4 teaspoon ground cinnamon
1/2 teaspoon whole black peppercorns
1/2 teaspoon fenugreek seeds
1 small onion, coarsely chopped
4 cloves garlic, peeled
1 cup water
14 small dried hot red chiles, such as piquins, seeds and stems removed
1 tablespoon cayenne
2 tablespoons paprika
1/2 teaspoon ground ginger
1/4 teaspoon ground allspice
1/4 teaspoon ground nutmeg
1/4 teaspoon ground cloves
3 tablespoons dry red wine
3 tablespoons vegetable oil

Originally used as the sauce for kifto, a fresh raw meat dish, berbere is now both an ingredient and a condiment in Ethiopian cooking. Like harissa, it is essentially a curry paste with an abundance of red chiles. Serve sparingly as a condiment with grilled beef and poultry or add to soups and stews. This paste will keep for a couple of months under refrigeration.

Toast the cardamom, cumin and coriander seeds, cinnamon, peppercorns, and fenugreek seeds in a hot skillet, shaking constantly, for a couple of minutes, until they start to toast and gain aroma. Grind these spices to form a powder.

Combine the onion, garlic, and 1/2 cup of the water in a food processor or blender and puree until smooth. Add the roasted spice powder, chiles, cayenne, paprika, ginger, allspice, nutmeg, and cloves, and continue to blend. Slowly add the remaining 1/2 cup water, wine, and oil, and blend until smooth.

Place the sauce in a saucepan and simmer for 15 minutes to blend the flavors and thicken.

Yield: About 2 cups

1 three-inch piece ginger, peeled
  and grated
1/2 cup minced onion
1 clove garlic, peeled and minced
2 pounds butter
1 two-inch piece cinnamon
1 tablespoon fenugreek seeds
2 teaspoons cumin seeds
1 tablespoon minced basil leaves
1 teaspoon cardamom seeds
1 tablespoon fresh oregano
1/2 teaspoon ground turmeric
1/4 teaspoon ground nutmeg
2 whole cloves

❀ *Ethiopian Curried Butter*

Known in Ethiopia as nit'ir qibe, *this interesting butter-oil is a basic ingredient in the preparation of traditional foods. It is also great spread on toasted breads of any kind.*

Combine the ginger, onion, and garlic, and pound to a coarse paste in a mortar. Set aside.

Melt the butter over low heat, stirring constantly, taking care that it does not darken. Skim off the foam as it rises and continue cooking until all the foam is gone.

Add the paste and all the remaining ingredients to the butter and simmer, uncovered, at the lowest possible heat, stirring occasionally, for 30 minutes.

Remove from the heat and allow to cool. Pour off the transparent top layer and reserve it, leaving behind as much of the milk solids and spices as possible. Strain the transparent layer through several layers of cheesecloth. The butter will usually be an oil at room temperature and will solidify in the refrigerator, where it can be kept, covered, for 3 or 4 months.

❀ *A Cluster of Cape Chutneys*

These delights range from the fruity Apple-Raisin Chutney and the blisteringly spicy Capricot Chutney to the peachy Curried Clingstone Chutney. All of the recipes are in quantities for canning. They reflect the variety of accompaniments to curries — including curried accompaniments!

Apple-Raisin Chutney

Combine all the ingredients in a large pot and simmer, uncovered, until thick, about 2 hours. Stir occasionally.

Spoon into sterilized jars and seal while hot. Serve at room temperature with curries.

Yield: 2 to 3 quarts

3 pounds apples, peeled, cored, and chopped
1/2 pound raisins, chopped
1 1/2 quarts wine vinegar
1 cup sugar
1 tablespoon salt
1 small green chile, such as serrano, seeds and stem removed
1 clove garlic, peeled and chopped
2 tablespoons minced ginger

Capricot Chutney

Soak the apricots and the raisins in the vinegar overnight. Transfer to a pot, add all the remaining ingredients, and boil slowly, stirring constantly, until the mixture is thick and drips off the spoon.

Spoon into sterilized jars and seal while hot. Serve at room temperature with mild curries.

Yield: 1 to 2 quarts

1/4 pound dried apricots, coarsely chopped
1/2 pound raisins
3 quarts vinegar
1/2 pound brown sugar
1 tablespoon salt
4 onions, chopped fine
1/4 cup grated ginger
2 tablespoons freshly ground coriander seeds
2 tablespoons freshly ground mustard seeds
1/2 cup small fresh red chiles, such as serranos, seeds and stems removed, chopped

Curried Clingstone Chutney

Tie the coriander seeds and the allspice in a cloth bag and place it along with the peaches and vinegar in a large pot. Boil for 5 minutes.

Puree together all the remaining ingredients, add this paste to the peach mixture, and simmer, uncovered, until thick, at least 1 1/2 hours. Remove the cloth bag, spoon into sterilized jars, and seal while hot. Serve at room temperature with mild curries.

Yield: 2 to 3 quarts

1 tablespoon coriander seeds
2 teaspoons whole allspice berries
3 pounds peaches, preferably clingstone, peeled, pitted, and chopped
3 cups white vinegar
2 onions, chopped
2 small green chiles, such as serranos, seeds and stems removed, chopped
1/4 cup sugar
2 teaspoons cornstarch
1 teaspoon salt
1 teaspoon ground turmeric

Nigerian Coconut-Curry Soup

Serves: 4 to 6

1 quart Coconut Milk (page 19)
1 tablespoon Malawi Curry Powder (page 179)
1 cup chicken stock
2 teaspoons cornstarch
Yogurt, toasted coconut, and
  chopped cilantro leaves for garnish

Although coconuts do not play much of a role in South African curries, they do in curry dishes from other parts of the continent. This curried coconut soup can be turned into a meal by the addition of cooked chicken or pumpkin.

Combine the Coconut Milk, Malawi Curry Powder, and chicken stock in a saucepan and bring to a boil. Reduce the heat and simmer for 10 minutes.

Mix the cornstarch with a little water to form a paste and slowly stir the paste into the soup until it thickens. Continue to simmer, stirring occasionally, for 5 minutes.

Remove from the heat, top with a dollop of yogurt, and sprinkle with the coconut and the cilantro leaves.

Cape Curried Fish Soup

Serves: 4

Head and bones of any large fish
1 large onion, minced
3 tablespoons olive oil
2 tablespoons Cape Curry Powder
  (page 179)
1 tablespoon freshly squeezed
  lemon juice
1 1/2 teaspoons brown sugar
1 large potato, peeled and cut into
  1/2-inch dice
2 carrots, peeled and cut into
  1/2-inch dice
1 large tomato, peeled and
  chopped fine
2 bay leaves

The Cape Malays in South Africa often combined seafood with the various spices they imported. Fish, abalone, periwinkles, and rock lobster were commonly curried and served as a dish with a souplike consistency.

Place the fish head and bones in a saucepan with a quart of salted water and boil slowly for 1 hour. Strain and reserve the stock.

Sauté the onion in the oil until soft. Combine with the Cape Curry Powder, lemon juice, and brown sugar, and mix well to make a paste.

Combine this paste and all the remaining ingredients with the reserved stock in a saucepan and simmer for 1 hour. Remove the bay leaves before serving.

Serve the soup in bowls garnished with hard-boiled egg slices, or over rice and garnished with lemon slices.

🌿 *Frikkadel Curry*

A frikkadel is a curried meatball that, in this case, is recurried in a sauce. It is usually served with white rice in South Africa. The heat of this curry is cut by the yogurt, so feel free to add more curry powder or chiles if you want a spicier result.

Combine the minced steak, peppercorns, salt, garlic, cinnamon, nutmeg, and egg, and mix well. Form the mixture into balls about 1 1/2 inches in diameter. Set aside.

Heat the oil in a large skillet and sauté the onions until golden, about 10 minutes. Add all the remaining ingredients except the yogurt and cook, covered, over medium heat for 15 minutes.

Add the *frikkadels* and cook, covered, over medium heat for 15 minutes, stirring once. Add the yogurt and cook, uncovered, over low heat for 15 minutes, stirring constantly. Remove the bay leaves before serving.

1 pound sirloin steak, minced
1 teaspoon freshly ground white peppercorns
1 teaspoon salt
2 cloves garlic, peeled and crushed
1 teaspoon ground cinnamon
1 teaspoon ground nutmeg
1 egg, slightly beaten
2 tablespoons vegetable oil
2 onions, sliced thin
1 large tomato, diced
2 cloves garlic, peeled and minced
1 tablespoon Cape Curry Powder (page 179)
2 small hot green chiles, such as serranos, seeds and stems removed, halved
2 bay leaves
1/2 cup water
1 cup plain yogurt

🌿 *Curried Beef and Bananas*

This Tanzanian specialty has the tantalizing aroma of cloves in addition to the curry spices. Make certain that you select green bananas for this dish, or your curry will be overly mushy. Chicken may be substituted for the beef and the cooking time reduced to a total of 40 minutes.

Heat the oil in a skillet and sauté the onion until it is light brown, about 5 minutes. Add the steak and sauté for 1 minute, then add the chiles, salt, Malawi Curry Powder, and cloves. Sauté for 10 minutes, stirring constantly.

Add the tomatoes and the water and simmer, uncovered, for 40 minutes, stirring occasionally. The sauce should be reduced considerably. Add the bananas and cook until both the meat and bananas are tender, 20 minutes or more.

Serve with white rice, sliced tomatoes, and curry condiments.

2 tablespoons vegetable oil
1 onion, chopped
1 pound sirloin steak (or substitute chicken), diced
3 small, hot green chiles, such as serranos, seeds and stems removed, chopped
Salt to taste
1 tablespoon Malawi Curry Powder (page 179)
1 teaspoon freshly ground cloves
3 large tomatoes, chopped
3 cups water
4 unripe bananas, quartered lengthwise and cut into 2-inch slices

Serves: 4

1/2 cup raisins
1/2 cup dates (or substitute
  prunes), chopped
1 cup dried apple sections
1 1/2 cups water
2 tablespoons vegetable oil
2 pounds sirloin steak, cut into
  3/4-inch cubes
1 large onion, chopped
2 tablespoons Malawi Curry
  Powder (page 179)
1 tablespoon freshly squeezed
  lemon or lime juice
2 tablespoons wine vinegar

🌸 Curry of Three Dried Fruits

This interesting curry, of South African origin, has a definite Arabian flavor, thanks to the raisins and dates. The Europeans added the apples, however, and the Cape Malays and Indians provided the curry. It should be served garnished with sliced bananas and chopped salted peanuts.

Combine the raisins, dates, apples, and water in a pot and simmer, uncovered, for 1 hour, stirring occasionally. Remove from the heat and reserve.

Heat the oil in a large skillet and brown the steak in batches, about 8 minutes per batch. Drain the steak and set it aside. Add the onion to the remaining oil and sauté until the onion is golden-brown, about 5 minutes.

Add the Malawi Curry Powder to the skillet, stir, and then add the reserved cooked fruits and their juice, steak, lemon or lime juice, and vinegar, and bring to a boil. Reduce the heat and simmer, uncovered, for about 1 hour or until the meat is tender, stirring occasionally. The sauce should be very thick.

Serves: 4 to 6

3 tablespoons vegetable oil
2 onions, chopped
2 pounds lamb spareribs, cut up
1/4 cup water
2 teaspoons Cape Curry Powder
  (page 179)
2 green chiles, such as serranos,
  seeds and stems removed,
  chopped
3 cloves garlic, peeled and minced
4 cups cooked kidney beans
1/4 cup freshly squeezed lemon
  juice

🌸 Kerrieboontjies Bredie

CURRIED KIDNEY BEANS

This Boer recipe translates as "curried bean stew," since the definition of bredie is any stew containing vegetables or legumes. However, this dish is more of a thick classic curry than a stew. Either lamb or beef ribs can be used, and possible bean choices include kidney, navy, and pinto. For a vegetarian version, simply omit the ribs.

Heat the oil in a large skillet and sauté the onions until golden, about 8 minutes. Add the lamb and sauté until lightly browned, turning often, and then add the water, reduce the heat, cover, and simmer for about 20 minutes.

Add the Cape Curry Powder, chiles, and garlic, and simmer, covered for about 10 minutes. Add the kidney beans and simmer, adding more water if necessary, for 15 minutes. Serve sprinkled with the lemon juice.

❧ Harira Kefta Tajine

Serves: 6 to 8

CURRIED LAMB BALLS

In this tajine, *the lamb* (harira) *is ground, combined with curry spices, made into balls (*keftas*), and then poached. These* keftas *are then added to a reduced vegetable sauce. In this way, the meatballs are curried but the sauce is not! Serve with couscous and* Harissa *(page 181) on the side to heat it up.*

Combine the lamb with the onion, mint leaves, marjoram, parsley, *Ras el Hanout*, Tunisian Five-Spice Powder, allspice, salt, and chile powder, and mix well. Form into balls about 1 1/2 inches in diameter.

Bring the 1 quart water to a boil and poach the *keftas* for 15 minutes, turning them constantly. Drain them on paper towels and refrigerate until ready to use.

Heat the olive oil in a large saucepan, add all the remaining ingredients except the water, and sauté for 10 minutes. Add the water and allow the mixture to simmer, covered, for 1 hour. Check the mixture and stir it occasionally.

Add the *keftas* to the mixture and cook, uncovered, for 20 minutes. The sauce should be very thick and should be ladled over the *keftas*.

2 pounds ground lamb
1 onion, chopped fine
4 mint leaves, minced
1/2 teaspoon fresh marjoram, minced
1 teaspoon minced parsley
2 teaspoons Ras el Hanout *(page 180)*
1 teaspoon Tunisian Five-Spice Powder (page 180)
1/4 teaspoon ground allspice
1 teaspoon salt
1 teaspoon hot red chile powder, such as cayenne
1 quart water
1/2 cup olive oil
2 pounds fresh tomatoes, chopped
2 onions, chopped
2 cloves garlic, peeled and chopped
1 fresh pimiento (or substitute bell) pepper, seeds and stem removed, chopped
1 cup water

Serves: 4

4 cloves garlic, peeled and minced
1/2 teaspoon salt
1 teaspoon ground turmeric
2 teaspoons Cape Curry Powder
   (page 179)
2 fresh orange leaves (or substitute
   bay leaves)
1 three-inch piece ginger, peeled
   and minced
2 tablespoons vinegar
1 teaspoon tamarind paste or 1
   tablespoon freshly squeezed
   lemon juice
1 teaspoon sugar
1 pound lamb, cubed
2 tablespoons vegetable oil
2 onions, sliced fine
1 cup water

Pinang-Kerrie

Perhaps the all-time favorite South African curry, this is a Cape Malay dish that should be served fairly dry. Some versions substitute lemon juice for the tamarind paste. Serve it with Saffron Rice (page 194).

Combine the garlic, salt, turmeric, Cape Curry Powder, orange leaves, ginger, vinegar, tamarind paste or lemon juice, and sugar to make a marinade. Toss the lamb in the marinade and allow to sit, covered, in the refrigerator for at least 2 hours.

Heat the oil in a skillet and sauté the onions until they are golden, about 10 minutes. Add the lamb with its marinade and the water and cook over low heat, uncovered, for about 45 minutes or until the lamb is tender. The sauce should be very thick, almost dry. If using the bay leaves, remove before serving.

Serves: 6

1 clove garlic, peeled and crushed
1 1/2 pounds leg of lamb, cut into
   1-inch cubes
1 onion, chopped
4 fresh lemon leaves (or substitute
   bay leaves), torn up
1 tablespoon brown sugar
1/2 cup milk
2 onions, chopped
3 tablespoons vegetable oil
2 tablespoons Cape Curry Powder
   (page 179)
1/2 cup vinegar
1 tablespoon sugar
2 tablespoons apricot jam
1/2 teaspoon tamarind paste (optional)
2 small hot green chiles, such as
   serranos, seeds and stems removed, chopped

Sosaties

The name of these interesting kababs is derived from the Malay word sate, *meaning grilled meat. There are a number of different marinades that can be used with* sosaties, *but one rule that seems to be always followed is that the cubes of lamb are marinated twice, so the recipe takes at least 2 days to prepare.*

Rub the garlic over the inside of a bowl. Add the lamb, onion, lemon leaves, brown sugar, and milk, and mix well. Marinate, covered, for 24 hours in the refrigerator.

In a saucepan, sauté the onion in the oil until it is soft. Add the Cape Curry Powder, vinegar, sugar, jam, and tamarind (if using), and bring to a boil. Remove from the heat, allow to cool, and add the chiles. Pour this mixture over the meat, toss well, and marinate, covered, for 24 hours in the refrigerator.

Remove the lamb from the marinade and place the mari-

A WORLD OF CURRIES

nade in a small pan. Add a little lemon juice and milk to increase the amount of marinade, and a little more Cape Curry Powder if you wish. Boil the marinade until reduced by half.

Meanwhile, thread the lamb cubes onto skewers and grill or broil them until done. Serve the *sosaties* with rice and the reduced marinade as a sauce.

🌼 *Bobotie*

Serves: 6

RAISIN-ALMOND CURRIED CASSEROLE

Care should be taken to not overcook this casserole or bake it in an oven that's too hot — otherwise it will dry out. This Boer adaptation of a Malay dish should be served moist, over rice, with additional chutney and grated coconut. Ground turkey, not a traditional South African ingredient, may be substituted for the lamb.

Soak the bread in the milk for about 5 minutes.

Melt the butter in a skillet and sauté the lamb for about 10 minutes, stirring constantly. Remove the lamb with a slotted spoon and reserve in a bowl.

Pour off all the butter and fat except for 2 tablespoons. Sauté the onion in this mixture over low heat for 5 minutes, taking care not to let it brown. Add the Cape Curry Powder, salt, sugar, and black pepper, and sauté for 2 minutes. Add the lemon juice and bring the mixture to a boil. As soon as it boils, remove from the heat and add to the lamb.

Drain the bread dry in a sieve, reserve the milk, and add the bread, 1 of the eggs, apple, raisins, almonds, and chutney to the lamb mixture and knead well. Transfer this mixture to a 3-quart baking dish. Place the lemon or lime leaves in the meat mixture and bake, uncovered, for 30 minutes at 300 degrees.

Combine the reserved milk and the other 2 eggs and beat with an electric mixer on high speed for about 2 minutes. Pour this mixture over the casserole and bake for another 15 minutes until a brown custard crust forms. Remove the lemon or lime leaves before serving.

Freshly squeezed lemon juice, milk, and Cape Curry Powder as needed

1 slice thick bread, torn up
1 cup milk
2 tablespoons butter
2 pounds ground lamb (or substitute beef or turkey)
2 cups onion, chopped
2 tablespoons Cape Curry Powder (page 179)
1 teaspoon salt
1/2 teaspoon sugar
1/2 teaspoon freshly ground black pepper
1/4 cup freshly squeezed lemon juice
3 eggs
1/2 cup freshly grated apple
1/2 cup golden raisins
1/4 cup blanched almond slivers
3 tablespoons chutney of choice (see A Cluster of Cape Chutneys, page 182)
4 fresh lemon or lime leaves (or substitute bay leaves)

Serves: 4 to 6

1 large tomato, chopped
1/2 teaspoon ground cinnamon
1 teaspoon ground cardamom
4 whole cloves, crushed
4 whole black peppercorns,
  crushed
1/2 teaspoon cumin seeds, crushed
4 small hot green chiles, such as
  serranos, seeds and stems removed, chopped
1/4 teaspoon ground turmeric
1 teaspoon cayenne
1 one-inch piece ginger, peeled and
  grated
2 cloves garlic, peeled and minced
1 cup plain yogurt
1 three-pound chicken, cut up
3 medium potatoes, peeled and cut
  into 1-inch cubes
1/4 cup vegetable oil
2 onions, sliced fine
1/2 cup water
Cilantro leaves for garnish

🌺 Chicken Curry with Yogurt

This dish, and variations on it, are sometimes termed kurma *curries. Although there are 4 chiles and 1 teaspoon cayenne in this recipe, the yogurt tends to cool it off somewhat.*

Combine the tomato, cinnamon, cardamom, cloves, peppercorns, cumin seeds, chiles, turmeric, cayenne, ginger, garlic, and yogurt to make a marinade. Toss the chicken pieces in the marinade to coat and allow the chicken to marinate, covered, for at least 2 hours in the refrigerator.

Place the potatoes in a pan and cover with water. Boil them for about 15 minutes, then drain. Heat the oil in a large skillet. Sauté the onions until they are golden-brown, about 10 minutes. Remove the onions and drain. Add the potatoes to the oil (adding more oil if necessary) and fry them until they are slightly crisp, at least 5 minutes. Remove the potatoes, drain, and reserve them.

Combine the onions, the marinated chicken, any remaining marinade, and the 1/2 cup water in a large skillet. Cook, covered, over low heat until the chicken is very tender, at least 35 minutes. During the last 15 minutes, add the potatoes and cook, stirring occasionally. Serve garnished with the cilantro leaves.

 # Doro W'et

1 three-pound chicken, cut into
 small pieces
3 tablespoons freshly squeezed
 lemon juice
1 large onion, chopped
2 cloves garlic, peeled and chopped
2 tablespoons butter
1/4 cup Berbere (page 181)
2 tablespoons paprika
2 teaspoons ground ginger
1 teaspoon freshly ground black
 pepper
1/4 teaspoon ground cardamom
1/4 teaspoon ground nutmeg
2 cups water
4 hard-boiled eggs, left whole

The most well known of the national dishes of Ethiopia is doro w'et, or chicken stew. It is traditionally served over injera, a sourdough bread.

Remove the skin from the chicken and score the meat so that the sauce will penetrate it. Rub the chicken with the lemon juice and let it marinate, covered, for 30 minutes at room temperature.

Sauté the onion and the garlic in the butter until browned. Add the Berbere, paprika, and remaining spices, and sauté for 2 to 3 minutes.

Add the chicken with its marinade to the pan and toss to coat. Stir in enough of the 2 cups water to form a thick sauce. Bring to a boil, reduce the heat, cover, and simmer for 30 minutes or until the meat starts to fall off the bone.

Using a fork, poke holes all over the eggs, then add them to the stew. Cover again and simmer for an additional 15 minutes.

Curried Prawns in Pineapple Boats

Serves: 4

4 quarts water
1 teaspoon salt
2 pounds uncooked prawns (or substitute jumbo shrimp)
Juice of 1 lemon
2 tablespoons vegetable oil
1 onion, chopped
2 green onions, chopped
2 tomatoes, chopped
2 teaspoons Malawi Curry Powder (page 179)
2 small pineapples
2 tablespoons butter
2 tablespoons flour

The presentation of this curry is spectacular. Try to arrange the prawns so that they appear to be jumping into the pineapple boat. The pineapple meat can be mixed with other fruits, topped with yogurt, and served as a salad on the side.

Bring the water to a boil, add the salt, and boil the prawns in their shells for 10 minutes. Remove the prawns, drain, and reserve 1 cup of the stock. Clean and devein the prawns, removing the shells and other undesirable parts. Sprinkle with the lemon juice and set aside.

Heat the oil in a skillet and add the onion, green onions, tomatoes, and Malawi Curry Powder. Cook, uncovered, over medium heat for 5 minutes, stirring constantly. Add the prawns and the 1 cup stock and simmer, uncovered, for 15 minutes.

While the curry is cooking, cut the pineapples lengthwise in half. Using a small knife or a fruit scoop, carve out each pineapple to make an oval hollow.

Combine the butter and the flour and stir into the curry. Continue to simmer, stirring occasionally, for 5 minutes.

Serve the curry in the hollows of the pineapples.

A WORLD OF CURRIES

Capetown Curried Lobster Tail

Serves: 6

The Cape Malays, who invented this dish, used the meat from lobster legs to make it. This version, using tails with the shells left on, approximates the original taste by giving the curry a strong seafood flavor, and it is a lot easier to eat. The addition of tomato is a European influence.

Heat the oil in a skillet and sauté the onions until they are soft, about 5 minutes. Add all the remaining ingredients and cook over low heat, uncovered, for about 30 minutes, stirring occasionally, until the sauce thickens. Remove the lemon or orange leaves before serving.

2 tablespoons vegetable oil
3 onions, chopped
6 frozen South African lobster tails, shells on, ventral plate removed, cut into 1-inch sections
1 tomato, chopped (optional)
1 tablespoon Cape Curry Powder (page 179)
1/2 teaspoon tamarind paste
3 cloves garlic, peeled and minced
1 tablespoon grated ginger
1 1/2 cups fish stock
2 fresh lemon or orange leaves (or substitute bay leaves)

Eggplant and Potato Curry

Serves: 4 to 6

This vegetarian curry is an East African favorite. The European influence is evident in the potatoes, tomatoes, and chiles — all New World crops transferred to Africa by colonists.

Toss the eggplant cubes with the salt and allow to sit for 10 minutes.

Heat the oil in a large skillet, add the onions and the garlic, and sauté for 8 minutes. Add the spices and the chiles and sauté for 2 minutes.

Drain the eggplant cubes on paper towels, pressing to extract any extra moisture from the cubes. Add the eggplant to the sautéed mixture and sauté until slightly golden, about 5 minutes. Add the potatoes, and more oil if necessary, and sauté them until lightly brown, about 15 minutes. Add the tomato, tomato paste, and water, and cook, uncovered, over low heat for about 15 minutes or until the potatoes are soft and the sauce is thick.

3 medium eggplants, peeled and cut into 1-inch cubes
2 teaspoons salt
1/4 cup vegetable oil
2 onions, chopped
2 cloves garlic, peeled and chopped
1 teaspoon cumin seeds, crushed
1 teaspoon coriander seeds, crushed
1 teaspoon ground cardamom
1 tablespoon grated ginger
1/2 teaspoon ground turmeric
3 small dried hot red chiles, such as piquins or santakas, seeds and stems removed, crushed
2 large potatoes, peeled and cut into 1-inch cubes
1 tomato, chopped
1 teaspoon tomato paste
1 cup water

Serves: 4

4 tablespoons butter or Ghee
  (page 17)
1 cup rice
2 cups stock of choice (beef,
  chicken, or fish)
1/4 teaspoon saffron or substitute
  1/2 teaspoon ground turmeric
1 cup raisins
1/2 teaspoon ground cinnamon
1 teaspoon brown sugar

Saffron Rice

This striking curry accompaniment can be prepared with either saffron or turmeric. The following version is made pilaf-style, but it can also be cooked on top of the stove.

Heat the butter or Ghee in a skillet and sauté the rice over medium heat until it is golden-brown, about 8 minutes. Add the stock and bring to a boil.

Immediately remove from the heat and stir in all the remaining ingredients. Transfer to a ceramic baking dish and bake, covered, at 350 degrees for 45 minutes. For a crispier rice, remove the cover during the last 15 minutes.

SEVEN

More Island Curries

One of the major legacies

of the British control of

India was the planting of

peoples of Indian origin

all over the British

Empire, including Britain

itself.

ROZINA VISRAM,

AUTHOR OF

AYAHS, LASCARS AND PRINCES

*E*ngland abolished its trade in African slaves in 1833, and the end of that abomination profoundly affected British colonies around the world. Plantation owners had great difficulty convincing freed slaves to work the sugarcane fields, so they were forced to turn elsewhere for labor. India, because of its huge, largely impoverished population, was considered a reservoir of cheap labor. In 1834 the first large-scale, organized emigration of Indian indentured laborers began, to Mauritius and British Guiana.

The plantation owners loved the new system because, as one put it, the cost of an indentured Indian "is not half that of a slave." Labor brokers could provide an indentured laborer for a mere twenty-one pounds, and over the next eighty-two years, until the system was abolished, Indian indentured laborers were sent all over the world, with particular emphasis on Trinidad, Jamaica, Ceylon, Malaya, Burma, South Africa, and Fiji.

In return for the promise of free land at the end of the term, or a free trip back to India, East Indians signed a bond to work for a particular planter for five years. Despite the fact that a small wage was paid, the indentured-labor system was the closest possible thing to slavery. It was a system, according to Dharam Dev, author of *Our Countrymen Abroad*, that "heaped upon our compatriots in India and abroad insults, hardships, suffering and humiliations that could ever have been conceived by the most fertile imagination."

After surviving the arduous voyage to their destination (about 12 percent died on the way), the laborers were forced to work from dawn until nearly midnight. Food was scarce, clothing was not provided, and men outnumbered women by at least ten to one. Another 10 percent or so of the laborers died during the first few years of plantation work.

Despite the horrendous conditions, the Indians survived and managed to create families and settlements in the colonies. The Indian diaspora established Indian customs and cuisines in many parts of the Western Hemisphere and the Pacific. By the 1920s and 1930s, shortly after the indenture system was abolished, the countries with the largest Indian populations were Mauritius, Burma, Malaya, British Guiana, Ceylon, Fiji, Jamaica, Trinidad, Kenya, and South Africa. We've covered Africa and the Spice

Islands in previous chapters, so now it's time to visit some other islands of curry.

From Fiji to Australia

The introduction of curries into the South Pacific was the result of both Indian immigration and the influence of the British, with their love of curries that was transplanted from the Raj. Fiji became a British colony in 1874 and began serious importation of Indian indentured laborers in 1879; another boom came in 1900. Between 1879 and 1916, when the indentured system was abolished, sixty thousand Indians arrived in Fiji, and for the most part these laborers worked for the Colonial Sugar Refining Company. After 1916, the Indian population soon reached more than ninety thousand, and these immigrants started moving away from sugarcane labor and became shopkeepers and hawkers. We have two interesting curry recipes from Fiji: Shrimp with Cardamom and Almonds (page 222), which points up the role of seafood in the country's cuisine, and Egg and Potato Curry (page 226), a tasty vegetarian entrée.

Another Pacific island with significant numbers of Indian immigrants was New Zealand, but these men and women were enticed not by the indentured-labor system but simply by the fact that jobs and careers awaited Indians who could circumvent the tight immigration controls. Today, many of New Zealand's more than ten thousand people of Indian descent work in food-related fields, such as market gardening, shopkeeping, and dairy farming. An unusual New Zealand curry is Codfish Curry Casserole (page 220), which combines curried seafood with apples and raisins.

No one really knows how curries spread across the Pacific and became popular in such far-flung locations as Hawaii and Australia, but we assume it was through trade and the assimilation of Indian people into other island cultures beyond Fiji. Interestingly enough, curries migrated to Hawaii without much of a British or Indian influence. Perhaps this is not unusual, though, for as food historian Howard Hillman has noted, "Hawaii has the most cosmopolitan admixture of cuisines, races, and cultural institutions in the world." We have included two Hawaiian curries, Hawaiian Chicken in Curried Cream Sauce (page 219) and Maui Curried Snapper (page 221).

Another reason, of course, for the spread of curries in the Pacific was the British presence, in Australia and elsewhere. Since the curry blends used in Australia tend to be commercial rather than homemade, it is the ingredients that are curried, rather than the curry spices, which make the curries interesting. Believe it or not, some Aussies love a dish called curried spaghetti, which in reality is an uninspired casserole of cooked spaghetti, ground beef, tomatoes, and a couple of teaspoons of commercial curry powder. Some of the more innovative curries served in Australia feature apples, which are a principal ingredient in Queensland Curry (page 216), along with raisins and bananas.

Also in Australia, in a dish for organ-meat lovers, ground lamb kidneys are combined with curry powder, ground lamb steak, tomato sauce, and bread crumbs in a curry called *kolendo;* the ingredients are placed in a billycan — a can with a tight-fitting lid — and the billycan is boiled in water for five hours, which sets the curry mixture into a mold.

Caribbean Curries

Although curries in some form appear in the cuisines of most of the Caribbean, they are particularly prevalent in the countries where the East Indian population is the greatest: Jamaica, Martinique, and Trinidad and Tobago (T&T).

In 1838, five years after slavery was proclaimed abolished in T&T, the food history of the two islands began to change profoundly. That year, the mandatory four-year postslavery apprenticeship ended, and some twenty thousand slaves who had worked the enormous sugarcane plantations left the estates and became squatters — causing an enormous labor shortage.

That shortage was filled by freed slaves from other islands, plus a huge influx of indentured laborers from India. Beginning in 1845, a mass migration of workers from India over the next seventy-two years increased the population of Trinidad by 145,000. By the 1940s, the East Indian influence was so pro-

A WORLD OF CURRIES

nounced that travel writer Patrick Leigh Fermor wrote: "Wide tracts of Trinidad are now, for all visual purposes, Bengal."

Typical Caribbean market scene, c. 1885.

Because the East Indians were thrown together in a strange land and were forced to share tasks equally, divisions of caste and religion were soon dissolved. The Hindus, who formed the bulk of the diaspora, began to eat beef out of necessity.

Unlike the Africans before them, the East Indian immigrants were allowed to keep their language, clothing, and food. Two animals that immigrated with them were the water buffalo — useful for heavy labor — and the white humped cattle, which provided the milk for butter, to be made into ghee, and their beloved yogurt.

Many East Indian foods and cooking techniques were introduced into T&T, notably curries and rice (rice is still grown on

Trinidad today). Curries have become enormously popular in the country, as noted by calypso writer Daisann McLane. "Without access to their curry," she writes, "Trinidadian cooks would be as lost as Sicilians without fresh garlic."

Several incarnations of curry exist. First there are *masala*s, which are spice blends usually without chile powder or turmeric. These are the mildest blends that are added to cooked meats and vegetables. The phrase *garam masala* literally means hot spices — see our West Indian *Masala* (page 211), in which both turmeric and allspice are optional. *Amchar masala*, a blend of coriander, fenugreek, fennel, mustard, and cumin, is commonly used to season cooked green mangoes (*amchar* is the Hindi word for mango).

Then there are commercial curry powders, such as the Raja Jahan brand, which contains coriander, cumin, turmeric, fenugreek, celery seed, fennel, and mangril, a mystery ingredient variously identified by the locals as curry leaf or poppy seeds. Most likely, the word is a corruption of the Hindi word *mangrail*, onion seed. Other popular commercial curry powders are Turban (manufactured since 1929), Chief (which contains black pepper), and Indi, a Guyanese brand containing some hot peppers.

A typical commercial mixture usually contains varying amounts of coriander, cumin, turmeric, fenugreek, celery seed, and fennel. The curry powder capital of Trinidad and Tobago is Tunapuna, a town on Trinidad about halfway between Port of Spain and Arima. Daisann McLane vividly described it in 1991: "Clouds of roasted cumin and turmeric, garlic, coriander, and those acidly hot Caribbean peppers . . . simply by breathing, one was exposed to hazardous levels of piquant longing."

Most of the curry powders made in T&T today are much milder than those of India because the early cooks lacked powdered hot peppers. However, hot pepper sauces are often added to curried dishes at the table. Some cooks still use old-fashioned curry pastes, which usually have Congo peppers (a habanero relative) added to them, and our recipe for Trinidadian Curry Paste (page 211) is a typical example.

Every imaginable foodstuff is curried in Trinidad and Tobago, including mangoes, pumpkins, eggplants, potatoes, green tomatoes, okra, chicken, fish, shellfish, beef, pork, goat, and lamb.

These curries are commonly served in *roti* shops, which dot the two islands. The curried mixture is placed on the flat, thin *roti* bread and then is wrapped up into an easy-to-eat package of curry.

Dave and Mary Jane toured Trinidad and Tobago in 1992 and dined on nine different curried fillings for the *roti* bread at the Patraj Roti Shop in San Juan: fish, beef, chicken, goat, conch, shrimp, liver, duck, and potato. The fillings were wrapped in the bread or were served in bowls accompanied by torn-up bread called buss-up-shut, slang for burst-up shirt, because the bread resembles torn cloth. The curry itself was not spicy, but the Congo pepper hot sauce served in squeeze bottles solved that problem.

They also received an extensive curry-cooking lesson from expert cook Nancy Ramesar, who demonstrated not only the methods for making T&T curries but also showed them how to make a variety of accompaniments, such as Curried *Pholouri* (page 213). Curried Chicken and *Roti* (page 220) is probably the most typical Trinidadian curried *roti* dish, while Trinidadian Curried Lobster (page 222) is reserved for more special occasions and is not served wrapped. The recipe for Ramesar Curried Mango (page 225) is another recipe given to Dave and Mary Jane during their cooking lesson with Nancy Ramesar in Port of Spain.

Sophisticated citizens of Trinidad who have traveled outside the country realize that there is more to curry than just the T&T style, but any changes are unlikely. One restaurant owner told Dave and Mary Jane she was quite disappointed when Gaylord's, a restaurant on Independence Square that served authentic East Indian curries, failed because the locals said: "This isn't curry." Noted food write Julie Sahni believes that "curry is such an integral part of Trinidadian cuisine that its Indian origin is actually being lost." She was amazed when a Trinidadian saleswoman in a curry factory asked her: "Are you from India? Do they have curry powder in India?"

The East Indian population of Jamaica is considerably smaller than that of T&T, but its curries are also esteemed. The first East Indians arrived in Falmouth aboard the *Athenium* in 1843, and within fifty years curries had risen to prominence on the island. *The Jamaica Cookery Book*, published in 1893, offered several curry recipes, including a simple but ingenious tropical

curry sauce: coconut jelly (the immature center of a green coconut) was boiled in coconut water with cinnamon and curry
powder until thick.

The most popular curry dish in Jamaica is curry goat (not
"curried goat"). In fact, according to Helen Willinsky, author

of *Jerk: Barbecue from Jamaica*, it is "one of our national dishes." She writes: "We always serve it for our special occasions, and it seems to be one of the best-remembered dishes by tourists."

The first time Dave tasted curry goat in Jamaica, in a restaurant frequented by locals in Ocho Rios in 1984, he had to be careful not to swallow numerous sharp slivers of bone. In a truly authentic recipe, the goat meat is chopped up — bones and all — because Jamaican cooks believe that the marrow in the bones helps to flavor the dish. The goat was cooked in a large cast iron kettle over a wood fire in the backyard of the restaurant.

In 1993, when Dave next tasted curry goat in Jamaica, the venue was a bit fancier but the taste was the same. That time, the goat was prepared by the chef of the Ciboney resort (also in Ocho Rios) and was served at a rather elegant buffet at a beach party.

In the early days, curry goat was considered a masculine dish, and there was a certain ritual involved in its serving. Zora Neale Hurston, an American anthropologist who traveled extensively in Jamaica in the 1930s, was fortunate enough to be invited to an all-male curry goat party. "On to the Magnus plantation and the curry goat feed," she writes. "This feast is so masculine that chicken soup would not be allowed. It must be soup from roosters. After the cock soup comes ram goat and rice. No nanny goat in this meal either. It is ram goat or nothing." In our recipe for Jamaican Curry Goat (page 218), rams are not so critical — either gender of goat is permissible.

In the French Antilles, the word for curry is *colombo*, named for the capital of present-day Sri Lanka. A typical *colombo*, such as the Christmas specialty Pork *Colombo* from Martinique (page 218), begins with a *colombo* paste that contains, in addition to some standard curry spices, crushed garlic, ginger, and habanero chile. Our recipe for Colombo Curry Paste appears on page 212. Coconut milk is used only in the meat *colombo*s, not in those featuring seafood. Another interesting recipe from the French Caribbean is Pumpkin-Curry Soup (page 215).

We are fortunate to have two creative curries provided by Jay Solomon, who teaches Caribbean cookery at cooking schools all over the United States. He has traveled extensively in the Caribbean and is the author of *A Taste of the Tropics*. His two favorite curries are Curried Blue Marlin and *Calabaza* Salad (page 215) and Scallops with Curried Chickpea Sauce (page 223). As for curry accompaniments, Caribbean Peas and Rice (page 224) makes a great addition to all kinds of island curries.

The Raj Reversed

While England was helping to spread curries around the globe through colonization and emigration, it was slowly becoming one of the curry capitals of the world. How ironic for a country infamous for its bland foods! We have already discussed in chapter 1 how the British were prepared for the word "curry" as early as 1390 with the appearance of the earliest version of the first English cookbook, *Forme of Cury*, meaning the art of cookery. The connection between "cury" and "curry" involves spices such as black pepper, galangal, cumin, coriander, cinnamon, cloves, and cardamom — the most popular spices found in that early cookbook.

These spices were readily available from grocers of the time. In her book *The Magic of Herbs*, C. F. Leyel explains:

> The grocers were descended from the pepperers of Sopers Lane and the spicers of cheap, who amalgamated in 1345, and in 1370 adopted the more comprehensive title of engrosser or grocer from the Latin *grossarius*. In a grocer's shop at that time was to be found every sort of medicine, root and herb, gums, spices, oils and ointments.

And cooks were buying them, according to recipes in cookbooks of the time.

Two untitled English cookery books, known as the Harleian Ms. 279 (c. 1430) and the Harleian Ms. 4016 (c. 1450), call for heavy spicing of 90 percent of the meat and fish dishes. The most common spices in those two books were ginger, black pepper, mace, cloves, cinnamon, and galangal.

These spices were so valuable and in such demand that around the end of the fifteenth century, Portuguese ships were smuggling black pepper and other Indian spices into England, along with olive oil and costly jeweled combs. When the ship *La Rose* was seized by the coast guard at the Poole harbor in England in

1486, she had 1,223 pounds of black pepper aboard and nearly that weight in cloves and ginger. Spices were still being smuggled into England as late as 1750.

In his play *Love for Love* (1695), William Congreve mentions the pocket nutmeg graters that eventually became very popular in the eighteenth century. During the Georgian period, it became fashionable in London for spices to be sprinkled over food from sterling silver cinnamon casters called muffineers.

The spices were not only added to foods and medicines, they were also blended. An early recipe for a currylike powder from 1682 called for 2 ounces of ginger and 1 ounce each of powdered black pepper, cloves, nutmeg, and cinnamon — but that whole blend was further mixed with another pound of pepper!

Perhaps the first published recipe for "currey" appeared in 1747, in Hannah Glasse's *Art of Cookery*. It was a stewed chicken spiced with turmeric, ginger, and fine black pepper. In 1780, *Forme of Cury* was finally printed in book form, and around this time recipes in other cookbooks called for premixed curry powder, which was just beginning to appear in the country. And no wonder! As Elizabeth David notes:

> In the case of curries, the complexity and the preparation of the correct spices must have been daunting for even the kitchen staffs of eighteenth and nineteenth century England, accustomed though they were to pounding and bashing, mashing and sieving. Some curry ingredients such as poppy seeds and fenugreek are so hard that it is impossible to pound them in an ordinary mortar. . . . Given the difficulties, it is not surprising that ready-prepared curry powders found and find such immediate acceptance.

Curry mixes were probably brought back to England by army officers and civil servants stationed in India; but by all indications, curry powder production was a small cottage industry at that time in India.

Indians themselves soon came to England. After African slavery ended, in the 1830s, Indians arrived in England, but not as indentured laborers as they were in the colonies. Rather, they were a relatively inexpensive source of labor and worked as ayahs (nannies), servants, and sailors. Some were students or civil ser-

The British Raj dines on curries in the mess tent.

vice exam takers, but no matter what their function, the Indians began to influence English food. In the 1840s, Charles Francatelli, chief cook to Queen Victoria, provided a recipe for "Indian Curry Sauce" in his book, *The Modern Cook*. The recipe called for "Cook's or Bruce's curry paste," so it is evident that English curry products were being made by that time.

According to Indian food expert Julie Sahni, the oldest curry powder factory in India, M. M. Ponjiaji and Company, was founded around 1868. She writes that its recipe, still a closely guarded family secret, has remained unchanged since its beginnings. The firm exported curry powders extensively to England, as did other entrepreneurs.

Near the end of the nineteenth century, a single dinner in India was responsible for a surge of interest in curry in England and elsewhere in Europe. As the story goes, an Englishman named Sharwood dined with the maharaja of Madras, and during their meal the maharaja mentioned a master curry maker named Vencatachellum, who sold his powder in his own shop. Sharwood later visited the shop and somehow obtained the secret recipe for what would later be called Madras curry powder: Chittagong saffron, turmeric, cumin, Kerala coriander, and Orissa chiles.

When Sharwood returned to England, he had a license to import Madras curry powder along with a pickle of fruits, ginger, sugar, vinegar, and chiles — the first imported chutney. As food historian Maguelonne Toussaint-Samat recounts, "Initially sold only in the best English grocers' shops, curry and chutney soon conquered Europe, and in 1889, at the time of the World Exhibition in Paris, the French Colonial Ministry fixed the legal composition of curry powder sold in France." Today, the Sharwood brand controls a significant market share of Indian foods sold in the United Kingdom.

During the heyday of the British Raj in India — roughly from 1858 to the end of World War I — Indian food became very popular in England, and its popularity reflected the English love affair with India. Food writer Mulk Raj Anand notes the "peculiar gastronomic enjoyment that curry seems to evoke in the English palate, and the warm associations which it brings into the English mind about India." For the English army aficionados of Indian cooking, the "finishing" of a particular dish with just the right mixture of spices became a hobby, and the former officers took pride in the special blends of spices they used to make the perfect curry. An example of an English spice blend is English Curry Powder (page 212).

One of the greatest proponents of curries around this time was Robert Christie. He entertained his friends at the Edinburgh Cap and Gown Club by preparing extensive, full-scale banquets from the regional cuisines of India, with a heavy emphasis on curries. There are more than thirty curries described in his section of *Banquets of the Nations*, published in England in 1911. Each of the recipes is individually spiced — no prepared curry powders are called for in the book.

One of the English curry favorites was Mulligatawny Soup (page 214). Countess Morphy, in her 1935 book *Recipes of All Nations*, cites an early British cookbook writer, Dr. Kitchener, on the subject of this soup: "Mullaga-tawny signifies pepper-water. The progress of inexperienced peripatetic Palaticians has lately been arrested by this outlandish word being pasted on the windows of English coffee-houses." There are literally dozens of different versions of mulligatawny, using chicken, veal, rabbit, and mutton as the basic meat.

There was at least one restaurant in London serving curries

around 1930. M.F.K. Fisher writes in *With Bold Knife and Fork* that the greatest curry she ever ate was in an unnamed "famous Indian restaurant" that served curries labeled mild and hot. Fisher, having been raised in Southern California "before Mexican cooking adjusted itself to the timid palates of invaders from Iowa," boldly said, "Oh, hot, of course." Soon after she tasted the curry, tears started streaming down her cheeks, and a thoughtful but ill-advised waiter placed a bowl of cracked ice by her bowl, "and every time I ate a mouthful of the curried whatever-it-was, I followed it with a mouthful of the temporary balm." And temporary it was, for "the next day," she writes, "the insides of my lips were finely and thoroughly blistered." The waiter should have served her yogurt, a surefire burn cure.

In the early 1930s, letters began appearing in the London *Times* that referred to curries, keeping the love of the subject alive. An Indian immigrant, Mulk Raj Anand, noted: "References to the files of that paper disclosed one or two other letters on the subject. . . . These were mainly tested recipes suggested by Englishmen and Englishwomen for the making of curry — some sensible, others totally inconsistent with the method of cooking curries in India." Anand was inspired by the recipes' lack of authenticity to write his own book, *Curries and Other Indian Dishes*, published in 1932.

Curry spices even played a minor role in World War II. A large number of Indians served in the British army, and the feeling arose that these troops were being turned into cannon fodder. For example, veterans claimed that the Indian wounded were being sent back to the trenches and that Indian troops were being sacrificed to spare English soldiers. Indian soldiers began sending messages back to India urging friends and family not to enlist for service on the western front. But because of wartime censorship restrictions, the Indians were forced to resort to curry code, referring to themselves as red pepper and the British as black pepper. Here is a verbatim message that did not get through, from the British army censored mails: "Further no black pepper is obtainable in this country. It has all been used up. There is a large quantity of red pepper, but they are living upon the black, day and night. Owing to the lack of black pepper we are having a hard time."

After the war, England was desperate for foreign workers to

assist the war-depleted workforce; however, Indians and Pakistanis were not among the hundreds of thousands of immigrants, mostly from Europe. In fact, the number of Indians and Pakistanis in England dropped from around 8,000 in 1949 to about 3,800 in 1958.

During the 1950s there were only six Indian restaurants in all of England, yet curry still held the interest of English cooks. Many cooks were influenced by Continental styles of cooking, and their curries reflected it. Curries were served at breakfast (they still are in some homes), and our Eggs Baked in Curry Sauce (page 224) is a breakfast dish that harkens back to the elegant curries of the fifties.

But Indian immigration picked up considerably in the late fifties, and by the time the Commonwealth Immigration Act slowed immigration in 1962, more than 100,000 Indians and Pakistanis had entered England — the first large-scale immigration to England from the Indian subcontinent. By 1991, the total population of Indians, Pakistanis, and Bangladeshis in the United Kingdom had exploded to 1.5 million.

"With this immigration came their infrastructure," explains England's Pat Chapman, founder of the Curry Club. "Their families came over, they brought their foodstuffs, and very shortly they were opening restaurants on the back streets." The appearance of Indian restaurants coincided with the beginning of a dining-out tradition among the middle class, which had never developed during the war years and the austere fifties.

"We have never experienced anything like this," Chapman adds. "The food was very, very tasty — and exotic." The food was also relatively inexpensive, and dining out at a curry restaurant soon became one of the nation's most popular social activities. As the Indian population grew, the number of restaurants increased, which dovetailed with the trend toward dining out. By 1991, there were 7,000 curry restaurants in the United Kingdom and 1,500 in London alone. In fact, England now has, after India, the largest number of Indian restaurants of any country in the world! It should be noted that in Great Britain and Northern Ireland the word "curry" is used interchangeably with "Indian food," so a curry restaurant means an Indian restaurant. These restaurants serve a variety of Indian foods, but they are judged by the quality of their curries.

During the eighties, fancier curry restaurants began to open, and even the upper class was dining on curries. Curries had conquered the United Kingdom. "The British Empire in India lasted the better part of two hundred years," writes Peter Chapman (no relation to Pat) in *Bon Appetit*, "but it's only in the past quarter century that curry houses have established themselves in the British culinary imagination. In that short time, they have played a huge role in breaking down the Brits' notorious resistance to all but the blandest of foods."

Pat Chapman has also played a large role in the immense popularity of curries in the United Kingdom. His grandfather had been in the British army in India and moved back to England when he retired. His enthusiasm for India was passed on to Pat, who was "weaned on curries" during the fifties at those original six restaurants, and cooking curries became his passion.

He turned his passion into a business when he founded the Curry Club, in 1982. Soon Pat became the "king of curry," ruling over a curry empire that included a membership of 13,000, a quarterly magazine, a mail order company with dozens of curry products, a guide to the top 1,000 curry restaurants in Great Britain and Northern Ireland, and numerous curry cookbooks in print.

There seems to be no end in sight for the popularity of curry in the region. The number of curry restaurants is projected to top 10,000 by the year 2000. In 1990, two and a half million households cooked curry at home at least once every two weeks, a rise of 80 percent since 1983, and Indian food accounted for fully half of the ethnic food market in the United Kingdom. Interestingly enough, the surveys that produced the above figures also came up with a surprising statistic about the Brits and their supposedly unadventurous palates: only about 5 percent of the people questioned liked their curries mild; the remainder said they liked theirs hot or medium-hot.

Courtesy of Pat Chapman and the Curry Club, we offer Lamb in Cashew Curry (page 217) and *Pakari* (Pineapple, Peanut, and Coconut Curry, page 226), a vegan recipe.

And so we've come full circle in our quest for world curries. All that remains is to select some favorite curries and cook them. In the words of the king of curry, Pat Chapman: "*Bon appétit,* and here's to good curries."

 West Indian Masala

Yield: Just over 1/2 cup

6 tablespoons coriander seeds
1 teaspoon fenugreek seeds
2 teaspoons fennel seeds
1 teaspoon mustard seeds
1 1/2 teaspoons cumin seeds
2 teaspoons ground turmeric (optional)
1 teaspoon ground Jamaican allspice (optional)

The lack of chiles in this blend is typical of the eastern Caribbean, where hot sauces rather than curry powder are expected to provide the bite. This recipe is superior to commercial masalas because the freshly ground seeds have not oxidized and lost their flavor. Generally speaking, in the West Indies, when turmeric is added to masala, the mixture is considered curry powder.

Roast all the seeds in a large pan in a 350-degree oven until they begin popping. Place a cookie sheet on top of the pan and roast for an additional 8 minutes, taking care not to burn the seeds. Cool the seeds and grind them together to a fine powder in a spice mill or with a mortar and pestle. Add the turmeric and allspice (if using) and mix well.

Trinidadian Curry Paste

Yield: 1 1/2 to 2 cups

6 tablespoons roasted coriander seeds
1 teaspoon roasted aniseed
1 teaspoon roasted whole cloves
1 teaspoon ground turmeric
1 teaspoon roasted cumin seeds
1 teaspoon roasted fenugreek seeds
1 teaspoon roasted whole black peppercorns
1 teaspoon roasted mustard seeds
2 cloves garlic, peeled and chopped
1 large onion, chopped
1/2 fresh habanero chile (or substitute 1 red jalapeño), seeds and stem removed, chopped
Water as needed

Many Caribbean curry powders lack chile peppers; however, this nineteenth-century recipe from Trinidad calls for the habanero chile, called Congo pepper there.

Grind all the ingredients into a paste with a mortar and pestle, or use a food processor and puree.

🌸 Colombo Curry Paste

Yield: 1/2 cup

1 1/2 tablespoons ground turmeric
1 1/2 tablespoons coriander seeds
1 1/2 tablespoons mustard seeds
1 1/2 tablespoons whole black peppercorns
1 1/2 tablespoons cumin seeds
3 cloves garlic, peeled and crushed
1 one-inch piece ginger, peeled and grated
2 fresh habanero chiles (or substitute 4 red jalapeños), seeds and stems removed, minced

This fiery-hot curry blend from Martinique is named after Colombo, the capital of Sri Lanka, which is appropriate considering the heat levels of the curries from that island. The habanero chile, the world's hottest, is recommended because of its unique fruity aroma.

Grind together the first 5 ingredients into a coarse powder. Add this powder to the garlic, ginger, and chiles, mix well, and allow to sit for at least 1 hour to blend the flavors.

🌸 English Curry Powder

Yield: About 4 cups

1 1/4 cups coriander seeds
2/3 cup cumin seeds
1/3 cup fenugreek seeds
1/2 cup gram flour (besan)
1/2 cup garlic powder
1/3 cup paprika
1/3 cup turmeric
1/3 cup garam masala
1 teaspoon dried powdered curry leaves
1 teaspoon asafoetida
1 teaspoon ground ginger
1 teaspoon red chile powder, such as New Mexican
1 teaspoon dry mustard
1 teaspoon freshly ground black pepper

From an English cookbook first published in 1870, here is the favorite curry mix of Pat Chapman's grandmother. The amounts of spices were calculated at a rate of 1 gram being approximately equal to 1 teaspoon. Pat advises that this powder "matures, or becomes better blended, the longer it is stored." It is best, he says, in about a month — but don't store it longer than eighteen months.

In a dry skillet, toast the coriander, cumin, and fenugreek seeds, then grind them together in a spice mill.
    Combine with the remaining ingredients and mix well.

🌺 Curried Pholouri

Serves: 6 to 10

1 yellow wax hot chile, seeds and
   stem removed, chopped
6 cloves garlic, peeled
1 pound split pea flour (see Note)
1 cup water
1 teaspoon salt
1/4 teaspoon ground cumin
1/4 teaspoon dried thyme
1 teaspoon West Indian Masala
   (page 211)
1 teaspoon baking powder
Soy or canola oil for frying (about
   1 inch deep in a frying pan)

Nancy Ramesar has mastered Trinidadian East Indian cooking
and has discovered that the way to her man's heart includes curries and other spicy delights, like this pholouri. She took Dave
into her kitchen, tied an apron around him, and directed him to
fry these little appetizers.

Place the first 8 ingredients in a blender and blend on high
speed until the mixture is thoroughly blended (about 90 seconds). Pour the batter into a mixing bowl and whisk in the
baking powder.

Pour a glass of cool water and test the batter by placing a
drop of it in the glass. If the batter floats, it is ready for frying.
If it sinks, whip more air into the batter and test again.

Heat the oil in a frying pan and drop the batter in, about 1
tablespoonful at a time. Fry until the batter is golden-brown,
about 2 to 3 minutes. Drain on paper towels and keep warm
in the oven until all the batter is fried. The *pholouris* can be
served with a dip like Ramesar Curried Mango (page 225).

Note: If split pea flour is not available at the local health food
store or natural foods supermarket, buy dried split peas and soak
them overnight in water. Drain off the liquid and grind the peas
in a blender, adding some water if necessary. Then add the
remaining ingredients and proceed. The peas can also be boiled
in water until barely soft and then ground in the blender.

Serves: 4

1 chicken, cut up
1 carrot, peeled and coarsely
  chopped
1 onion, sliced
3 stalks celery, coarsely chopped
1 teaspoon thyme leaves
1 bay leaf
3 tablespoons chopped parsley
1/2 teaspoon ground mace
3 whole cloves
1 quart chicken stock
2 tablespoons butter
1 small apple, peeled, cored, and
  chopped
2 onions, sliced
2 tablespoons flour
2 tablespoons English Curry
  Powder (page 212)
1/2 teaspoon cayenne
1 cup Coconut Milk (page 19)
2 cups cooked white rice

🌸 Mulligatawny Soup

There are so many versions of this dish that the total number of possible ingredients probably tops fifty. Charles Baker, writing in The Gentleman's Companion, *describes his version this way: "More Often Is Actually a Stew & Not a Soup; which Is a Curry, yet Not Strictly a Curry; Is Made of Fowls, coconut milk, Herbs, Curry & Lentils." Our version lacks lentils, and it also lacks some of the ingredients suggested by other cookbooks: mushrooms, turnips, ham, and oysters. Some recipes add a little cream at the end to thicken the soup; others suggest squeezing a whole lemon or lime into the soup.*

In a large kettle, combine the chicken, carrot, onion, celery, thyme leaves, bay leaf, parsley, mace, cloves, and chicken stock. Bring to a boil, then reduce the heat and simmer, uncovered, for 1 hour. Strain the mixture, reserving the chicken and the broth. Place the broth in the freezer. When it has cooled sufficiently, skim the fat off the top. Remove the meat from the bones, remove the skin, and mince the meat.

Heat the butter in a soup kettle and sauté the apple and onions until the onions are soft, about 5 minutes. Stir in the flour, English Curry Powder, and cayenne, and continue sautéing for 3 more minutes, stirring often. Add the reserved broth and the Coconut Milk, bring to a boil, then reduce the heat and simmer, uncovered, for 15 minutes.

Remove the soup from the heat and strain through a fine sieve. Return the soup to the heat and add the reserved chicken. Simmer gently until the chicken is heated through, about 5 minutes.

Place 1/2 cup of rice in the center of each of 4 soup bowls. Pour the soup around the rice and serve.

Pumpkin-Curry Soup

Serves: 6

This curried soup, a variation on a dish from Guadeloupe, in the French West Indies, also features the West Indian "pumpkin," or calabaza. *Do not use American pumpkins, which are too soft; Hubbard or acorn squash are the best substitutes.*

Heat the butter and the oil together in a saucepan, add the bacon, and cook for 5 minutes over low heat. Add the onion, bell pepper, tomatoes, and garlic, and cook over medium heat for another 5 minutes.

Add the *calabaza*, Colombo Curry Paste, cloves, and water. Stir, cover, and simmer until the *calabaza* is tender, about 30 minutes, stirring occasionally.

Remove the mixture from the heat, transfer it to a food processor or blender, and puree, adding a little water if necessary. Strain the pureed mixture through a strainer or colander and return it to the saucepan. Add the half-and-half, stir, and cook the soup over low heat until it thickens slightly, taking care not to let it boil.

2 tablespoons butter
2 tablespoons vegetable oil
1/4 pound bacon, chopped
1 onion, chopped
1 bell pepper, seeds and stem removed, chopped
2 tomatoes, chopped
2 cloves garlic, peeled and minced
1 pound calabaza, peeled and diced
1 tablespoon Colombo Curry Paste (page 212)
1/4 teaspoon ground cloves
1/2 cup water
2 cups half-and-half

Curried Blue Marlin and Calabaza Salad

Serves: 4

This recipe is a personal favorite of Jay Solomon, the chef and former owner of Jay's Cafe at Clinton Hall in Ithaca, New York, and now a traveling cooking instructor. He notes: "The curry is a nice gustatory stimulant for the mild flavor of the calabaza, and warmly complements the fish as well." Calabaza is the West Indian name for a squashlike pumpkin; in the United States, winter squash is a better substitute than pumpkin.

Place the fish steaks in boiling water to cover and cook for 10 minutes or until the fish is done in the center. Drain the

1 pound blue marlin, swordfish, or tuna steaks
2 cups peeled and diced calabaza (or substitute Hubbard or acorn squash)
1 egg yolk
1 teaspoon Dijon mustard
2 tablespoons freshly squeezed lemon juice
3/4 cup olive oil
1 tablespoon minced ginger
2 cloves garlic, peeled and minced
1 tablespoon West Indian Masala (page 211)
1/4 teaspoon ground cloves
1/4 teaspoon cayenne

1/4 teaspoon salt
7 broccoli florets, parboiled for 2
  minutes and drained
1 cup minced celery
1 lemon, quartered

steaks and chill under running water. Shred the fish with a fork and refrigerate for 1 hour.

Place the *calabaza* in boiling water to cover and cook for 12 minutes or until it is tender but not mushy. Drain and chill under running water. Refrigerate for 1 hour.

Meanwhile, blend the egg yolk for 15 seconds in a food processor or blender. Scrape the sides down, add the mustard and the lemon juice, and process for another 10 seconds. With the motor still running, slowly drizzle in half the olive oil. Stop the machine, scrape down the sides, then start it again and drizzle in the remaining oil. Add the ginger, garlic, West Indian *Masala*, cloves, cayenne, and salt, and process for another 15 seconds or until all the ingredients are incorporated smoothly.

In a large bowl, combine the fish, *calabaza*, broccoli, and celery. Add the curry mayonnaise and toss thoroughly. Serve the salad on a bed of lettuce, either immediately or after refrigerating. Squeeze the lemon over the salad.

🌸 Queensland Curry

A hallmark of curries from Australia and New Zealand is the presence of fruits. But unlike the dried-fruit curries of South Africa, these curries feature predominantly fresh fruits. And unlike the exotic fruits incorporated in the curries of India and the Spice Islands, the fruits used in Australia and New Zealand are fairly familiar to Americans — namely apples, raisins, and bananas. With the addition of pineapple and coconut, this fruit curry offers a delicious blend of flavors from around the world.

Serves: 6

1/4 cup butter
1 1/2 pounds sirloin steak, cut
  into 1-inch cubes
2 onions, chopped
1 banana, sliced
1 green apple, peeled, cored, and
  chopped
2 tomatoes, peeled and chopped
1 1/2 tablespoons English Curry
  Powder (page 212)
1/4 cup flour
1/4 cup pineapple juice
1 cup water
Salt and pepper to taste
1 cup fresh pineapple, cut into
  1/2-inch cubes
1/2 cup freshly grated coconut
1/4 cup golden raisins
2 tablespoons freshly squeezed
  lemon juice
Apple slices for garnish

Heat the butter in a large skillet and brown the sirloin cubes in it uniformly, cooking and stirring for about 5 minutes. Remove the cubes and reserve. Sauté the onions, banana, apple, tomatoes, and English Curry Powder in the remaining butter for 3 minutes. Add the flour, stir, and simmer for 2 minutes. Add the pineapple juice and the water and bring to a boil. Reduce the heat, return the meat to the skillet, add salt and pepper to taste, and simmer, covered, for 1 1/2 hours.

A WORLD OF CURRIES

Add the pineapple cubes, coconut, raisins, and lemon juice, and simmer, uncovered, for 15 minutes, stirring occasionally until the sauce thickens. Serve with rice, garnished with the apple slices and the following condiments: almonds, cashews, carrot sticks, celery sticks, and grated coconut.

🌸 Lamb in Cashew Curry

Serves: 4 to 6

3 ounces unsalted cashews, preferably raw
3 dried red New Mexican chiles,
seeds and stems removed
1 three-inch piece ginger, peeled
and chopped
1 four-inch piece cinnamon
1/2 teaspoon cardamom seeds
5 whole cloves
4 cloves garlic, peeled
1/4 cup poppy seeds
1 tablespoon coriander seeds
1 teaspoon cumin seeds
2 teaspoons ground turmeric
1/4 cup water
1/2 cup Ghee (page 17)
1 onion, chopped
1/2 cup plain yogurt
2 pounds lamb, cut into 1-inch
cubes
1/2 cup cilantro leaves, chopped
Salt to taste
1 lemon, quartered, seeds removed

This recipe, courtesy of Pat Chapman, appeared in the Curry Club Magazine in an article about the Gurkhas, "the world's most natural of fighting men." It is interesting because it is one of the few curry recipes we uncovered that depend on cashews, which are native to India.

In a food processor or blender, combine the cashews, chiles, ginger, cinnamon, cardamom seeds, cloves, garlic, poppy seeds, coriander seeds, cumin seeds, turmeric, and water, and puree into a smooth paste.

Heat the Ghee in a large skillet, add the onion, and fry to a golden-brown, about 8 minutes. Stir in the cashew-curry paste and the yogurt and cook over medium heat, stirring often, for 5 minutes. Add the lamb, stir it to coat well, then cover the skillet and cook the lamb over low heat for 20 minutes.

Remove the cover and add 1/4 cup of the cilantro leaves and the salt. Stir, re-cover, and cook over low heat for 10 minutes.

Place the contents of the skillet in a heated serving dish, sprinkle with the remaining cilantro leaves, and squeeze the lemon over the dish.

2 pounds goat meat, cut into
  1/2-inch cubes
3 tablespoons West Indian Masala
  (page 211)
1/2 teaspoon salt
1/2 teaspoon ground cardamom
1/2 teaspoon freshly ground black
  pepper
2 cloves garlic, peeled and minced
2 onions, sliced
2 tomatoes, chopped
2 green onions, chopped
2 fresh habanero chiles (or substitute 4 red jalapeños), seeds and
  stems removed, chopped
2 tablespoons butter
1/4 cup vegetable oil
3 cups water

🌸 Jamaican Curry Goat

*Here is a classic Jamaican dish that is much beloved in that
country. Lamb may be substituted for the goat, but the taste will
not be quite the same. Note the West Indian traits of using a
masala without chile powder and then adding chiles to the curry.
The dish is traditionally served with white rice, mango chutney,
and grated coconut.*

In a large bowl, combine the goat meat, West Indian *Masala*,
salt, cardamom, black pepper, garlic, onions, tomatoes, green
onions, and chiles, and mix well. Allow the meat to marinate,
covered, for 1 hour in the refrigerator.

Remove the meat from the marinade and reserve the marinade. Sauté the meat in the butter and the oil in a large skillet
until lightly browned. Add the water, cover, and simmer until
the meat is very tender, about 1 hour, adding more water if
necessary.

Return the marinade to the meat mixture, cover, and simmer for 15 minutes.

Serves: 4

2 pounds lean pork, diced
1/4 cup butter
1 cup chopped cabbage
2 onions, chopped
1 green (or slightly ripe) mango,
  skin and seed removed, sliced
1 cup white wine or Coconut Milk
  (page 19)
2 tablespoons Colombo Curry
  Paste (page 212)
2 teaspoons tamarind paste or
  pulp
3 cloves garlic, peeled and crushed
1 fresh habanero chile (or substitute 2 red jalapeños), seeds and
  stem removed, minced
2 medium eggplants, peeled and
  chopped

🌸 Pork Colombo from Martinique

This recipe, curried with colombo *paste, illustrates the Bengal influence in Martinique, particularly the northern part of the island. Why the Bengalis named their curry after Colombo, so far
from Calcutta, is not known. The dish is notable for some ingredients not usually found in curries, such as wine, beans, and cabbage. (The cabbage is a substitute for the green tops of malanga,
a tropical tuber.) Cooks have their choice of preparing this curry
with wine or coconut milk. A rather spicy dish, it is traditionally
served with fried plantains.*

In a large skillet, brown the pork in the butter for 4 minutes
over medium heat. Add the cabbage, onions, and mango, and
stir-fry for 3 more minutes. Add the wine or Coconut Milk

A WORLD OF CURRIES

and enough water to cover the meat mixture and bring to a boil. Immediately reduce the heat, stir in the Colombo Curry Paste, tamarind, garlic, and chile, and cook, covered, over low heat for 1 hour, stirring occasionally.

Remove the cover and add the eggplants, chayotes, and navy beans. Cook, uncovered, over low heat for 1 hour, stirring occasionally. The curry sauce should be fairly thick.

2 chayotes, peeled and chopped (or substitute Hubbard squash)
1 cup cooked navy beans

🏵 *Hawaiian Chicken in Curried Cream Sauce*

Here is an elegant and refined curry from Hawaii, "one of the famous curries of the Pacific Islands," according to curry expert Florence Brobeck. She recommends serving it with finely chopped bell peppers, chopped hard-boiled eggs, mango chutney, finely chopped roasted peanuts, and shredded Bombay duck.

Soak the coconut in 2 cups of the milk for 30 minutes.

Melt the butter in a saucepan and sauté the onion, garlic, and ginger for about 6 minutes. Add the Classic Indian Curry Powder and continue sautéing for 1 minute. Add the remaining 1 cup milk, a little at a time, stirring constantly. Cover and simmer for 5 minutes, then add the milk-coconut mixture, cover, and simmer for 20 minutes, taking care not to let the mixture boil.

Strain through a fine sieve or several layers of cheesecloth and discard the solids. Return the strained mixture to a saucepan and heat. Combine the flour and water into a paste and add it to the saucepan. Cook on low heat, uncovered, stirring occasionally, until slightly thickened, about 5 minutes. Add the chicken and simmer for 15 minutes. Stir in the lemon juice just before serving.

Serves: 4

3 cups freshly grated coconut
3 cups milk
2 tablespoons butter
1 medium onion, chopped
2 cloves garlic, peeled and minced
1 two-inch piece ginger, peeled and grated
2 tablespoons Classic Indian Curry Powder (page 73), or more to taste
2 tablespoons flour
3 tablespoons water
3 cups chopped cooked chicken
1 tablespoon freshly squeezed lemon juice

Serves: About 4, depending on the size of the bread and the amount of filling

1/4 cup vegetable oil
1 onion, chopped
4 cloves garlic, peeled and minced
1/4 fresh habanero chile (or substitute 1/2 red jalapeño), seeds and stem removed, minced
1 chicken, cut up
6 tablespoons Trinidadian Curry Paste (page 211) or commercial curry powder
4 cups water
Roti (page 227)

Curried Chicken and Roti

Roti *shops are as common in Trinidad as McDonald's is in the United States. Here is a typical Trinidadian chicken curry, but virtually any other meat can be substituted. Diced potatoes may also be added to any recipe for curried* roti *fillings.*

Heat the oil in a large skillet and sauté the onion, garlic, and chile. Add the chicken and brown it. Add the Trinidadian Curry Paste and cook for 3 minutes, stirring occasionally.

Add the water, stir, and cover the skillet. Cook over low heat until the chicken is tender, about 45 minutes. Remove the cover for the last 15 minutes so the sauce will thicken.

Remove the chicken and cut the meat off the bones. Continue to cook the curry sauce until it is quite thick. Return the meat to the sauce and heat through.

Fold up the curried chicken in the *Roti* (page 227) and serve warm, accompanied by any of the chutneys in this book.

Serves: 4

1 pound codfish (or other firm whitefish) fillets, cubed
1/2 cup freshly squeezed lime juice
1 cup flour
1/2 cup butter
1 large apple, peeled, cored, and sliced thin
1/4 cup golden raisins
1 onion, diced
1 bay leaf
2 teaspoons Classic Indian Curry Powder (page 73)
1/3 cup flour
1/2 cup cream
1 egg, beaten
1/2 cup milk
Chopped parsley for garnish

Codfish Curry Casserole

This New Zealand combination of fruits and fish, seasoned with curry powder and baked in a casserole dish, makes a tasty and easy-to-prepare entrée.

Soak the cod cubes in the lime juice for 30 minutes. Remove the cod, pat dry, and roll in the flour. Sauté the cod cubes in the butter in a skillet until they are light brown, about 5 minutes, then remove and reserve.

Sauté the apple, raisins, onion, and bay leaf in the remaining butter until the onion is soft, about 5 minutes. Remove the bay leaf and then remove the apple-onion mixture from the skillet.

Grease a casserole dish and sprinkle some of the Classic Indian Curry Powder on the bottom. Place a layer of cod on the bottom, then a layer of the apple-onion mixture, then more

220   A WORLD OF CURRIES

Classic Indian Curry Powder. Repeat until all the cod, apple-onion mixture, and Classic Indian Curry Powder are used up.

Combine the flour, cream, and egg, and pour over the casserole. Cover and bake at 350 degrees for 30 minutes.

Remove the casserole from the oven, pour the 1/2 cup milk over it, cover, and return to the oven to bake for another 15 minutes. Serve garnished with the parsley.

❀ Maui Curried Snapper

Serves: 4

1 1/2 pounds red snapper fillets
1 cup freshly squeezed lime juice
1 cup freshly grated coconut
4 cups milk
2 tablespoons vegetable oil
1/4 cup chopped onion
1 two-inch piece ginger, peeled and grated
2 tablespoons Classic Indian Curry Powder (page 73)

Here is an easy fish curry from Hawaii, with coconut again as a major complementary flavor to the curry powder. Serve it with other Hawaiian condiments, such as pineapple slices, dried squid, coarse salt, and crisp, finely chopped bacon.

Combine the snapper with the lime juice and marinate, covered, for 30 minutes in the refrigerator. Meanwhile, combine the coconut and the milk and marinate, covered, for 30 minutes in the refrigerator.

Heat the oil in a saucepan and sauté the onion and the ginger until the onion is soft, about 5 minutes. Add the Classic Indian Curry Powder and stir well. Strain the milk from the coconut and add the coconut to the saucepan. Strain the fillets, reserving any marinade that might remain, and add them to the saucepan.

Cook, uncovered, over low heat for 20 minutes. Just before serving, stir in the reserved marinade or 1 tablespoon lime juice.

Shrimp with Cardamom and Almonds

Serves: 4

3 tablespoons Ghee *(page 17)* or vegetable oil
2 bay leaves
1 three-inch piece cinnamon
Seeds from 5 cardamom pods (about 1 tablespoon), coarsely crushed
1 1/2 pounds large uncooked shrimp, shelled and deveined
1 one-inch piece ginger, peeled and grated
1 onion, chopped
4 cloves garlic, peeled and minced
1 tablespoon flour
3 tablespoons ground almonds
1/2 teaspoon ground turmeric
2 1/2 cups thick Coconut Milk *(page 19)*
3 small hot green chiles, such as serranos, seeds and stems removed, chopped
1 teaspoon sugar
Salt to taste
1 tablespoon freshly squeezed lemon or lime juice
Cilantro leaves for garnish
Slivered almonds for garnish

This recipe is similar to others from Fiji that combine the elements of seafood, curry spices, coconut milk, and chiles. Feel free to substitute lobster or crabmeat for the shrimp.

Heat the Ghee or oil in a skillet and add the bay leaves, cinnamon, and cardamom seeds. Sauté for 2 to 3 minutes. Add the shrimp and cook for 2 minutes over low heat, stirring constantly. Remove the shrimp and set aside.

Add the ginger, onion, and garlic, and sauté until the onion is soft, about 3 minutes. Add the flour, almonds, and turmeric, and cook over low heat for 2 minutes, stirring constantly. Add the Coconut Milk, chiles, and sugar, and simmer for 10 minutes.

Return the shrimp to the curry, add salt to taste, and simmer for about 8 minutes. Add the lemon or lime juice, stir, and remove from the heat. Remove the bay leaves and the cinnamon. Serve over rice garnished with the cilantro leaves and the almonds, or as a filling for *Roti* (page 227).

Trinidadian Curried Lobster

Serves: 4

3 tablespoons vegetable oil
3 tablespoons butter
3 tablespoons Trinidadian Curry Paste *(page 211)*
2 onions, chopped
2 cloves garlic, peeled, crushed, and minced
1 tablespoon grated ginger
3 medium tomatoes, chopped
2 tablespoons freshly squeezed lime juice
2 pounds cooked lobster meat

The firm meat of the lobster holds up well in this curry, a Trinidadian example of the East Indian influence in the West Indies. Some cooks add vegetables such as potatoes to this dish, but we prefer to keep it pure and to serve it in the traditional manner — over steamed rice.

Place the vegetable oil and the butter in a large skillet and heat. Add the Trinidadian Curry Paste, onions, garlic, ginger,

A WORLD OF CURRIES

tomatoes, and lime juice, and cook for about 30 minutes, stirring occasionally. This sauce should be very thick.

Add the lobster, stir well, and simmer for about 10 minutes. Serve over steamed rice.

🏵 Scallops with Curried Chickpea Sauce

Serves: 4

2 tablespoons butter
1 medium red onion, diced
1 medium red bell pepper, seeds and stem removed, chopped fine
2 cloves garlic, peeled and minced
2 teaspoons minced ginger
2 tablespoons Colombo Curry Paste (page 212)
1 teaspoon ground cumin
1/2 teaspoon ground cloves
1/2 teaspoon black pepper
1/4 teaspoon salt
2 sweet potatoes, peeled and chopped
2 cups water
1 sixteen-ounce can chickpeas (garbanzo beans)
2 pounds sea scallops, washed
2 tablespoons butter
1 cup cooked okra, stems removed, chopped

Another curry favorite of Jay Solomon, this recipe combines scallops with chickpeas, okra, and sweet potatoes. Jay is the author of A Taste of the Tropics *(Crossing Press, 1991).*

Heat the butter in a deep skillet. Add the onion, bell pepper, garlic, and ginger, and sauté for 5 or 6 minutes over medium heat. Add the Colombo Curry Paste, cumin, cloves, black pepper, and salt, and sauté for another 2 minutes. Add the sweet potatoes and the water and simmer for about 15 minutes or until the sweet potatoes are soft. Lower the heat, add the chickpeas, and cook for another 10 minutes. Remove this sauce from the heat and set aside.

In another skillet, sauté the scallops in the butter over moderately high heat for 4 to 6 minutes. Add the okra, cook for another 2 minutes, and then add the curried chickpea sauce. Simmer for 4 to 5 minutes, stirring frequently.

Serves: 6

1/4 cup Ghee (page 17) or vegetable oil
1 onion, chopped fine
1 tablespoon English Curry Powder (page 212)
1 tablespoon flour
1 1/2 cups chicken stock
1 tablespoon currant jelly or apricot jam
1 teaspoon freshly squeezed lemon juice
2 tomatoes, peeled, seeded, and chopped
6 eggs

🌼 Eggs Baked in Curry Sauce

This recipe from England illustrates a refined use of curry that was popular during the 1950s. Use egg molds to make certain that the eggs have eye appeal, and serve this dish for breakfast or brunch accompanied by rice and a chutney of choice.

Heat the Ghee in a skillet and sauté the onion until it is soft, about 4 to 5 minutes. Add the English Curry Powder and continue to sauté for 1 minute. Stir in the flour, mix well, and add the chicken stock. Bring to a boil, stirring constantly, then reduce the heat and simmer, uncovered, for 20 minutes.

Add the jelly or jam and the lemon juice and simmer for 5 minutes. Add the tomatoes, stir well, cover the pan, and remove it from the heat.

Place 6 greased egg molds or ramekins on a baking sheet and carefully break the eggs into them. Top each egg with curry sauce. Place the molds in the oven and bake for 8 to 10 minutes at 350 degrees. Do not overcook. Heat any remaining curry sauce and serve it on the side.

Serves: 6 to 8

3/4 cup kidney beans, soaked in water overnight and then drained
4 cups Coconut Milk (page 19)
1/2 teaspoon dried thyme
1 fresh habanero chile (or substitute 2 red jalapeños), stem removed, left whole
4 green onions, minced, including the tops
3 cloves garlic, peeled and minced
1/2 teaspoon salt
1/4 teaspoon freshly ground black pepper
2 1/2 cups long-grain white rice
1 cup water

🌼 Caribbean Peas and Rice

Here is a classic dish from the West Indies that makes a great accompaniment to curry. It is usually associated with Jamaica ("peas" are kidney beans there), but variations on it appear all over the region. For a Trinidadian version, substitute pigeon peas or black-eyed peas for the kidney beans.

Combine the beans and the Coconut Milk in a large saucepan and bring to a boil. Lower the heat, cover the pan, and simmer for 45 minutes or until the beans are tender.

A WORLD OF CURRIES

Add all the remaining ingredients and bring to a boil. Reduce the heat and simmer, covered, until all the liquid has been absorbed and the rice is tender, about 20 minutes.

Remove the chile, fluff together the rice and beans with a fork, and serve.

Ramesar Curried Mango

Serves: 6 to 8 as a side dish

4 green mangoes, only about half-ripe
2 tablespoons vegetable oil
1 cup water
2 cloves garlic, peeled and mashed
2 tablespoons West Indian Masala (page 211)

This recipe is from Dave and Mary Jane's cooking lesson with Nancy Ramesar in Port of Spain. She includes the mango seed as part of the recipe because, as she says, it's great to pick it up and suck the flavor off it. Nancy uses the famous Chief brand Amchar Masala, but a good substitute is to roast 6 tablespoons coriander seeds, 1 teaspoon fenugreek seeds, 2 teaspoons fennel seeds, 1 teaspoon mustard seeds, and 1 1/2 teaspoons cumin seeds, and grind them all together.

Scrub the mangoes thoroughly, leave the skins on, and cut into 2-inch slices, leaving some mango meat on the seeds. Heat the oil in a large, heavy casserole. Add the water, garlic, and West Indian *Masala*, and cook for 2 to 3 minutes over medium heat.

Add the mango slices and stir to coat them with the mixture. Reduce the heat, cover, and simmer until tender, about 30 to 40 minutes.

Check the mixture about halfway through the cooking time and add more water if it is dry. Taste the mixture when it's done and add 1 teaspoon sugar if it's too sour.

Mangoes are commonly curried in the Caribbean.

Serves: 4 to 6

3 small hot green chiles, such as
  serranos, seeds and stems removed, minced
1/2 teaspoon mustard seeds
6 cloves garlic, peeled
1/2 teaspoon cumin seeds
1/2 teaspoon whole black peppercorns
1 teaspoon coriander seeds
1/4 teaspoon ground cinnamon
1/2 teaspoon ground turmeric
1 tablespoon water
3 tablespoons Ghee (page 17) or
  vegetable oil
2 onions, chopped
1 medium piece ginger, peeled and
  grated
2 boiled potatoes, peeled and diced
2 cups Coconut Milk (page 19)
8 hard-boiled eggs, halved
1 tablespoon freshly squeezed
  lemon or lime juice
Cilantro leaves for garnish

🌸 Egg and Potato Curry

*The combination of hard-boiled eggs, potatoes, coconut, and curry
spices is quite popular in Fiji, where it is usually served with
salads and pickles. It also can be wrapped in Roti (page 227).*

In a food processor or blender, combine the chiles, mustard
seeds, garlic, cumin seeds, peppercorns, coriander seeds, cinnamon, turmeric, and water, and process to a thick paste.

Heat the Ghee or oil in a large skillet and sauté the onions
until they are soft, about 5 minutes. Add the ginger and the
spice paste and continue sautéing, stirring well, for 3 minutes.
Add the potatoes and cook over low heat for 2 minutes. Add
the Coconut Milk and bring to a boil, then reduce the heat
and simmer, uncovered, until the sauce thickens and the potatoes are tender, about 10 to 15 minutes.

Add the eggs and the lemon or lime juice, stir gently, and
heat through, about 2 minutes. Serve garnished with the cilantro leaves.

Serves: 4

4 ounces freshly shredded coconut
1 cup Coconut Milk (page 19)
1/4 cup vegetable oil
4 ounces raw unsalted peanuts
3 cloves garlic, peeled and minced
1 onion, chopped fine
2 teaspoons ground coriander
1 teaspoon ground cumin
1/2 teaspoon ground cassia or cinnamon
1/2 teaspoon ground turmeric
1/2 teaspoon freshly ground black
  pepper

🌸 Pakari

PINEAPPLE, PEANUT, AND COCONUT CURRY

*Courtesy of Pat Chapman, this Indonesian vegetarian recipe,
transplanted to London, emphasizes sweetness. "Pineapple is
added to a creamy, coconut-based sauce," Pat says, "which itself
is lightly spiced and enhanced with peanuts."*

Take half the shredded coconut and roast it under the broiler
in the oven until it turns light brown. Place the other half of
the coconut in a food processor or blender with the Coconut
Milk and process to make a paste.

In a wok, heat the oil and stir-fry the peanuts for 2 minutes, then remove and drain. Stir-fry the garlic in the same oil for 1 minute, add the onion, and stir-fry for 3 minutes.

Combine the coriander, cumin, cassia or cinnamon, turmeric, black pepper, and sugar, and add this spice mixture to the garlic-onion mixture in the wok. Stir-fry for 2 minutes. Add the coconut paste and stir-fry until the mixture thickens, about 3 to 5 minutes.

Add a little water to thin the mixture, add the pineapple cubes, and bring to a simmer. Cook for 2 minutes, add the peanuts, and cook for 1 minute. Serve garnished with the roasted coconut.

2 teaspoons sugar
Water as needed
1 pineapple, peeled, cored, and cut into 1-inch cubes

Roti

This Indian bread is ubiquitous in Trinidad. The curried filling is wrapped up in the bread, or the bread is torn up and dipped into the curry.

Yield: 4 roti

3 cups flour
3 teaspoons baking powder
1/2 teaspoon salt
1 cup water
Vegetable oil

Sift together the flour, baking powder, and salt. Add the water and mix to form a dough. Knead the dough for 10 minutes and let sit for 30 minutes. Knead again for 10 minutes and divide into 4 balls. Roll out each ball on a floured surface to a diameter of about 8 to 10 inches, making each *roti* as thin as possible.

Grease a large skillet or griddle with vegetable oil and heat. Fry each *roti* for about 90 seconds per side, adding a little more oil to the pan as you flip it over. Remove carefully and drain on paper towels. The *roti* can be left whole for stuffing or torn up for dipping.

Mail Order Sources

Adriana's Bazaar
2152 Broadway at 75th St.
New York, NY 10023
(212) 877–5757
Prepared curries, including Jaffna Curry and Sinhala Curry; many curry spices; various chile peppers.

Blake's Natural Herbs and Spices
505 North Railroad
Ellensburg, WA 98926
(800) 932–HERB
Prepared curry powders and spice blends.

Cinnabar
1134 W. Haining St.
Prescott, AZ 86301
(602) 778–3687
Specialty foods and seasonings from India, Thailand, and the Caribbean.

Colorado Spice Company
5030 Nome St., Unit A
Denver, CO 80239
(303) 373–0141
Curry spices and prepared curry mixes.

Cosmopolitan Foods, Inc.
138 Essex Ave.
Glen Ridge, NJ 07028
(201) 680–4560
Indonesian sauces and spices.

Dean and DeLuca
Mail Order Department
560 Broadway
New York, NY 10012
(212) 431–1691
Exotic herbs and spices from around the world.

DeWildt Imports
R.D. 3
Bangor, PA 18013
(215) 588–0600
Spices and ingredients from Indonesia, Malaysia, Vietnam, and Thailand.

G. B. Ratto & Co.
821 Washington St.
Oakland, CA 94607
(510) 836–2250
Spices and foods from India, Indonesia, and Africa.

Golden Bow Gift Baskets
P.O. Box 27778
Honolulu, HI 96827
Curry pastes from Thailand.

House of Spices
76–17 Broadway
Jackson Heights, NY 11373
(718) 476–1577
Curry spices and other Indian and Pakistani foodstuffs.

Le Saucier
Faneuil Hall Marketplace
Boston, MA 02109
(617) 227–9649
Curry pastes, oils, powders, and sauces.

Mikael Theodros Co.
P.O. Box 12761
Tucson, AZ 85732
Ethiopian spices and *berbere*.

Nancy's Specialty Market
P.O. Box 327
Wye Mills, MD 21679
(800) 462–6291
Spices, herbs, hot sauces, coconut extract, coconut milk, curry pastes, and Indian pickles and chutneys.

Nature's Key Products
P.O. Box 1146
New Hyde Park, NY 11040
(516) 775–5279
Various packaged Sri Lankan curries and curry pastes, including black curries for fish.

Spices of Vermont
Rt. 7, P.O. Box 18
North Ferrisburg, VT 05473
(802) 425–2555
Indian-oriented curry spices and mixes.

Illustration Credits

Marco Polo (page 5): Thomas W. Knox, *The Boy Travellers in the Far East*. New York: Harper and Brothers, 1881.

Black pepper (page 6): William Dufougere, *Madinina, Reine des Antilles*. Paris: Editions Berger-Levrault, 1929.

Gathering coconuts (page 18): Reverend W. Urwick, *Indian Pictures Drawn with Pen and Pencil*. London: Religious Tract Society, c. 1890.

The cashew (page 22): F. A. Ober, *The Knockabout Club in the Antilles*. Boston: Estes and Lauriat, 1888.

Vasco da Gama (page 32): *Indian Historical Pictures*. Bombay: K. and J. Cooper, c. 1900.

Jackfruit (page 39): F.H.H. Guillemard, *The Cruise of the Marchesa to Kamschatka and New Guinea*. London: John Murray, 1886.

Chiles (page 64): D. Bois, *Les Plantes Alimentaires*. Paris: Editions Paul Lechevalier, 1927.

Transport carts (page 65): North Wind Picture Archives.

Turmeric (page 73): D. Bois, *Les Plantes Alimentaires*. Paris: Editions Paul Lechevalier, 1927.

Mandalay, Burma (page 107): North Wind Picture Archives.

Rice fields, Mekong Delta (page 113): Thomas W. Knox, *The Boy Travellers in the Far East*. New York: Harper and Brothers, 1881.

Ginger (page 114): D. Bois, *Les Plantes Alimentaires*. Paris: Editions Paul Lechevalier, 1927.

Nutmeg (page 137): F.H.H. Guillemard, *The Cruise of the Marchesa to Kamschatka and New Guinea*. London: John Murray, 1886.

Borneo women (page 139): Julia A. Stone, *Illustrated India: Its Princes and People*. Hartford: American Publishing Company, 1877.

Okra (page 156): D. Bois, *Les Plantes Alimentaires*. Paris: Editions Paul Lechevalier, 1927.

Cape Town, c. 1885 (page 167): Bayard Taylor, *Travels in South Africa*. New York: Charles Scribner's Sons, 1887.

Tamarind (page 168): F. A. Ober, *The Knockabout Club in the Antilles*. Boston: Estes and Lauriat, 1888.

Street in Tangier (page 171): North Wind Picture Archives.

Bananas (page 174): Thomas W. Knox, *The Boy Travellers in the Far East*. New York: Harper and Brothers, 1881.

Caribbean market scene (page 199): F. A. Ober, *The Knockabout Club in the Antilles*. Boston: Estes and Lauriat, 1888.

On the way to the market in Jamaica (page 202): North Wind Picture Archives.

Dinner in a mess tent (page 206): North Wind Picture Archives.

Mangoes (page 225): Thomas W. Knox, *The Boy Travellers in the Far East*. New York: Harper and Brothers, 1881.

Bibliography

Ammal, S. Meenakshi. *Cook and See*. Mylapore, Madras: Alliance Press, 1968.

Amin, Fawziah. "Rich and Fiery." *Wine and Dine* (Singapore) 6, no. 4 (August/September 1991): 32.

Anand, Mulk Raj. *Curries and Other Indian Dishes*. London: Desmond Harmsworth, 1932.

Andersen, Juel. *Juel Andersen's Curry Primer*. Berkeley, Calif.: Creative Arts Communications, 1984.

Anderson, E. N. *The Food of China*. New Haven, Conn.: Yale University Press, 1988.

Athenaeus. *Deipnosophistai* (The Gastronomers). Reprinted as *The Deipnosophists* or *Banquet of the Learned*. Translated by C. D. Yonge. London: George Bell and Sons, 1909.

Ayto, John. *The Glutton's Glossary: A Dictionary of Food and Drink Terms*. London and New York: George Routledge and Sons, 1990.

Aziz, Khalid. *The Encyclopedia of Indian Cookery*. London: Park Lane Press, 1983.

Babbar, Purobi. *Rotis and Naans of India with Accompaniments*. Bombay: Vakils, Feffer and Simons, 1992.

Baker, Charles H., Jr. *The Gentleman's Companion, Being an Exotic Cookery Book*. New York: Crown Publishers, 1946.

Banik, Sambhu, and Elizabeth A. Esch. *Sampling the Cuisine of India*. Bethesda, Md.: American Cooking Guild, 1991.

Bastyra, Judy. *Caribbean Cooking*. Kingston, Jamaica: Heinemann Publishers, 1987.

Benghiat, Norma. *Traditional Jamaican Cookery*. London: Penguin Books, 1985.

Bhatti, A. Nisa. *Modern Muslim Cooking of Indo-Pakistan*. Lahore, Pakistan: Indus Publishing House, 1964.

Bois, D. *Les Plantes Alimentaires*. Paris: Editions Paul Lechevalier, 1927.

Brennan, Jennifer. *The Cuisines of Asia*. London: Macdonald, 1984.

—— . "Tantalizing Thai Curries." *Food and Wine*, May 1986, 77.

—— . *Curries and Bugles: A Memoir and a Cookbook of the British Raj*. New York: HarperCollins, 1990.

Brissenden, Rosemary. *Joys and Subtleties: South East Asian Cooking*. New York: Pantheon, 1970.

Brobeck, Florence. *Cooking with Curry*. New York: M. Barrows and Company, 1952.

Burt, Elinor. *Far Eastern Cookery*. Boston: Little, Brown and Company, 1947.

Campbell, Marjorie Pringle, and John Kenneth Pringle. *A Collection of 19th Century Jamaican Cookery and Herbal Recipes*. 1893. Reprint. Kingston, Jamaica: Mill Press, 1990.

Carpenter, Frank G. *Carpenter's Geographical Reader: Asia*. New York: American Book Company, 1897.

Chablani, Mohan, and Brahm Dixit. *The Bengal Lancers Indian Cookbook*. Chicago: Henry Regnery, 1976.

Chakravarty, Indira. *Saga of Indian Food*. New Delhi: Sterling Publishers, 1972.

Chandan, Amarjit. *Indians in Britain*. New Delhi: Sterling Publishers, 1986.

Chapman, Pat. *Curry Club Favourite Middle Eastern Recipes*. London: Judy Piatkus, 1989.

—— . *The Curry Club Vegetarian Cookbook*. London: Judy Piatkus, 1990.

—— . *The Cobra Good Curry Restaurant Guide*. London: Curry Club/Judy Piatkus, 1991.

—— ."250 Favourite Curries and Accompaniments." *Curry Club Magazine* (London) 31 (Summer/Autumn 1992): 8.

—— . Telephone interview with Dave DeWitt, personal correspondence, February 1993.

Chapman, Peter. "The Curry Houses of London." *Bon Appetit*, October 1992.

Cherian, Antony. "Spices Face New Challenges." Madras: *The Hindu Survey of Agriculture*, 1990.

Christie, Robert H. "Twenty-two Authentic Banquets from India." In *Banquets of the Nations*. 1911. Reprint. New York: Dover, 1975.

Clark, E. Phyllis. *West Indian Cookery*. Walton-on-Thames, England: Nelson Caribbean, 1976.

Coelho, C. J. *The Chef*. Mangalore, India: Codialbail Press, 1974.

Coetzee, Renata. *The South African Culinary Tradition*. Cape Town: C. Struik Publishers, 1977.

Coyle, L. Patrick. *Cook's Books*. New York: Facts on File, 1985.

Cranwell, John Philips. *The Hellfire Cookbook*. New York: Quadrangle, 1975.

"Curry." In *Oxford English Dictionary*. 2d ed. London: Clarendon Press, 1989.

"The Curry Mystery." *Sunset*, February 1977, 78.

"Cury." In *Oxford English Dictionary*. 2d ed. London: Clarendon Press, 1989.

Daniels, Roger. *History of Indian Immigration to the United States*. New York: Asia Society, 1989.

David, Elizabeth. *Spices, Salt and Aromatics in the English Kitchen*. Middlesex, England: Penguin Books, 1970.

David, Julia, ed. *Flavours of Malaysia* (special ed., *Wine and Dine*). Singapore: Couture Publishing, 1991.

Day, Harvey, with Sarojini Mudnani. *Curries of India*. Bombay: Jaico Publishing House, 1963.

DeWit, Antoinette, and Anita Borghese. *The Complete Book of Indonesian Cooking*. New York: Bobbs-Merrill, 1962.

DeWitt, Dave. "Singapore Fling." *Chile Pepper* 6, no. 3 (May/June 1992): 22.

——. "Down de Islands." *Chile Pepper* 7, no. 1 (January/February 1993): 18.

DeWitt, Dave, and Nancy Gerlach. *The Whole Chile Pepper Book*. Boston: Little, Brown and Company, 1990.

Douglas, Luther A. *The Explorer's Cookbook*. Caldwell, Ida.: Caxton Printers, 1971.

Drake, William, Jr. *The Connoisseur's Handbook of Marijuana*. San Francisco: Straight Arrow Books, 1971.

Dufougere, William. *Madinina, Reine des Antilles*. Paris: Editions Berger-Levrault, 1929.

Ekambaram, Manorama. *Hindu Cookery*. Bombay: D. B. Taraporevala Sons and Company, 1963.

Fernandez, Rafi. *Malaysian Cookery*. London: Penguin Books, 1985.

Fernando, Juliet. *Gunasena Cookery Book*. Colombo, Sri Lanka: M. D. Gunasena and Company, 1970.

Fisher, M.F.K. *With Bold Knife and Fork*. New York: G. P. Putnam's Sons, 1968.

Gardner, Brian. *The East India Company*. New York: McCall Publishing Company, 1972.

Gerber, Hilda. *Traditional Cooking of the Cape Malays*. Cape Town: A. A. Balkema, 1957.

Glasse, Hannah. *The Art of Cookery Made Plain and Easy*. 9th ed. London: privately printed, 1765.

Guigno, Sam. "Sri Lanka Has Fiery Cuisine for Export." *Kansas City Star*, August 30, 1989.

Guillemard, F.H.H. *The Cruise of the* Marchesa *to Kamschatka and New Guinea*. London: John Murray, 1886.

Gupta, Pranati Sen. *The Art of Indian Cuisine*. New York: Hawthorn Books, 1974.

Hachten, Harva. *Kitchen Safari: A Gourmet's Tour of Africa*. New York: Atheneum, 1970.

Hall, Captain Basil. *Travels in India, Ceylon, and Borneo*. London: George Routledge and Sons, 1931.

Handy, Ellice. *My Favorite Recipes*. Singapore: MPH Publications, 1960.

Hare, R.A.P. *Tasty Dishes of India*. Bombay: D. B. Taraporevala Sons and Company, 1965.

Herbst, Sharon Tyler. *Food Lover's Companion*. New York: Barron's, 1990.

Hillman, Howard. *The Book of World Cuisines*. New York: Penguin Books, 1979.

Hodgson, Moira. *The Hot and Spicy Cookbook*. New York: McGraw-Hill, 1977.

Hoii, James. *The Guide to Singapore Hawker Food*. Singapore: Hospitality Host, 1985.

Hultman, Tami, ed. *The Africa News Cookbook*. New York: Penguin Books, 1986.

Hurston, Zora Neale. *Tell My Horse*. Philadelphia: J. B. Lippincott Company, 1938.

Indar, Polly, ed., et al. *Naparima Girls' High School Diamond Jubilee Recipe Book*. San Fernando, Trinidad and Tobago: Naparima Girls' High School, 1988.

Indian Historical Pictures. Bombay: K. and J. Cooper, 190?.

Jaffrey, Madhur. An Invitation to Indian Cooking. New York: Vintage, 1975.

——. "A Taste of India: Kerala." Gourmet, April 1986, 68.

Jain, Girilad, ed. Times of India Directory and Yearbook. Bombay: Times of India Press, 1983.

Johns, Yohanni. Dishes from Indonesia. Philadelphia: Chilton Book Company, 1971.

Kaufman, William, and Saraswathi Lakshmanan. The Art of India's Cookery. Garden City, N.Y.: Doubleday and Company, 1964.

Khinduka, Manorama. Jalpaan: A Treasury of Indian Recipes. Chesterfield, Mo.: Khinduka Publishing, 1991.

Knox, Thomas W. The Boy Travellers in the Far East. New York: Harper and Brothers, 1881.

Krochmal, Connie and Arthur. Caribbean Cooking. New York: Quadrangle, 1974.

Kurup, K.K.N. History of the Tellicherry Factory (1683–1794). Calicut University, India: Sandhya Publications, 1985.

Laas, William. Cuisines of the Eastern World. New York: Golden Press, 1967.

Lesberg, Sandy. The Art of African Cooking. New York: Dell, 1971.

Leyel, Mrs. C. F. The Magic of Herbs. London: Jonathan Cape, 1926.

Lingeman, Richard R. Drugs from A to Z: A Dictionary. New York: McGraw-Hill, 1969.

MacKie, Christine. Life and Food in the Caribbean. New York: New Amsterdam Books, 1991.

Maharani of Jaipur (Gayatri Devi). Gourmet's Gateway. Bombay: Thacker's Press, 1969.

Mahindru, S. N. Spices in Indian Life. New Delhi: Sultan Chand and Sons, 1982.

Majupuria, Indra. Joys of Nepalese Cooking. Gwalior, India: S. Devi, 1980.

Marks, Copeland. The Indonesian Kitchen. New York: Atheneum, 1981.

——. The Varied Kitchens of India. New York: M. Evans and Company, 1986.

——. The Burmese Kitchen. New York: M. Evans and Company, 1987.

——. The Exotic Kitchens of Indonesia. New York: M. Evans and Company, 1989.

Mathew, K. M. Kerala Cookery. Kottayam, India: Manorama Publishing House, n.d.

Meakin, Budgett. The Moors. New York: Macmillan, 1902.

Merchant, Ismail. Ismail Merchant's Indian Cuisine. New York: Fireside, 1986.

Merson, Annette. African Cookery. Nashville: Winston-Derek, 1987.

Mesfin, Daniel J. Exotic Ethiopian Cooking. Falls Church, Va.: Ethiopian Cookbook Enterprises, 1990.

Moore, Thomas, and David Eldredge, eds. India Yesterday and Today. New York: Bantam, 1970.

Morphy, Countess. Recipes of All Nations. New York: William H. Wise and Company, 1935.

Morton, Julia. Herbs and Spices. New York: Golden Press, 1976.

Muthachen, Rachel. Regional Indian Recipes. Bombay: Jaico Publishing House, 1970.

Narasimhan, Chakravarthi (trans.). The Mahabharata. New York: Columbia University Press, 1965.

Negre, Andre. Caribbean Cooking. Papeete: Les Editions du Pacifique, 1978.

Nev, Dharma. Our Countrymen Abroad: A Brief Survey of the Problems of Indians in Foreign Lands. Allahabad, India: All India Congress Committee, 1940.

Newman, Graeme. The Down Under Cookbook. New York: Harrow and Heston, 1987.

Norman, Jill. The Complete Book of Spices. New York: Viking Studio Books, 1991.

Ober, F. A. The Knockabout Club in the Antilles. Boston: Estes and Lauriat, 1888.

Ortiz, Elisabeth Lambert, ed. The Encyclopedia of Herbs, Spices and Flavorings. New York: Dorling Kindersley, 1992.

Pais, Arthur. "A Gust of Ethiopian Restaurants." American Visions, February 1992, 59.

Peiris, Doreen. A Ceylon Cookery Book. Colombo, Sri Lanka: Lanka Trading Company, 1967.

Pruthi, J. S. Spices and Condiments: Chemistry, Microbiology, Technology. New York: Academic Press, 1980.

Rau, Santha Rama. The Cooking of India. New York: Time-Life Books, 1969.

Reejsinghani, Aroona. The Art of South Indian Cooking. Bombay: Jaico Publishing House, 1973.

———. *Cooking the Punjabi Way*. Bombay: Jaico Publishing House, 1978.

———. *Oil-Less Cooking*. Bombay: Jaico Publishing House, 1988.

———. *The Great Art of Mughlai Cooking*. New Delhi: Vikas Publishing, 1993.

Ritchie, Carson I. A. *Food in Civilization*. Sydney: Methuen Australia, 1981.

Root, Waverly. *Food*. New York: Simon and Schuster, 1980.

Sahni, Julie. *Classic Indian Cookery*. New York: William Morrow, 1980.

———. "An Indian Spice Sampler." *Gourmet*, May 1984, 42.

———. "Curry Classics." *Bon Appetit*, April 1988, 117.

———. "Fire and Spice — Indian Home Cooking." *Cook's*, January/February 1989, 42.

———. "Madras Curry Powder." *Bon Appetit*, April 1993, 36.

Samaroo, Brinsley. "East Indian Life and Culture." In *David Frost Introduces Trinidad and Tobago*. London: Andre Deutsch, 1975.

Sandler, Bea. *The African Cookbook*. New York: World Publishing, 1970.

Sattin, Anthony, ed. *An Englishwoman in India: The Memoirs of Harriet Tytler*. Oxford, England: Oxford University Press, 1986.

Shaxon, Annabel, et al. *The Cook Book*. Zomba, Malawi: Government Printer, 1974.

Sheth, Aruna. *The New Indian Cook Book*. Delhi: Orient Paperbacks, 1968.

Simonds, Nina. *Classic Chinese Cuisine*. Boston: Houghton Mifflin Company, 1982.

Singapore Tourist Promotion Board. *Singapore: 101 Meals*. Singapore: Tourist Promotion Board, n.d.

Singh, Dharamjit. *Classic Cooking from India*. Boston: Houghton Mifflin Company, 1956.

———. *Indian Cookery*. Middlesex, England: Penguin Books, 1970.

Singh, Manju Shivraj. *The Spice Box*. Freedom, Calif.: Crossing Press, 1981.

———. *Royal Indian Cookery*. New York: McGraw-Hill, 1987.

Skinner, Gwen. *The Cuisine of the South Pacific*. Auckland, New Zealand: Hodder and Stoughton, 1983.

Sokolov, Raymond. "A Portable Feast." *Natural History*, May 1991, 84.

Solomon, Charmaine and Reuben. *The Complete Curry Cookbook*. New York: McGraw-Hill, 1980.

Steinberg, Rafael. *Pacific and Southeast Asian Cooking*. New York: Time-Life Books, 1970.

Stobart, Tom. *The Cook's Encyclopedia*. New York: Harper and Row, 1980.

Stone, Julia A. *Illustrated India: Its Princes and People*. Hartford: American Publishing Company, 1877.

Subramanian, Aruna. *Aruna's Vegetarian Recipes*. Port of Spain: Indian Women's Group of Trinidad and Tobago, 1988.

Taik, Aung Aung. *Under the Golden Pagoda: The Best of Burmese Cooking*. San Francisco: Chronicle Books, 1993.

Tang, Tommy. *Tommy Tang's Modern Thai Cooking*. New York: Doubleday, 1992.

Tannahill, Reay. *Food in History*. New York: Crown Publishers, 1988.

Taylor, Bayard. *Travels in South Africa*. New York: Charles Scribner's Sons, 1887.

"Thai Cooks Heat Up Things with Curry Paste." *Sunset*, November 1984, 232.

Tinker, Hugh. *A New System of Slavery: The Export of Indian Labour Overseas, 1830–1920*. Oxford, England: Oxford University Press, 1974.

Toussaint-Samat, Maguelonne. *History of Food*. Cambridge, Mass.: Blackwell Publishers, 1992.

Uberoi, Pritam and Nimmi. *Pure Vegetarian Indian Cookery*. New Delhi: Sterling Publishing, 1991.

Urwick, the Reverend W. *Indian Pictures Drawn with Pen and Pencil*. London: Religious Tract Society, 189?.

U.S. Department of Agriculture. *Composition of Foods: Spices and Herbs (Raw, Processed, and Prepared)*. Washington, D.C.: Handbook no. 8-2 (January 1977).

Van Der Post, Laurens. *African Cooking*. New York: Time-Life Books, 1970.

———. *First Catch Your Eland*. New York: William Morrow, 1978.

Veach, William B. T., and Helen Evans Brown. *A Book of Curries and Chutneys*. Pasadena, Calif.: Ward Ritchie Press, 1963.

Visram, Rozina. *Ayahs, Lascars and Princes: Indians in Britain 1700–1947*. London: Pluto Press, 1986.

Waldo, Myra. *The Complete Round-the-World Cookbook*. New York: Greenwich House, 1973.

Wason, Betty. *Cooks, Gluttons and Gourmets*. New York: Doubleday and Company, 1962.

Waun, Sime Ee. "Tiffin Break?" *Wine and Dine* (Singapore) 6, no. 4 (August/September 1991): 20.

Whiteman, Joan, ed. *Craig Claiborne's New York Times Food Encyclopedia*. New York: Times Books, 1985.

Williams, Fadela. *The Cape Malay Cookbook*. Cape Town: C. Struik Publishers, 1988.

Williams, Neville. *Contraband Cargoes: Seven Centuries of Smuggling*. London: Longmans, Green and Company, 1959.

Willinsky, Helen. *Jerk: Barbecue from Jamaica*. Freedom, Calif.: Crossing Press, 1990.

Wilson, C. Anne. *Food and Drink in Britain*. London: Constable, 1973.

Wilson, Ellen. *A West African Cookbook*. New York: M. Evans and Company, 1971.

Wilson, John. *Australia and New Zealand Fish Cookbook*. Sydney: Paul Hamlyn, 1977.

Wolfert, Paula. *Couscous and Other Good Foods from Morocco*. New York: Harper and Row, 1973.

Index

meatball(s)
   Curried Lamb (*Harira Kefta Tajine*), 187
   Frikkadel Curry, 185
   and Radish Curry (*Shabril*), 78
Meenu Kootu, 48–49
Mewaii Kabab, 80
Moghlai cuisine, 69–70
Mohinga, 130–131
Moru Kolambu, 57
Mulligatawny Soup, 214
Murgh Achar, 74
Muslim Curry Paste, 116–117
mustard seed, 2, 9, 10, 12, 30, 64, 166
Mutton Soup, Indonesian Curried, 151

Naan, 102
Nam Prik Gaeng Ped, 116
Nasi Kunyit, 163
Nasi Lemak, 163
Nepalese cuisine, 70
   Gurkha Pork Curry, 84
New Zealand cuisine, 197
   Codfish Curry Casserole, 220–221
   Queensland Curry, 216–217
Nga Baung Doke, 128
Ngapi Ye, 108–109, 117
Nigerian cuisine, 173–174
   Coconut-Curry Soup, 184
Nimbu Masala Murgh, 86
noodle(s), 109
   Curried Fish with (*Mohinga*), 130–131
   Soup with Prawns, Curried (*Laksa Kari*), 152
North Indian cuisine, 63–104
   Aromatic Fish (Fish *Kalia*), 93
   Banana Chutney, 76
   Banik's Nehru Chicken, 89
   Bengali-Style Fish (*Macher Jhol*), 90–91
   Biryani, 87
   Bitter Gourd Curry (*Shukto*), 99
   Chapatti, 103
   Chicken Pickle (*Murgh Achar*), 74
   Chicken with Apricots (Stendhal's *Aru Murgh*), 85
   Classic Indian Curry Powder, 73
   Curried Lamb Shanks (*Raan Shahnshahi*), 81
   Curried Rice (Sant's *Korma Chawal*), 100
   Deep-Fried Bread (*Bhatura*), 101
   Fish Baked in Chutney (*Chutney Machi*), 92
   Fish Cooked in Banana Leaves (*Elish Macher Paturi*), 90

Fish Roe with Okra (*Bhinda Gharbano Patio*), 94
Flat Bread (*Naan*), 102
Fried Spareribs with Potatoes, 78–79
Hot Spinach Bread (*Palak Paratha*), 104
Ismail Merchant's Baked Salmon for Paul Newman, 95
Ismail Merchant's Ginger Chicken for Anthony Hopkins, 88
Kababs with *Prantha* Bread (*Bangri Kabab* with *Prantha*), 77
Kashmiri Gosht, 82
Lamb with Grains (*Kichida*), 83
Moghul and European invasions and, 64–68
regional trends and, 69–72
Ribs with Rose Petals (*Yakhni*), 82–83
Shrimp in Yogurt Sauce (*Dahi Chingree*), 96
Smoked Eggplant (*Baingan Burtha*), 98
Spiced and Baked Fish (*Masala Dum Machchi*), 91
Spicy Lime Chicken (*Nimbu Masala Murgh*), 86
Spicy Yogurt Salad, 76
see also Pakistani cuisine
nutmeg, 11, 12, 26, 30, 32, 67, 137, 138, 139, 205
nuts, 69
   Curried Lamb from Sind with (*Sindhi Gosht*), 79
   Egg Curry with Cashews (*Tantiychi Kadi*), 52
   Eggplant with (*Baingan Mewaa Ke Saath*), 98–99
   Lamb in Cashew Curry, 217

okra, 26
   Fish Roe with (*Bhinda Gharbano Patio*), 94
onions, 12, 14, 26, 136

Pakari, 226–227
Pakistani cuisine, 69–70
   Curried Dried-Fruit *Kababs* (*Mewaii Kabab*), 80
   Eggplant with Nuts (*Baingan Mewaa Ke Saath*), 98–99
   Lamb with Grains (*Kichida*), 83
   Nutty Curried Lamb from Sind (*Sindhi Gosht*), 79
   Peshawari *Biryani*, 97
   Prune Chutney, 75
Palak Paratha, 104

pancakes
   Lace (*Roti Djala*), 164
   with Stuffing (Arthur's *Masala Dosai*), 60
Pannang Beef Curry, 121
papaya, 26
   Salad (*Som Tum*), 119
Paratha, Palak, 104
peaches, in Curried Clingstone Chutney, 183
peanut(s), 226–227
   Pineapple, and Coconut Curry (*Pakari*), 226–227
peas
   Caribbean Rice and, 224–225
   Sambhar, 61
Penang Fish Curry, 157
pepper, 6, 8, 32, 33, 66
   black, 6, 11, 12, 22, 30, 31, 65, 68, 137, 139, 204–205
   red, 9, 10, 11
   white, 10
   see also chile peppers
Peshawari *Biryani*, 97
Phan Sin Fahn, 122–123
Pholouri, Curried, 213
pickle(d)(s)
   Chicken, 74
   Eggplant, 41
   Ginger Salad, Burmese (*Ghin Thoke*), 120
   Vegetable, Malaysian, 149
Pinang-Kerrie, 188
pineapple
   Boats, Curried Prawns in, 192
   Curry (*Kalan*), 54
   Peanut, and Coconut Curry (*Pakari*), 226–227
Pisang Kari, 160
poppy seed, 26, 64
pork, 36
   Colombo from Martinique, 218
   Countryside Curry (*Gaeng Bah*), 122
   Curried Sausages, 45–46
   Curry (*Whethar Thayathee Thanut Hin*), 121
   Curry, Devil's, 154
   Curry, Goan (*Shikar Vindaloo*), 46
   Curry, Gurkha, 84
   Fried Spareribs with Potatoes, 78–79
   Salad, Hanoi, 118
   and Yam Curry (*Dukor Ani Batate*), 46–47
potato(es), 138
   Coconut Curry (*Ubi Kentang Kari*), 161–162